ACHIEVING IMPLEMENTATION AND EXCHANGE

The science of delivering evidence-based practices to at-risk youth

Lawrence A. Palinkas

P

First published in Great Britain in 2019 by

Policy Press
University of Bristol
1-9 Old Park Hill
Bristol BS2 8BB
UK
t: +44 (0)117 954 5940
e: pp-info@bristol.ac.uk
www.policypress.co.uk

North American office:
Policy Press
c/o The University of Chicago Press
1427 East 60th Street
Chicago, IL 60637, USA
t: +1 773 702 7700
f: +1 773-702-9756
e:sales@press.uchicago.edu
www.press.uchicago.edu

© Policy Press 2019

British Library Cataloguing in Publication Data
A catalogue record for this book is available from the British Library.

Library of Congress Cataloging-in-Publication Data
A catalog record for this book has been requested.

ISBN 978-1-4473-3813-0 paperback
ISBN 978-1-4473-3812-3 hardcover
ISBN 978-1-4473-3815-4 ePub
ISBN 978-1-4473-3816-1 Mobi
ISBN 978-1-4473-3814-7 ePdf

Cover design by Hayes Design
Front cover: image kindly supplied by Abstract Technology © Freepik

Dedication

To my dear friends and colleagues, John, Patti, Lisa, Kimberly and Sally, from whom I learned so much about implementation, collaboration, and why this work is so important.

Contents

Tables and figures

Figures

Tables

Abbreviations

ACS	Administration for Children's Services (New York City)
ADHD	attention deficit/hyperactivity disorder
ARC	Availability, Responsiveness and Continuity program
ASD	autism spectrum disorders
BHS	Behavioral Health Services (San Diego County, California)
BPT	behavioral parent training
CAFÉ	Computer Assisted Fidelity Environment
CAL-OH	the California–Ohio study
CASRC	Child and Adolescent Services Research Center
CBT	cognitive behavioral therapy
CDT	community development team
CEI	Cultural Exchange Inventory
CFIR	Consolidated Framework for Implementation Research
CIMH	California Institute of Mental Health
CSAP	Center For Substance Abuse Prevention
CSNYC	Child Success New York City
CTAC	community technical assistance center
CTP	Clinic Treatment Project
CWS	Child Welfare Services (San Diego County, California)
D&I	dissemination and implementation
EBDM	Evidence-Based Decision Making model
EBP	evidence-based practice
EPIS	Exploration, Preparation, Implementation and Sustainment framework
GBG	Good Behavior Game
IDEAS	Center for Implementation-Dissemination of Evidence-Based Practices among States
IND	individualized implementation
KEEP	Keeping Foster Parents Trained and Supported
KMb	knowledge mobilization
KT	knowledge translation

KTE	knowledge transfer and exchange
LC	learning collaborative
LOCI	leadership and organizational change for implementation
MATCH	Modular Approach to Therapy with Children
MMT	modular manualized treatment
MOST	multiphase optimization strategy
MST	Multisystemic Therapy
NICE	National Institute for Health and Care Excellence
NIDA	National Institute on Drug Abuse
NIH	National Institutes of Health
NIMH	National Institute of Mental Health
NIRN	National Implementation Research Network
NPT	normalization process theory
OJJDP	Office of Juvenile Justice Delinquency Prevention
OMRU	Ottawa Model of Research Use
OMH	Office of Mental Health (New York State)
OSLC	Oregon Social Learning Center
PTC	Parenting Through Change
PTSD	posttraumatic stress disorder
QI	quality improvement
QIC	quality improvement collaborative
RCT	randomized controlled trial
RE-AIM	reach, effectiveness, adoption, implementation, and maintenance
RPPP	research–practice–policy partnerships
SAMHSA	Substance Abuse and Mental Health Services Administration
SIC	Stages of Implementation Completion
SIEU	Structured Interview for Evidence Use
SMT	standard manualized treatment
SMART	sequential multiple assignment randomized implementation trial
SOCE	System of Care Evaluation (San Diego County, California)
TFCO	Treatment Foster Care Oregon
TF-CBT	Trauma Focused Cognitive Behavioral Therapy
UC	usual care
URE	use of research evidence

Preface

Implementation science is one of a number of "sciences" to have emerged in the past few decades to tackle one of the most important problems associated with the delivery of health and social services in our time, that is, the 17-year gap between the identification of a priority for service delivery that promises better outcomes at less cost, and the routine use of that service. People in need of such services generally cannot afford to wait that long to receive them. Even then, we devote so much time, energy and resources to developing these services and then creating an evidence base using costly randomized controlled trials, only to have the routine use of these services more the exception than the rule. The problem often lies in a failure to understand and address the potential barriers to the implementation and sustainment of these evidence-based services and policies, known in this book as evidence-based practices or EBPs.

The task of changing the behavior of individual practitioners and service organizations for the sake of EBP implementation has drawn upon a number of theoretical traditions associated with an array of disciplines, including rural sociology, cultural anthropology, social work, organizational psychology, management science, public health, and social psychology. The model introduced in this book draws from transactional theory as represented in the work of anthropologist Frederick Bailey. However, while Bailey focused on transactions as a source of political gain and competitive struggle, the model advanced in this book sees social change as a bidirectional process in which both parties in a transaction exchange one thing in order to receive something else. In this instance, the social change is successful implementation observed in research conducted in child welfare and child mental health by the author in the past decade. The argument advanced in this book is that in order to change the behavior of the individual practitioners and organizations in these systems of care, or in any health and social service system for that matter, researchers and EBP developers must be willing and able to change themselves. Further, that change manifests itself through a series of transactions in knowledge, attitudes and practices that occur through social relationships between researchers, practitioners and policymakers, and the emergence of a set of shared understandings or common "culture of implementation" linking all participants in this endeavor. These transactions are not always easy to achieve and the process often requires a good deal of negotiation, debate and compromise; but the results are well worth the effort, especially when lives hang in the balance.

I wish to acknowledge the support received through funding from the National Institute of Mental Health (P30 MH074678-03, John Landsverk, P.I.; and R01MH07658, Patricia Chamberlain, P.I.), National Institute on Drug Abuse (R34037516-01A1, Lawrence Palinkas, P.I.; 5P50DA035763-04, Patricia Chamberlain, P.I.; and 2P30DA027828-06 Hendricks Brown, P.I.), the John D. and Catherine T. MacArthur Foundation (John Weisz, P.I.), and the William T. Grant Foundation (No. 9493 and No. 10648, Lawrence Palinkas, P.I.). I also wish to acknowledge my colleagues engaged in implementation research, whose invaluable advice and support helped to shape the ideas contained in this book. Among others, this distinguished group of scholars includes the following: Greg Aarons, Hendricks Brown, Bruce Chorpita, Mary McKay, Enola Proctor, Cherrie Short, John Weisz, and Marleen Wong. I am especially grateful to those to whom this book is dedicated: John Landsverk, Patti Chamberlain, Sally Horwitz, Kimberly Hoagwood, and Lisa Saldana. A special thanks goes to Vivien Tseng and Kim DuMont of the William T. Grant Foundation, who were supportive of most of the research described in this book. I am also thankful to Catherine Gray, Policy Press commissioning editor, and anonymous reviewers for valuable comments and guidance.

1

Introduction

I think that we have to be careful about using the term evidence-based practice and really defining it in different ways. And I think of the three Ps, I think of evidence-based practices, I think of evidence-based programs, and I think of evidence-based principles. And I think principles are more interchangeable. But, the difference between a program that is a canned program that needs to be done just this way, versus having components of principles that people do. And so, for example, Motivational Interviewing is a skill that can be incorporated into many settings. It doesn't have to be rolled out like a canned curriculum. So, like I said, we need to put that back out to think about evidence-based practices and principles as different things, or programs and principles as different things. And also, I think we need to be clear about what really has evidence behind it and what not, and what the quality of that evidence is. I think that we need to be careful, because I'm afraid everyone is going to say "Oh well, I do evidence-based practice," but it doesn't look like it when you break it down. That, again, is why I like principles. So, how are the staff delivering it? How are the kids receiving it, you know, or the adults? So, I guess I have a lot of concern about, you know, getting on the bandwagon with this and not being really thoughtful both from the practitioner's side and the researcher's side. (Chief probation officer)

Evidence provided by single studies, systematic reviews, and government statistics suggests that mental health problems affect up to one-quarter of all youths worldwide at any one point in time and about one-third across their lifetimes (Merikangas, 2009). Half of all lifetime cases of mental health problems begin before age 14 and 75 percent by age 24 years (Kessler et al, 2005) if not sooner (Kim-Cohen et al, 2003). These problems include depression, anxiety, traumatic stress, conduct disorders, and substance abuse. Youth involved in child welfare systems are at even higher risk, with as many as 50 percent having behavioral and mental health problems (Burns et al, 2004).

There are numerous evidence-based practices (EBPs) for the prevention and treatment of mental health and behavioral problems among children and adolescents (Henggeler et al, 1998; Burns, 2003; Webster-Stratton et al, 2004; Weisz et al, 2004). The beneficial effects of these psychotherapeutic and pharmacologic interventions for children and adolescents have been repeatedly demonstrated through clinical trials of treatment efficacy (Weisz and Jensen, 1999). However, these practices are not widely used in clinical practice (Bickman et al, 2000; Chorpita et al, 2002; Hoagwood and Olin, 2002; Hanson et al, 2016). In fact, it has been estimated that 90 percent of publicly-funded child-serving systems do not use EBPs (Hoagwood and Olin, 2002). In the United Kingdom, 70 percent of children and adolescents who experience mental health problems have not had appropriate interventions at a sufficiently early age (Children's Society, 2008).

There remains a large gap between the development of services shown to be effective in the prevention and treatment of child abuse and neglect and child and adolescent mental health and behavioral problems and the routine use of these services (Burns et al, 2004; Costello et al, 2014). As a result, the majority of youth in need receive services lacking evidence to support their effectiveness and lack access to services supported by such evidence (Weisz et al, 1995; Hoagwood and Olin, 2002; Raghavan et al, 2010). As many as 50 percent of these youth will grow up to be adults who continue to suffer from clinically significant mental and behavioral health problems that will have a substantial social and economic impact due to poor parenting, loss of productivity, and expenditures for treatment (Kessler et al, 2012). In 2010, mental and substance use disorders constituted 10.4 percent of the global burden of disease and were the leading cause of years lived with disability among all disease groups (Whiteford et al, 2013). The global direct and indirect economic costs of mental disorders that year were estimated at US$2.5 trillion, 68 percent of which were attributed to indirect costs (US$1.7 trillion) (Trautman et al, 2016). Studies conducted in Europe, the United States and the United Kingdom estimate annual costs of €21.3 billion, $247 billion and £1.47 billion, respectively associated with childhood attention-deficit hyperactivity disorder, autism spectrum disorders, and conduct disorders alone (O'Connell et al, 2009; Olesen et al, 2012; Snell et al, 2013).

Scaling up the use of EBPs in child and adolescent mental health services remains one of the greatest challenges of our time. Many in the field agree that a great deal of research will be needed to identify factors that facilitate or impede EBP implementation in service sectors that cater to children and adolescents, including specialty mental health, schools, juvenile justice, primary care, and child welfare (Hoagwood et al, 2001; Schoenwald and Hoagwood, 2001; Fixsen et al, 2005; Aarons and Palinkas, 2007; Beidas and Kendall, 2014).

The gap between research and practice is by no means limited to child welfare. In 2001, the Institute of Medicine published a report, *Crossing the quality chasm*, focusing on closing the quality gap between what we know to be good healthcare and the healthcare that people actually receive. As described by the Committee on Quality of Health Care in America that wrote the report: "The lag between discovery or more efficacious forms of treatment and their incorporation in routine patient care is unnecessarily long, in the range of about 15 to 20 years (Balas and Boren, 2000). Even then, adherence of clinical practice to the evidence is highly uneven" (p. 145).

The elimination or narrowing of this gap is the focus of implementation science. Implementation research is "the scientific study of methods to promote the systematic uptake of research findings and other evidence-based practices into routine practice, and, hence, to improve the quality and effectiveness of health services" (Eccles and Mittman, 2006, p. 1). At the outset, implementation scientists focused on understanding the barriers and facilitators to implementing EBPs in service systems such as child welfare and child mental health. More recently, the focus has shifted to designing and evaluating strategies and other tools to overcome these challenges and promote successful implementation and sustainment. Implementation science may be viewed as one of a number of efforts to bridge the gap between research and practice by focusing on the transfer or translation of knowledge. "The terms knowledge translation, knowledge exchange, knowledge transfer, knowledge integration and research utilization are used to describe overlapping and interrelated research on putting various forms of knowledge, including research, to use" (Nilsen, 2015, p. 4).

Evidence-based practices

As illustrated by the statement of a county chief probation officer at the beginning of this chapter, EBP is often used to refer to a variety of products, including interventions, programs, policies, and treatments, that are supported by empirical evidence. It also is used to refer to the process of applying research evidence in general and evidence-based interventions, policies and programs in particular in a specific sociocultural context (Soydan and Palinkas, 2014). This notion of EBP as a process can be traced to the development of the evidence-based medicine movement in the 1990s. As defined by Sackett and colleagues (1996, p. 71), "Evidenced-based medicine is the conscientious, explicit and judicious use of current best evidence in making decisions about the care of individual patients. The practice of evidence-based medicine means integrating individual clinical expertise with the best available external clinical evidence from systematic research." Later, patient preferences were included as one of three primary sources of evidence for EBP (Haynes et al, 2002).

As suggested by the definition of evidence-based medicine, the evidence supporting EBPs comes in many forms. Usually, this evidence is arranged in hierarchical fashion, ordered by scientific standards of rigor and validity (Atkins et al, 2004). According to the U.S. Preventive Services Task Force (Atkins et al, 2001), the highest form of evidence is derived from randomized controlled trials (RCTs), followed by non-randomized control studies, case-control and cohort studies, uncontrolled time series, and expert opinion. Another hierarchical arrangement, adapted from Shadish et al (2002), places systematic reviews and meta-analyses at the top of the hierarchy, followed by RCTs, cohort studies, cross-sectional surveys, case reports, expert opinions, and anecdotes. Unfortunately, the preference for experimental designs such as the RCT tends to minimize the potential value of studies that may have limited internal validity due to small sample size, weak statistical power, and design issues, but may have greater external validity due to their being conducted in more typical, less controlled populations and settings (Green et al, 2009).

Why is implementing EBPs so important? Evidence-based programs, policies and practices are important because they aim to provide the most effective care that is available, with the aim of improving service user outcomes. Service users (clients, patients, consumers) seek care in the belief that what is provided will be effective in addressing their needs. Of course, evidence of effectiveness is not a guarantee that a particular program, policy or practice will work in every instance. Benefits are related to the effect size of the EBP and whether it was implemented well. A particular practice may have a small effect size or be poorly implemented in a particular setting, yet still be considered evidence-based. However, the knowledge that what is provided is based on the best available evidence offers reassurance and validation of the decision to seek care. For service providers, such knowledge provides similar reassurance that the services delivered are the best available. The process of EBP also promotes ongoing assessment of the latest evidence in the context of self-assessment of performance.

EBP also plays a role in ensuring that finite resources are used wisely and that relevant evidence is considered when decisions are made about funding health and social services (Hoffman et al, 2013). Although the use of EBPs to maximize the quality and quantity of life for individual patients may raise rather than lower the cost of their care (Sackett et al, 1996), by improving health outcomes, use of EBPs can also lead to cost savings in treatment of physical and mental health problems, as well as savings in the costs associated with these problems, such as unemployment and reduced economic productivity. For instance, a study of youths receiving trauma-focused cognitive-behavioral therapy (TF-CBT) (Cohen et al, 2004) compared to control youths diagnosed with PTSD receiving state outpatient mental health services as usual found that the cost of providing low-end, evidence-based treatment is more than offset by reductions in the utilization of high-end mental health services for traumatized youth (Greer et al, 2013).

EBPs also have the potential of breaking the cycle of child and adult dysfunction. As will be explained in greater detail in Chapter Two, a significant percentage of behavioral and mental health problems experienced in adulthood can be linked to childhood adversities (Green et al, 2010; Kessler et al, 2010). Many of these adversities, in turn, can be traced to the behavioral and mental health problems of adults. Thus, the adversities experienced by one generation may ultimately contribute to the adversities experienced by succeeding generations.

Goal of the book

If EBPs are so beneficial, then why are they not being used in routine practice and what can we do about it? The answers to these two questions are the central focus of implementation science and the focus of this book. They lie at the heart of some of the major debates in the field. One such debate revolves around how best to accommodate two potentially conflicting aims when implementing an EBP: exercising fidelity in delivering the EBP as planned, and making adaptations to the EBP to make it work for a specific or new use, setting, or population. Fidelity is the extent to which the intervention was delivered as planned (Allen et al, 2018). It represents the quality and integrity of the intervention as conceived by developers (Schoenwald et al, 2011). Adaptation is the extent to which the intervention is modified to make it fit for a specific or new use, setting, or population (Allen et al, 2018). It refers to changes that are planned and based on a specific rationale. It does not refer to changes due to poor quality of implementation (that is, drift). While there is the expectation that the intervention is implemented with strict adherence to standards that were developed for efficacy trials, the implementation of EBPs in real world settings often require modification of these standards. This is because implementing an intervention as designed by the developers may be impractical, undesirable, and/or ineffective.

A related debate revolves around how best to insure both the internal and external validity of an EBP during its implementation. As described by Brownson and colleagues (2018, p. 483):

> what is fundamental to D&I research and is often missing is a body of evidence that can help to determine the generalizability of an intervention from one population and/ or setting to another, that is, the core concepts of external validity. There are many remaining research questions related to external validity – for example: What factors need to be taken into account when an internally valid program or policy is implemented in a different setting or with a different population subgroup? How does one balance the concepts of fidelity and adaptation (reinvention)? If the adaptation processes change the original intervention so that the original efficacy data no longer apply, then the program may be viewed as a new intervention under very different contextual conditions.

Although implementation researchers are in general agreement as to the need for such a body of evidence related to external validity, a third related debate revolves around the question of what constitutes research evidence when implementing an EBP. As described by Soydan and Palinkas, there are two potentially competing forms of evidence used in EBP implementation:

Global evidence originates outside of an agency or jurisdiction; it is based on standards for scientific rigor (e.g., RCTs) and it places emphasis on the generalizability or transferability of findings from one setting to another. In contrast, local evidence originates within an agency or jurisdiction, may include administrative data, is based on personal experience (either involvement in data collection and analysis or familiarity with population studied), and places emphasis on the uniqueness of a population and its needs. Social work practitioners may be more inclined to make decisions based on local evidence because it is more intimate and familiar, even if it does not always adhere to the same standards of rigor and is certainly lacking in terms of external validity. It also represents a measure of individual control over the decision-making process rather than surrendering control to researchers, who are often perceived as being outsiders with little understanding of the local context. (2014, p. 92)

The suggestion provided by the county chief probation officer quoted at the beginning of this chapter, that researchers and practitioners must be very thoughtful in deciding what constitutes an EBP and the evidence upon which it is based, points to a possible resolution to all three of these debates through the development of relationships and the exercise of debate and compromise. Both of these activities play a critical role in developing and implementing EBPs.

This book has two aims. The first aim is to examine how implementation science is being used to enable youth to receive high quality services for the prevention and treatment of behavioral and mental health problems. The second aim is to introduce a model for EBP implementation that has emerged from a decade of research on the experiences of implementation in child welfare and child mental health settings. It is a response to a call issued by Proctor and colleagues for "'transactional' models in which all stakeholders equally contribute to and gain from the collaboration and where cultural exchange is encouraged. Such collaborations can move beyond traditional, unidirectional models of 'diffusion' of research from universities to practice, to a more reciprocal, interacting 'fusing' of science and practice" (2009, p. 31). The model introduced in this book traces its roots to the transactional theories of anthropologists Fredrik Barth (1959) and Frederick Bailey (1973). However, rather than seeing transactions primarily as a tool to gain political power as they did, the model introduced here views transactions as the operation of mutual self-interest where social change is more likely to result from cooperation than from competition. Although the model is drawn from the experience of implementing EBPs in child welfare and child mental health, it can be used to provide guidance to implementing EBPs in any service setting or any setting where the adoption and implementation of innovative practices is critical to achieving goals and maximizing performance.

Structure of the book

The remainder of this book begins with a broad overview of the problem being addressed by the implementation of EBPs in child welfare and child mental health, the challenges faced in addressing this problem, and the tools for overcoming these challenges. It then proceeds to an examination of five specific components of this transactional model: the use of social networks, research evidence, the integration of global and local models of evidence and implementation, research–practice–policy partnerships and cultural exchanges. These components are then examined in light of a common thread of building and maintaining social relationships and shared understandings among those intimately involved in mental and behavioral health services delivery to children and adolescents in need of such services, especially those involved in child welfare systems.

Chapter Two begins with a description of the prevalence and distribution of mental and behavioral health problems of children worldwide and a review of the literature identifying major risk factors for these problems, including genetic, social and environmental factors. The chapter then turns its attention to a segment of the youth population that is especially vulnerable to these problems, that is, those who are involved in child welfare systems. The number of youth in child welfare systems in the United States and the problems faced by these youth, including abuse and neglect, multiple placements, and specific mental and behavioral health problems are examined in detail. The second part of this chapter focuses on existing EBPs for screening, prevention, and treatment of behavioral and mental health problems. The term 'evidence-based practice' in this context refers to individual interventions, treatments, practices and programs that represent an integration of the results of rigorous scientific research with clinical experience and consumer preference. This section profiles several exemplary practices designed to prevent and treat youth mood, trauma and conduct disorders, detail how these practices became 'evidence-based' or 'evidence-informed', explain the difference between evidence-based and 'promising' interventions, and describe standards used by agencies and clearinghouses for identifying and promoting the use of EBPs for youth. The third part of the chapter then documents the lack of routine use of these EBPs.

Chapter Three provides a detailed examination of the literature documenting barriers to EBP implementation in child welfare and child mental health, as well as efforts to overcome these barriers. The chapter introduces some of the major theories, models and frameworks that guide implementation research, such as the Diffusion of Innovation Theory (Rogers, 2003), Ottawa Model of Research Use (Graham and Logan, 2004), and the National Implementation Research Network (NIRN) framework (Fixsen et al, 2005). Efforts to address these barriers highlighted in this chapter include the availability, responsiveness and continuity (ARC) intervention that is designed to prepare organizations for implementing EBPs by focusing on barriers related to organizational culture and climate (Glisson and Schoenwald, 2005), continuous quality improvement strategies like learning collaboratives and the Institute for Healthcare Innovation Breakthrough Series model (IHI, 2003), cascading diffusion (Chamberlain et al, 2012), train-the trainer models (Tobias et al, 2012), and leadership development interventions (Aarons et al, 2017). Measures for assessing outcomes such as the Stages of Implementation Completion scale (Chamberlain et al, 2012) and the RE-AIM framework (Glasgow et al, 1999) and innovative methods for implementation science such as mixed methods, alternative experimental designs, and systems science methods are also introduced in this chapter.

Chapter Four introduces a model for implementing EBPs in child welfare and child mental health based on the author's own experience of conducting research to understand and reduce the gap between research and practice in these youth-serving systems of care. This model is founded on five primary components, listed in Box 1.1:

Box 1.1: Components of a transactional model of EBP implementation

1. The *social networks* of service providers and the agencies and organizations they represent
2. The *use of research evidence* (URE) in deciding whether or not to adopt EBPs

3. The *integration of global and local cognitive frameworks or models of evidence and implementation* used by policymakers and practitioners
4. The role of *research–practice–policy partnerships* in EBP implementation
5. The *exchanges* that occur between partners, and the transformations in the organizational cultures of these stakeholders resulting from those exchanges

---

The objective of this chapter is to explain why these five components are believed to be critical to EBP implementation, how they are linked together by the principle that social relationships and shared understandings are critical to EBP implementation, and how they inform both research and practice in child welfare and child mental health. The chapter provides an overview of four major studies of EBP implementation in child welfare and child mental health that serve as the foundation for the proposed model.

Chapter Five examines in detail the first of the five components of a model for successful implementation of EBPs. It begins with an examination of how current implementation theories, models and frameworks highlight the role of social networks in implementation process and outcomes. Two of these frameworks are profiled in this chapter, the Exploration, Preparation, Implementation and Sustainment (EPIS) framework developed by Aarons and colleagues (2011), and the Consolidated Framework for Implementation Research (CFIR) developed by Damschroder and colleagues (2009). It also explains how intra- and inter-organizational networks can facilitate EBP implementation and how the absence of such networks can serve as a barrier to implementation. The chapter then summarizes research on the influence of social networks and inter-organizational collaborations in implementing Treatment Foster Care Oregon (TFCO) (Chamberlain et al, 2007), an EBP designed to meet the behavioral health needs of youth in foster care, in California and Ohio. This research also demonstrates how community development teams, a continuous quality improvement strategy developed by the California Institute of Mental Health, can be used to build and sustain such networks.

One of the reasons why social networks are important to implementation is that they facilitate the flow of information among network members, including information gained from research on the EBP itself and on the best means to implement and sustain the EBP in routine practice settings. Chapter Six begins with an examination of how current implementation theories, models and frameworks highlight the role of use of research evidence in implementation process and outcomes. It also explains how the use of research evidence facilitates EBP implementation and how the lack of such use serves as an implementation barrier. The chapter then summarizes research on the role of use of research evidence acquisition, evaluation, application and total engagement in the scaling up of TFCO in California and Ohio, and in the adoption of innovative and EBPs in state-supported mental health clinics and agencies serving youth in New York State. This research summary highlights three lessons learned from this research: 1) use of research evidence does inform policy and practice in child welfare and child mental health; 2) priority is given with respect to how evidence is accessed, evaluated and applied; and 3) systems leaders use three other types of evidence when considering whether to seek and apply research evidence in making decisions: evidence of resources necessary and available for making use of research evidence (supply), evidence of the need for research evidence, usually obtained from local conditions of client and service needs (demand), and evidence gained from personal experience (that is, is the research evidence consistent with practice experience or personal observation).

One of the ways of defining and distinguishing the two types of research evidence described in Chapter Six is by their origin or source. Evidence acquired through the application of rigorous scientific methods such as randomized controlled trials (RCTs) and systematic reviews that is intended to be generalizable across a range of settings with similar characteristics is described in this book as being 'global' in character. Evidence acquired through personal experience in a specific setting through the application of methods ranging from nonsystematic observations to more rigorous procedures is described as being 'local' in character. In Chapter Seven, the difference between global and local models of EBP implementation is examined, along with the principles underlying the decision-making process related to EBP implementation. It explains why an understanding of local models facilitates EBP implementation and why a lack of such an understanding can serve as an implementation barrier. It then presents the findings of research on policymaker and practitioner decision-making related to the adoption of innovative and EBPs for treatment of youth mental and behavioral problems in New York State. This research illustrates a decision-making model that is anchored by concerns related to the costs associated with, capacity for, and acceptability of the EBPs and their adoption. This research also illustrates the importance of certain principles of behavioral economics such as orientation to the present rather than the future (temporal discounting), concern about losing something one possesses rather than about gaining something one has not yet experienced (loss aversion), and use of heuristics or rules of thumbs to make complex decisions rather than going through all possible choices.

One of the key venues for the transfer of research evidence from producer to consumer and the integration of global and local models of implementation is the partnerships between researchers and practitioners. Not every effort to implement a new EBP involves researchers or a research component (Nieva et al, 2005); nevertheless, such efforts benefit when researchers are engaged as collaborators whose function extends beyond dissemination and evaluation (Palinkas and Soydan, 2012). Chapter Eight has four aims: 1) to describe the structure and operation of successful research–practice–policy partnerships for child welfare and child mental health, with a particular focus on disseminating and implementing EBPs; 2) to explain why such partnerships are critical facilitators of EBP implementation; 3) to identify barriers to successful partnerships; and 4) to identify the core features of successful partnerships. The chapter profiles three successful models of such partnerships, each of which illustrates variations in leadership, knowledge generation and dissemination, and research and technical assistance. Core features of these partnerships are grouped into intra-personal, interpersonal, organizational, environmental and cultural categories. The exercise of flexibility, sensitivity to the needs of partners, transparency, the pursuit of mutual self-interest, and willingness to engage in teaching and learning are characteristics of all three models of successful partnerships.

Following from the last chapter, Chapter Nine examines in detail the transformation of research, policy and practice resulting from such partnerships. It describes cultural exchange as a theory and a method for conducting translational research and facilitating research translation. It explains why some form of cultural exchange is necessary for successful EBP implementation. Cultural exchange involves a transaction and transformation of knowledge, attitudes and practices of individuals or groups representing different cultural systems. In the context of child welfare and child mental health, this transaction is between researchers, policymakers and practitioners. The product of this exchange is the transformation and integration of the researcher's global culture of EBP and the practitioner/policymaker's local culture of practice-based evidence. What is most important is that this transaction and transformation is both a process and product of debate and compromise. The chapter then summarizes research on the role of cultural exchange in the implementation of a modular approach to EBPs for treatment of child anxiety, depression and conduct disorders in Massachusetts and

Hawaii and an EBP for treatment of behavioral problems in foster care youth in California and Ohio.

The final chapter summarizes the five components of a model for successful implementation of EBPs and explains how these components are related to one another. It also examines the implications of this framework in the design and implementation of three implementation 'facilitators' or support systems: 1) the development of policies that promote EBP use; 2) the development and use of strategies that facilitate EBP implementation; and 3) the formation and maintenance of partnerships that promote ongoing quality improvement in services delivery. It concludes by describing an agenda for future research and practice that will contribute to reducing the gap between these two important elements of child services.

Summary

- There is an average 17-year lag between the development of efficacious forms of treatment and their incorporation in routine patient care.
- Implementation research is the scientific study of methods to promote the systematic uptake of research findings and other EBPs into routine practice, and, hence, to improve the quality and effectiveness of health services.
- The practice of evidence-based medicine means integrating individual clinical expertise with the best available external clinical evidence from systematic research and patient preferences.
- In this book, evidence-based practice (EBP) is used to refer to a variety of products, including interventions, programs, policies, and treatments, that are supported by empirical evidence.
- The evidence supporting EBPs comes in many forms, arranged hierarchically according to scientific standards of rigor and validity.
- Evidence-based programs, policies and practices are important because they aim to provide the most effective care available, with the aim of improving service user outcomes.
- This book has two aims: 1) examine how implementation science is being used to address the needs of youth to receive high quality services for the prevention and treatment of behavioral and mental health problems; and 2) introduce a model for EBP implementation that has emerged from a decade of research on the experiences of implementation in child welfare and child mental health settings.

2

The need for evidence-based practice

And I know that their interventions have been tested on populations similar to the populations that we're working with. And so, and I have found that they're good interventions for our clients, that they're not rigid, that they have flexibility to them. That fidelity to the model is important. But that there's sort of bobbing and weaving with clients, which is a really important thing when you're working with folks that have multi-stressors and not a lot of supports. That being able to be responsive to the needs of clients and not having to have the sort of rigidity to a model is very useful. (Clinic director)

Evidence-based practices (EBPs) are designed to address specific needs. In many cases, the extent to which these practices successfully address those needs, as evidenced by improved and desired outcomes, determines whether or not they will be sustained. Often, programs will be sustained despite lack of evidence of positive outcomes. In either case, the decision whether or not to adopt a specific program or practice is determined by the availability or supply of services to address a specific need, the demand (that is, number of clients or patients) for that service, and the fit between the practice, the organization responsible for its use, and the patients or clients who are its intended beneficiaries.

In this chapter, we begin with an examination of the need for evidence-based mental health services among youth in general and child-welfare involved youth in particular. We begin with a review of the current state of our understanding of this need among youth in general, focusing on the prevalence of mental and behavioral health problems in this population and the risk of these problems associated with the experience of childhood adversities such as child maltreatment, poverty, racism and discrimination, and involvement in criminal justice systems. We then narrow our focus to youth involved in the child welfare system and examine both the scale and severity of their mental and behavioral health problems and limited access to services to address these problems. The chapter then introduces some of the current evidence-based programs and practices designed to address these problems, focusing on their prevention and treatment, and then concludes with a brief review of the extent to which they are utilized for this purpose.

Mental and behavioral health problems experienced by youth

As noted in the last chapter, numerous studies, meta-analyses and systematic reviews using data collected from nationally representative cohorts and community surveys have concluded that one fourth of youth experience a mental disorder during the past year, and about one third across their lifetimes (Merikangas et al, 2009). A meta-analysis of 41 studies conducted in 27 countries reported a 13.4 percent pooled prevalence of any mental disorder in children and adolescents (Polanczyk et al, 2015). The prevalence of any anxiety disorder was 6.5 percent, any depressive disorder was 2.6 percent, attention-deficit/hyperactivity disorder (ADHD) was 6.5 percent, and any disruptive disorder was 3.4 percent. In a nationally representative survey conducted by the Office of National Statistics in the United Kingdom, 10 percent of 5–16-year-olds were reported to have a clinically diagnosable mental health problem (Green et al, 2005). Using data from the National Comorbidity Survey – Adolescent Supplement, a nationally representative face-to-face survey of 10,123 adolescents aged 13–18 years in the United States, Merikangas and colleagues (2010) found anxiety disorders to have the highest lifetime prevalence of any mental health condition (31.9%), followed by behavior disorders (19.1%), mood disorders (14.3%), and substance use disorders (11.4%), with approximately 40 percent of those with one class of disorder also meeting criteria for another class of disorder. Using data from the National Comorbidity Survey Replication Adolescent Supplement, Kessler and colleagues (2012) found the 12-month prevalence of any mental disorder in 13–17-year-olds to be 40.3 percent and the 30-day prevalence to be 23.4 percent. Anxiety disorders were the most common (24.9%) followed by behavior (16.3%), mood (10.0%), and substance abuse disorders (8.3%).

Anxiety disorders are the most prevalent mental disorder among children and adolescents worldwide, involving 10–20 percent of this group (Beesdo et al, 2009). In a national survey of 10,123 American adolescents aged 13–18 years, Burstein et al (2014 and 2011) reported that around 3 percent of the participants had generalized anxiety disorder in six months' duration, and 9 percent social phobia in their lifetime. Generalized anxiety disorder and social anxiety disorder are the two most prevalent disorders in youth (Merikangas et al, 2009). In the United Kingdom, the prevalence of any anxiety disorder is 3.3 percent (Merikangas et al, 2009).

Depressive disorder is another leading mental health problem faced by youth. In 2014, 11.4 percent of 12–17-year-olds living in the United States had at least one depressive episode and 8.2 percent had at least one major depressive episode with severe impairment (SAMHSA, 2015). Another study reported an increase in the 12-month prevalence of major depressive episodes from 8.7 percent in 2005 to 11.3 percent in 2014 in adolescents (Mojtabai et al, 2016). A 2006 meta-analysis of 26 epidemiologic studies of children and adolescents born in Britain between 1965 and 1996 found that the one-year prevalence of depression in mid- to late adolescence was between 4 percent and 5 percent (Costello et al, 2006).

Suicide is the fourth leading cause of death in 5–14-year-old children in the United States (Hoyert and Xu, 2012) and the second leading cause of death for 10–24-year-olds, resulting in 5,178 deaths in 2012 (CDC, 2015a). In the United States, suicide accounted for 17 percent of all deaths among 10–24-year-olds in 2014 (CDC, 2015b). Further, the 2015 Youth Risk Behavior Surveillance System survey of private and public high school students reported that 17.7 percent had seriously considered attempting suicide; 14.6 percent had made a plan for how they would attempt suicide; 9.6 percent had attempted suicide one or more times within the past year; and 3.2 percent had made a suicide attempt that resulted in an injury, poisoning, or an overdose that had to be treated by a doctor or nurse (Kann et al, 2016). In the United Kingdom, there were 201 intentional deaths among 10–19-year-olds in 2014, a 14 percent increase from 2012 (n=176) (Stallard, 2016).

Alcohol abuse is another problem for children and adolescents, especially in high-income countries like the United States and the United Kingdom. In 2014, there were 679,000 12–17-year-olds in the United States with a past year alcohol use disorder, or 2.7 percent of all adolescents. However, the percentage of adolescents in 2014 with an alcohol use disorder was roughly half the percentages in 2002 to 2004 (SAMHSA, 2015). Among school pupils aged 11–15 in the United Kingdom, 57 percent do not drink and 10 percent report that they drank in the last week. Among the 15-year-olds, over a quarter report drinking in the previous week (Fuller, 2013). Self-reported accounts of being drunk at least twice in their lives suggest that this has happened to approximately a quarter of 15-year-olds in England, and more than a third in Scotland (Brooks et al, 2011).

Despite notable declines in the past ten years, substance abuse among adolescents in the United States remains high; a third of tenth-graders and half of twelfth graders have used an illicit drug, one in 15 high school seniors use marijuana daily and a quarter of seniors have had five or more drinks at one time in the last two weeks, a 10 percent increase from 2011 to 2012 (Johnston et al, 2013). Excessive drinking accounted for approximately 4,300 deaths each year among persons aged <21 years during 2006–2010, and underage drinking cost the United States $24.3 billion in 2010 (Sacks et al, 2015). Adolescent drug abuse represents a substantial economic burden to society. Annually, drug abuse costs $600 billion in the United States, and while drug abuse treatment is cost effective (NIDA, 2012), prevention programs are even more cost effective than treatment (O'Connell et al, 2009). An estimated 867,000 adolescents or 3.5 percent of all adolescents had an illicit drug use disorder in 2014 (SAMHSA, 2015). In the United Kingdom, 26 percent of 13–15-year-old males and 21 percent of females reported some experimentation with illegal drugs in 2011 (Fuller, 2013).

ADHD is perhaps the most prominent of the category of conduct or behavior problems in children and adolescents. In a nationally representative study in 2001–2004, some 8.9 percent of 8–15-year-olds in the United States met the Diagnostic and Statistical Manual of Mental Disorders (DSM)-IV criteria for ADHD (Froehlich et al, 2007). By 2007, the rate had risen to 9.5 percent (Visser et al, 2010). A more recent study, however, reported a nationwide prevalence of 5.7 percent (Gupta-Singh et al, 2017). In the United Kingdom, analysis of a primary care database indicated that the administrative prevalence of ADHD in 6–17-year-olds had risen from 0.19 percent in 1998 to 0.51 percent in 2009 (Holden et al, 2013). When families were surveyed to ask if they had *ever* received a diagnosis from any source, the rate was about 1.2 percent (Russell et al, 2014). This was in contrast to the reported 2.5 percent prevalence in 8–12-year-olds in a representative population survey in 1999 (Ford et al, 2003). The rise may be attributed to National Institute for Health and Care Excellence (NICE) guidance, public awareness and continuing professional education (Taylor, 2017).

Another increasingly common neurodevelopmental disorder is autism or autism spectrum disorders (ASD). For 2010, the overall prevalence of ASD in the United States among 8-year-olds was estimated to be 14.7 per 1,000 (one in 68). Approximately one in 42 boys and one in 189 girls were identified as having ASD. Non-Hispanic white children were approximately 30 percent more likely to be identified with ASD than non-Hispanic black children and were almost 50 percent more likely to be identified with ASD than Hispanic children (CDC, 2014). Approximately 1 percent of schoolchildren in the United Kingdom are estimated to have ASD (Baron-Cohen et al, 2009). The total costs per year for children with ASD in the United States were estimated to be between $11.5 billion and $60.9 billion (2011 US dollars) (Buescher et al, 2014). This significant economic burden represents a variety of direct and indirect costs, from medical care to special education to lost parental productivity (Lavelle et al, 2014).

Posttraumatic stress disorder (PTSD) is another mental health problem which can develop after experiencing or witnessing a very stressful, frightening or distressing event, or after a prolonged traumatic experience, or otherwise feeling seriously threatened (Pynoos et al, 2009). The reported overall lifetime prevalence of PTSD in the general youth population of the United States is 3–9 percent and varies by gender with approximately 4 percent of male adolescents and 7 percent of female adolescents meeting full diagnostic criteria for PTSD (Breslau et al, 1991; Copeland et al, 2010). The one-month post trauma incidence of PTSD is 15.9 percent (Alisic et al, 2014). In clinical pediatric samples, symptoms of traumatic stress have been found in approximately 90 percent of sexually abused children, 75 percent of children exposed to school violence, 50 percent of children who are physically abused, and in 35 percent of children exposed to community violence (Schneider et al, 2013). Between 60 percent and 90 percent of children presenting for outpatient mental health treatment may have been exposed to at least one traumatic stressor (Schneider et al, 2013).

Certain segments of the population of children and adolescents in the United States and worldwide are at particular risk for mental and behavioral health problems such as those outlined above. It has long been recognized that many psychiatric disorders tend to run in families, suggesting potential genetic roots. Such disorders include ASD, ADHD, bipolar disorder, major depression and schizophrenia, which have been found to be associated with specific single-nucleotide polymorphisms (Cross-Disorder Group of the Psychiatric Genomics Consortium, 2013).

Genetic factors alone, however, do not account for all child and adolescent mental health problems; rather, it is the interaction between genes and environmental factors that account for the majority of these problems. "There is growing appreciation that epigenetic modifications to genes that regulate the stress response are a likely mechanism by which the early environment has a long-lasting impact on stress biology" (Tyrka et al, 2016, p. 1319).

In general, childhood adversities, including interpersonal loss (parental death, parental divorce, and other separation from parents or caregivers), parental maladjustment (mental illness, substance abuse, criminality, and violence), maltreatment (physical abuse, sexual abuse, and neglect), and life-threatening childhood physical illness and extreme childhood family economic adversity are associated with 44.6 percent of all childhood-onset disorders and with 25.9–32.0 percent of later-onset disorders (Green et al, 2010; Kessler et al, 2010).

Exposure to childhood maltreatment has been consistently shown to increase the lifetime risk for many psychiatric disorders, including mood (Kendler et al, 2004; Widom et al, 2007) and anxiety disorders (Phillips et al, 2005), and has also been recognized as an independent risk factor for suicidal behavior (Hoertel et al, 2015; Peyre et al, 2017). In 2015, approximately 3.4 million children in the United States were the subjects of at least one report of abuse or neglect, 12.5 percent were the subject of two reports, and 3.6 percent were the subject of three or more reports (Children's Bureau, 2017). In 2015, there were approximately 683,000 victims of child abuse and neglect. Children in their first year of life had the highest rate of victimization at 24.2 per 1,000 children of the same age in the national population. The majority of victims were white (43.2%), Hispanic (23.6%), or African American (21.4%). As in prior years, the greatest percentages of children suffered from neglect (75.3%) and physical abuse (17.2%).

Poverty is another form of childhood adversity associated with an increased risk for mental and behavioral health disorders. Children under 18 years of age are disproportionately affected by poverty, making up 33 percent of all people in poverty in the United States (Hodgkinson et al, 2017). Living in a poor or low-income household or neighborhood has been linked to poor health and increased risk for mental health problems in both children and adults that can persist across the life span (Yoshikawa et al, 2012; Evans, 2016; Hodgkinson et al, 2017). Twenty-one percent of low-income 6–17-year-olds have mental health disorders (Howell, 2004). Fifty-seven percent of these low-income children and youth come from households with incomes at or below the federal poverty level (Howell, 2004). Children from families living in poverty are three times more likely, on average, to suffer from psychiatric conditions, including both externalizing disorders such as ADHD, oppositional defiant disorder, and conduct disorder, and internalizing disorders such as depression, anxiety, and poor coping skills (Costello et al, 1996).

Racism and discrimination represent another form of childhood adversity from a mental health perspective. Youth of color experience disparities in prevalence and treatment for mental health problems. In the United States, 88 percent of Latino children and youth have unmet mental health needs, compared to 77 percent for African Americans and 76 percent for white children and youth (Kataoka et al, 2002). Twenty percent of female Latino high school students seriously considered attempting suicide and 15.4 percent made a suicide plan, compared to 16.1 percent of white female high school students who considered it and 12.3 percent who made a suicide plan (CDC, 2015a).

Another form of childhood adversity is delinquent behavior and involvement in criminal justice systems. Approximately 50–75 percent of the two million youth encountering the juvenile justice system in the United States meet criteria for a mental health disorder (Teplin et al, 2002; Gottsman and Schwarz, 2011). Approximately 40–80 percent of incarcerated juveniles have at least one diagnosable mental health disorder (Teplin et al, 2002; Wasserman et al, 2002). An additional 10 percent also meet criteria for a substance use disorder (Wasserman et al, 2002; Teplin et al, 2006). Approximately 15–30 percent have diagnoses of depression or dysthymia (Weiss and Garber, 2003), 13–30 percent have diagnoses of ADHD, 3–7 percent have diagnoses of bipolar disorder (Teplin et al, 2002), and 11–32 percent have diagnoses of PTSD (Abram et al, 2004).

Youth involved in the child welfare system are among those most likely to experience childhood adversity. At the present time, there are an estimated 415,000 children in the child welfare systems in the United States (Children's Bureau, 2017), and approximately six million children are referred to child welfare agencies annually (Horwitz et al, 2012). During 2014, approximately 702,000 children were confirmed to be victims of maltreatment (Children's Bureau, 2017). In the United Kingdom, there are currently 94,000 children in the child protection systems (Bentley et al, 2017). There were 621,470 referrals relating to 547,300 children in England alone for the year ending March 31, 2016. Studies conducted in the United States have reported that an estimated 50 percent of children and youth in the child welfare system have mental health disorders (Burns et al, 2004). A systematic review and meta-analysis of data from international studies conducted in the United States and Europe found a similar pooled estimate (49 percent), with the most common disorders being conduct disorder (20%; 95% CI = 13–27), anxiety disorders (18%; 95% CI = 12–24), oppositional defiant disorder (12%; 95% CI = 10–14), ADHD (11%; 95% CI = 6–15), depressive disorders (11%; 95% CI = 7–15), and PTSD (4%; 95% CI = 2–6) (Bronsard et al, 2016).

Estimates are even higher for youth who have been placed into foster care or residential treatment. A study by dosReis and colleagues (2001) found that 57 percent of youth placed in foster care have a mental disorder. A study of youth in residential youth care in Norway found that over 76 percent of adolescents received at least one three-month DSM-IV diagnosis (Josefiak et al, 2016). The risk for mental health problems, especially traumatic stress, is greatly increased for children who are living in foster care as a result of abuse and neglect.

Nevertheless, despite the high levels of mental and behavioral health problems of child welfare involved youth, not all receive services to address these needs. Burns and colleagues (2004) reported that less than half of youth involved in child welfare with mental health needs received services to address those needs. Horwitz and colleagues (2012) found that one third of a nationally representative cohort of youth who had been investigated for alleged maltreatment received some mental health services. Although foster care youth aged 17–18 years are two to four times more likely to experience lifetime and/or past year mental health disorders compared to transition-aged youth in the general population, mental health service use declines at ages when the prevalence of such disorders is peaking (Havlicek et al, 2013).

Untreated mental and behavioral health problems have important implications for later life as most adult mental disorders begin in childhood or adolescence. A study conducted by Kim-Cohen and colleagues (2003) found that among adult cases defined via the Diagnostic Interview Schedule, 73.9 percent had received a diagnosis before 18 years of age and 50.0 percent before 15 years of age. Among treatment-using cases, 76.5 percent received a diagnosis before 18 years of age and 57.5 percent before 15 years of age. Among cases receiving intensive mental health services, 77.9 percent received a diagnosis before 18 years of age and 60.3 percent before 15 years of age.

EBPs in child welfare and child mental health

There are numerous EBPs that have been developed to address the mental and behavioral health needs of youth in general and high-risk youth involved in child welfare in particular. Descriptions of these practices, summaries of the evidence supporting them, and independent evaluations of the evidence can be found on a number of websites. Two of the best-known sources of information on EBPs for child welfare and child mental health are the National Registry of Effective Programs, hosted by the Substance Abuse and Mental Health Services Administration (SAMHSA) of the United States Department of Health and Human Services (SAMHSA, 2016) and the California Evidence-Based Clearinghouse for Child Welfare (CEBC, n.d.) hosted by the California Department of Social Services (CDSS) Office of Child Abuse Prevention and Rady Children's Hospital, San Diego. Each website describes guidelines for determining whether or not a practice is evidence based. For example, the CEBC website defines practices as being evidence based if they meet the criteria outlined in Box 2.1. In contrast, practices described as promising have the criteria listed in Box 2.2:

Box 2.1: Criteria for practices well-supported by research evidence

1. Multiple site replication and follow-up:
   a. At least two rigorous RCTs [randomised controlled trial] in different usual care or practice settings have found the practice to be superior to an appropriate comparison practice.
   b. In at least one of these RCTs, the practice has been shown to have a sustained effect at least one year beyond the end of treatment, when compared to a control group.
2. The RCTs have been reported in published, peer-reviewed literature.
3. Outcome measures must be reliable and valid, and administered consistently and accurately across all subjects.
4. If multiple outcome studies have been published, the overall weight of the evidence supports the benefit of the practice.
5. There is no case data suggesting a risk of harm that: a) was probably caused by the treatment and b) the harm was severe or frequent.
6. There is no legal or empirical basis suggesting that compared to its likely benefits, the practice constitutes a risk of harm to those receiving it.

7. The practice has a book, manual, and/or other available writings that specify components of the service and describe how to administer it.
    Source: CEBC, 2018

Box 2.2: Criteria for practices supported by promising research evidence

1. At least one study utilizing some form of control (for example, untreated group, placebo group, matched wait list study) has established the practice's benefit over the control, or found it to be comparable to a practice rated a 1, 2, or 3 on this rating scale or superior to an appropriate comparison practice. The study has been reported in published, peer-reviewed literature.
2. Outcome measures must be reliable and valid, and administered consistently and accurately across all subjects.
3. If multiple outcome studies have been conducted, the overall weight of evidence supports the benefit of the practice.
4. There is no case data suggesting a risk of harm that: a) was probably caused by the treatment and b) the harm was severe or frequent.
5. There is no legal or empirical basis suggesting that compared to its likely benefits, the practice constitutes a risk of harm to those receiving it.
6. The practice has a book, manual, and/or other available writings that specify the components of the practice protocol and describe how to administer it.
    Source: CEBC, 2018

Despite the wide use of registries such as the NREPP and the CEBC are widely used by child welfare and child mental health systems leaders in identifying and selecting potential EBPs for use with their clients. For instance, as stated by one such leader:

> So, if I'm looking at something, let's say at a particular population, I go to SAMHSA's website and they have all the disorders and all the practices that are evidence-based, and you can look up the practices or you can look up the disorder, attention-deficit disorder or whatever. You can go find out what are the practices that have been 'normed',

that have been tested on different populations and what populations have then tested out on and what the results have been, and then they rate them and they rate the practices. (Child welfare services director)

They are not without their limitations, however. For instance, systematic reviews that are considered by many to be the best source of evidence (Shadish et al, 2002) are not included in the criteria for evaluation of a specific program or practice. In a review of 113 newly previewed programs added to the NREPP website, 16 (14%) were supported by a non-peer-reviewed report that was either unpublished or available online (Gorman, 2017). An additional 51 (45%) of programs were supported by evidence contained in a single journal article and 27 (24%) of programs were supported by evidence contained in two journal articles. Further, 87 (78%) involved some form of conflict of interest on the part of the investigators reporting the evidence. In 2018, the Substance Abuse and Mental Health Services Administration (SAMHSA) decided to no longer support the NREPP. As explained by Assistant Secretary McCance-Katz (SAMHSA, 2018):

> We at SAMHSA should not be encouraging providers to use NREPP to obtain EBPs, given the flawed nature of this system. From my limited review – I have not looked at every listed program or practice – I see EBPs that are entirely irrelevant to some disorders, 'evidence' based on review of as few as a single publication that might be quite old and, too often, evidence review from someone's dissertation. This is a poor approach to the determination of EBPs. As I mentioned, NREPP has mainly reviewed submissions from 'developers' in the field. By definition, these are not EBPs because they are limited to the work of a single person or group. This is a biased, self-selected series of interventions further hampered by a poor search-term system.

In child welfare and child mental health, EBPs can be classified into prevention programs and treatment interventions. Examples of each of these two forms of EBPs are provided below.

Prevention EBPs

The **Good Behavior Game (GBG)** is an environmental intervention used in the classroom with young children to create a learning-conducive environment. The intervention is designed to reduce off-task behavior, increase attentiveness, and decrease aggressive, disruptive, shy, and withdrawn behavior. The intervention also aims to improve academic success and reduce mental health and substance use problems later in life. GBG includes a set of evidence-based strategies and a classroom game intended to increase self-regulation and cooperation and decrease unwanted behaviors. Children are rewarded for displaying appropriate on-task behaviors during instructional times. The class is divided into two to five teacher-selected teams and a point is given to a team for any inappropriate behavior displayed by one of its members. The team with the fewest number of points at the game's conclusion each day wins a group reward. If both teams keep their points below a preset level, then both teams share in the reward (Intervention Central, 2017). A booklet for parents and children explains the game and provides guidance on how parents can use elements of the game at home.

Several studies conducted since 1969 have demonstrated the effectiveness of the GBG in increasing the rate of on-task behaviors while reducing classroom disruptions (Harris and Sherman, 1973; Medland and Stachnik, 1972). Several studies have also found the Good Behavior Game to be cost effective in preventing drug and alcohol abuse and dependence disorders (Kellam et al, 2008), criminal behaviors and antisocial personality disorder (Petras et al, 2008), suicide ideation and behavior (Wilcox et al, 2008), and HIV risk behavior (Poduska et al, 2009; Kellam et al, 2014).

The Incredible Years® is a set of three training programs for children and their parents and teachers. These programs are guided by developmental theory on the role of multiple interacting risk and protective factors in the development of conduct problems. The three programs are designed to work jointly to promote emotional and social competence and to prevent, reduce, and treat behavioral and emotional problems in young children. The parent, teacher, and child programs can be used separately or in combination. There are treatment versions of the parent and child program as well as prevention versions for high-risk populations.

Short-term goals of The Incredible Years® include improved parent–child interactions, building positive relationships and attachment, improved parental functioning, less harsh and more nurturing parenting, and increased parental social support and problem solving; improved teacher–student relationships, proactive classroom management skills, and strengthened teacher–parent partnerships; prevention, reduction, and treatment of early onset conduct behaviors and emotional problems; and promotion of child social competence, emotional regulation, positive attributions, academic readiness, and problem solving. Long-term goals include the prevention of conduct disorders, academic underachievement, delinquency, violence, and drug abuse.

The positive effects on The Incredible Years® intervention have been repeatedly demonstrated in numerous studies. For instance, child training (CT) alone, the CT + teacher training (TT), and the CT + TT + parent training (PT) conditions, relative to controls was associated with a reduction in conduct problems at school and at home with mother (Webster-Stratton et al, 2004). Children had lower mother-rated internalizing and depressed mood symptoms than a control group at posttest (Webster-Stratton and Herman, 2008). Independent replications of the parent program in the United Kingdom and throughout Europe found significant improvement in treatment children as compared to control children for antisocial behavior, hyperactive behavior, conduct problems, externalizing behavior, and social skills, as well as significant reductions in negative parenting practices and increases in perceptions of self-efficacy among treatment caregivers as compared to control caregivers (Hutchings et al, 2007; Gardner et al, 2006; Little et al, 2012). RCTs found significant positive program effects on both mother and father parenting behaviors when the child training component was included with the parent intervention, significant reductions in children's problem behaviors, less mother-reported aggression and parent stress, and significant improvements in observer-reported child total deviant behaviors, children's emotional vocabulary and problem-solving abilities, and teacher-reported externalizing behavior in preschool children with ADHD (Webster-Stratton et al, 2004; Webster-Stratton et al, 2011). An RCT assessing the additive benefit of teacher training (Parent + Teacher) showed fewer child conduct problems at school and at home with both mothers and fathers, a decrease in mother and father negative parenting and increase in mother positive parenting, and a reduction in negative feelings among teachers (Webster-Stratton et al, 2004). A meta-analysis found a significant average effect size across 50 studies for reductions in child disruptive behavior and increases in child prosocial behavior (Menting et al, 2013).

The Incredible Years® was selected as a model 'Strengthening Families' program by the Center for Substance Abuse Prevention (CSAP), as an 'exemplary' program by the Office of Juvenile Justice Delinquency Prevention (OJJDP), and as a 'Blueprints' program by OJJDP. The Incredible Years® program series have also been recommended by the Home Office in the United Kingdom as one of the evidence-based interventions for antisocial behavior and by Sure Start as a recommended program for families with children under five years (Incredible Years, 2017).

Treatment EBPs

Trauma-Focused Cognitive Behavioral Therapy (TF-CBT) is a psychosocial intervention designed to treat posttraumatic stress and related emotional and behavioral problems in children and adolescents aged 3–18 years. Initially developed to address problems associated with childhood sexual abuse, TF-CBT has been modified and tested with children who have experienced a wide array of traumas, including domestic violence, traumatic loss, war, commercial sexual exploitation, and the often multiple and complex traumas experienced by children who are placed in foster care (Cohen et al, 2006).

The intervention integrates cognitive, behavioral, interpersonal, and family therapy principles as well as trauma interventions. It is designed for use by trained and certified TF-CBT therapists. Initially, therapists provide parallel individual sessions with children and their parents or primary caregivers; joint parent–child sessions then become increasingly incorporated over the course of treatment. Each TF-CBT session is aimed at building the therapeutic relationship while also providing education and skills development in a safe environment, in which the child is able to address and process traumatic memories. Joint parent–child sessions are aimed at helping parents and children practice the skills learned during therapy and enabling the children to share their stories of trauma, while also nurturing more effective parent–child communication about the abuse and related issues.

Several RCTs have been conducted in the United States, Europe, and Africa, comparing TF-CBT to other active treatment conditions. All of these studies have demonstrated TF-CBT to be superior in reducing child traumatic symptoms and negative responses (Cohen et al, 2004; Smith et al, 2007; Cohen et al, 2011; Diehl et al, 2015; Murray et al, 2015). A recent RCT found youth receiving TF-CBT maintained their symptom improvement at 18 months' follow-up with scores below clinical cut-off on all symptom measures. The most depressed youth had also a significant decline in symptoms that were maintained at follow-up. Symptom trajectories differed as the TF-CBT group reported a more rapid symptom reduction compared to the treatment as usual condition (Jensen et al, 2017).

Treatment Foster Care Oregon (TFCO), previously known as Multidimensional Treatment Foster Care, is a model of foster care treatment for 12–18-year-olds with severe emotional and behavioral disorders and/or severe delinquency. TFCO was developed as an alternative to group home treatment or state training facilities for youth who have been removed from their homes due to conduct and delinquency problems, substance use, and/or involvement with the juvenile justice system. As noted by the county mental health services director quoted at the beginning of this chapter, such placements typically cost the county a lot of money and increase the likelihood that these youth will end up in other systems. Youth are typically referred to TFCO after previous family preservation efforts or other out-of-home placements have failed. Referrals primarily come from juvenile courts and probation, mental health, and child welfare agencies. TFCO aims to help youth live successfully in their communities while also preparing their biological parents (or adoptive parents or other aftercare family), relatives, and community-based agencies to provide effective parenting and support that will facilitate a positive reunification with the family (Chamberlain and Reid, 1998).

TFCO is based on social learning theory and is characterized by four key elements: 1) providing youth with a consistent reinforcing environment where he or she is mentored and encouraged to develop academic and positive living skills; 2) providing daily structure with clear expectations and limits, with well-specified consequences delivered in a teaching-oriented manner; 3) providing close supervision of youth's whereabouts; and 4) helping youth to avoid deviant peer associations while providing them with the support and assistance needed to establish prosocial peer relationships. The goals of TFCO include eliminating or reducing youth problem behaviors, increasing developmentally appropriate normative behavior in youth, transitioning youth to a birth family or lower level aftercare resource, improving youth peer associations, improving parent–child interaction and communication, improving youth coping and social skills, and improving behavior in school and providing academic support. TFCO also has versions for preschoolers and children.

TFCO typically lasts 6 to 9 months and relies on coordinated, multimethod interventions conducted in the TFCO foster home, with the youth and their biological or aftercare family. Youth are individually placed with highly trained and supervised foster parents and are provided with intensive support and treatment in a setting that closely mirrors normative life. Progress is tracked through daily telephone calls with the foster parents. A program supervisor with a caseload of 10 or fewer youth oversees and coordinates the interventions and supervises and supports the foster parents throughout treatment through the daily telephone calls and weekly foster parent group meetings. The supervisor also coordinates the work of family and individual therapists (for therapy conducted with the youth and his or her parents), skills trainers, and a foster parent liaison/trainer.

Several studies conducted in the United States, England, Norway and Sweden have demonstrated the effectiveness of TFCO relative to other forms of group care or services as usual. In one of the first evaluations, 20 boys were randomly assigned to receive either TFCO or to community-based group care. Boys assigned to TFCO ran away less frequently, completed their programs more often, and were referred to detention or training schools less frequently. They also had fewer criminal referrals and had fewer self-reported delinquent acts, and violent or serious crimes. Finally, they spent more days living with their families in follow-up (Chamberlain and Reid, 1998). In another study, 153 12–17-year-old girls and boys were randomly assigned to the TFCO condition or to a group care condition. TFCO youth had fewer associations with delinquent peers than did those in the group condition (Leve and Chamberlain, 2005). A third study randomly assigned 81 girls to the TFCO condition or to a group care control condition. The one-year effects for TFCO were maintained at two years on all measures. Older girls showed less delinquency over time for both the TFCO and group care conditions (Chamberlain et al, 2007). A more recent study examined 12-month outcomes for girls enrolled in an implementation trial of TFCO in England compared with girls enrolled in a RCT of TFCO in the United States. The England TFCO sample included 58 12–16-year-old girls in foster care. The United States TFCO intervention sample included 81 13–17-year-old girls who were referred to out-of-home care due to chronic delinquency. Results indicated a reduction in offending, violent and risky sexual behavior, self-harm, and improvement in school activities for girls enrolled in the England implementation trial with effect sizes similar to those obtained in the United States RCT (Rhoades et al, 2013).

Underutilization of EBPs

Despite the numerous EBPs for screening, preventing and treating behavioral and mental health problems, it is estimated that only 20 percent of youth receive the services they need (Kataoka et al, 2002). Youth of color and youth living in poverty with mental and behavioral health problems are even less likely to receive services (Kataoka et al, 2002; Hodgkinson et al, 2017). Moreover, many of the services they do receive lack an evidence base to support their effectiveness. EBPs have not been incorporated into most everyday clinical practice (Strupp and Anderson, 1997; Bickman et al, 2000; Weisz et al 2004; Chorpita et al, 2002).

In publicly-funded child welfare, mental health and juvenile justice systems of care, it is estimated that 90 percent do not use EBPs (Hoagwood and Olin, 2002). Only half of all children in child welfare receive care consistent with any one national standard and less than 10 percent receive care consistent with all 10 national standards (Raghavan et al, 2010). Using a nationally representative sample of child welfare systems in the United States, Horwitz and colleagues (2014) found that almost all agencies (94%) had started a new program or practice but only 24.8 percent of these programs were evidence-based.

Summary

- One fourth of youth in general experience a mental disorder during the past year, and about one third across their lifetimes.
- The most common mental and behavioral health problems experienced by these youth are anxiety disorders, followed by behavior disorders such as ADHD, depressive disorders, and substance use disorders.
- Childhood adversities such as interpersonal loss, maltreatment, poverty, racism and discrimination, and juvenile justice involvement account for slightly less than half of all child-onset disorders.
- An estimated 50 percent of children and youth involved in child welfare systems have mental health disorders.
- Less than half of these youth receive services to prevent and treat these disorders.
- Fewer than 20 percent of these youth receive services that are evidence-based.
- There are numerous EBPs for the prevention and treatment of youth mental and behavioral health problems.
- These EBPs are being underutilized in systems of care that deliver services to youth in need.

3

Understanding and reducing the gap

So, the key to these systems is not the clinical work, necessarily, it is the implementation process to make sure, first of all, that they are correctly diagnosed, and second of all, that the model is correctly implemented and people are well trained and they do it correctly, not doing part of it. Do part of it and you can't measure it, and you don't know why they got better. And so that is why I think we implement these models, when we're doing it correctly, I see people get really excited and they get really good at doing it, and they start understanding why it has to be done correctly and people start getting better, and it's an amazing thing to watch because you're doing a particular model and the kid actually gets better, when you're a probation officer or a social worker and you've done it for thirty years and you've never seen anybody get better because of something somebody did, it's an amazing thing to watch. (Mental health services director)

As noted in the last chapter, despite the existence of numerous EBPs for prevention and treatment of mental and behavioral health problems in youth, fewer than one in five youth in need of such EBPs actually receive them. Given that one in every three to five youth are in need of such services at some point in their lives, the disconnect between supply of EBPs and demand for them is concerning. Identifying the barriers to successful EBP implementation and sustainment and application of evidence-based strategies to overcome these barriers are the aims of implementation science.

In this chapter, we examine common barriers to EBP implementation found in most systems of care that help to explain why EBP implementation has enjoyed limited success in child welfare and child mental health to date. We then introduce the four pillars underlying implementation science; 1) theories, models and frameworks that identify and explain the associations between potential predictors and outcomes of implementation efforts; 2) discrete and multifaceted strategies for achieving positive implementation outcomes; 3) measures for assessing implementation process and outcomes; and 4) innovative methods for implementation science such as mixed methods, hybrid and alternative experimental designs, and systems science methods.

Barriers to successful implementation

The limited use of EBPs by children and adolescents for prevention and treatment of mental and behavioral health problems can be attributed to several factors. Melnyk and colleagues (2015), for instance, cite the shame and fear that deter those in need of services from seeking help; inadequate screening by primary care providers, due to a lack of timely access to mental health services for their patients; trouble finding treatment, due to the severe shortage of mental health providers across the country; an overreliance on medications rather than other evidence-based treatments, such as cognitive-behavioral or interpersonal psychotherapy; and the slow implementation of research findings, often taking many years between the publishing of research findings and their implementation in real world settings.

In any system of care, the adoption, implementation and sustainment of evidence-based and innovative practices is often confronted by numerous obstacles and challenges. Perhaps the most often cited barrier is the limited availability of time and resources for practitioners to learn about such practices. Acquiring expertise in such practices often requires time spent at training workshops. Inevitably, this means less time spent seeing clients and generating revenues for the organization, unless the practitioner is willing to assume a personal cost by participating in training on his or her own time (Palinkas et al, 2017a). Even then, training is often inadequate if not accompanied by ongoing supervision by someone with expertise in the practice or participation in one or more booster sessions. Practitioners perceive themselves to be inadequately prepared to implement a new program or practice.

A second barrier is the lack of time and resources available to utilize such practices. Manualized evidence-based treatments for mental health problems like depression or anxiety requiring 12 sessions of therapy may be impractical when insurance will only pay for four weeks or when the clinician is confronted with other unanticipated client issues during the time available for treatment (Palinkas et al, 2008; Weisz et al, 2012).

Lack of access to information about innovative EBPs is another obstacle to successful implementation. As we will see later, in Chapter Six, practitioners often access a variety of sources in striving to learn about new treatments and interventions. Unfortunately, the primary mode of dissemination of the details about these treatments and interventions for researchers is the peer-reviewed research journal. Practitioners, on the other hand, rarely have access to research journals and rarely use them even when they do have access (Lavis et al, 2006).

Another barrier to successful implementation is the lack of feedback and incentives for use of EBPs. Even when a decision is made to adopt an evidence-based or innovative practice as the standard of care, organizations rarely offer clinicians incentives to obtain training in the practice or to use the practice with fidelity (Armstrong et al, 2016; Palinkas et al, 2017a). How well a therapist uses a particular practice is rarely a feature of clinical supervision or performance evaluation (Glasgow et al, 2003).

The logic and assumptions behind the design of efficacy and effectiveness research trials is another important barrier to successful implementation. In an effort to insure rigor and the internal validity of research, interventions are tested in artificially controlled conditions that do not mirror real world practice (Glasgow et al, 2003; Brown et al, 2017). Study participants are subjected to inclusion and exclusion criteria to maximize effect sizes on the one hand and, on the other hand, to rule out confounding influences that might constitute alternate explanations for outcomes having little to do with the intervention itself. EBP protocols are typically designed for single or homogeneous clusters of disorders, developed and tested with recruited youth who differ from patients seen in everyday clinical practice, and involve a pre-determined sequence of prescribed session contents, limiting their flexibility (Westen et al, 2004; Weisz and Gray, 2008). For many of the psychosocial interventions used to address child and adolescent mental and behavioral health problems, context, adaptability, and external validity become as important as experimental control, fidelity of implementation, and internal validity (Green et al, 2009).

Strict inclusion and exclusion criteria also have the disadvantage of generating an evidence base from clients who bear little resemblance to the kinds of clients that practitioners see in the real world. For instance, clients rarely present with only one specified mental or behavioral health problem that can be effectively addressed with only one EBP (Chorpita et al, 2005). Clients frequently present with a multitude of problems and are not always readily available for treatment, thus complicating the use of a particular protocol for treatment. Practices must be adapted to meet the needs of clients who reflect a different age, gender, or race/ethnicity from those who provided the evidence supporting the effectiveness of the intervention. Such adaptation is perceived to be necessary to insure the intervention is age, gender or culturally appropriate.

Another barrier to implementation is the concern of practitioners over a perceived lack of control and disruption of therapeutic process. Therapists are often presumed to resent EBPs because they tend to overemphasize a positivistic view of treatment as a science and underemphasize a humanistic, constructivist view of treatment as an art (Palinkas et al, 2008; Palinkas et al, 2013a). Rather than facilitate a therapeutic alliance between practitioners and clients, EBPs are perceived to act as barriers to such an alliance.

Finally, the infrastructure and systems organization to support implementation is often inadequate. This may include a lack of available funding for EBP training or program administration, lack of qualified staff, the absence of a mandate requiring the implementation of a specific EBP, the absence of leadership support for implementation, limited access to information about the EBP, and lack of fit between the EBP and the organization implementing it (Greenhalgh et al, 2004; Fixsen et al, 2005; Damschroder et al, 2009; Aarons et al, 2011).

Pillars of implementation science

The goal of implementation science is to overcome these barriers. To accomplish this goal, it relies on four pillars or sets of tools: theories, models and frameworks; strategies; measures of implementation process and outcomes; and innovative methods. Each of these is examined below.

Theories, models and frameworks

The first pillar of implementation science is the generation and application of theories, models and conceptual frameworks that identify potential barriers, facilitators, the process, and outcomes of program, practice, and policy implementation. Although these are often used interchangeably in implementation research, there are important distinctions between theories, models and frameworks. The distinctions are highlighted in Box 3.1.

Box 3.1: Distinction between theories, models and frameworks

Theory: a set of analytical principles, statements or principles designed to structure our observation, understanding and explanation of the world. It helps us understand why something happens the way it does. Most accepted theories have been repeatedly tested by experiments and can be used to make predictions about natural phenomena.

Models: theories with a more narrowly defined scope of explanation. A model is descriptive, whereas a theory is explanatory as well as descriptive. Models offer a systematic description of an object or phenomenon and a simplified version of a concept, phenomenon, relationship, structure, system, or an aspect of the real world.

Frameworks: a structure, overview, outline, system or plan consisting of various descriptive categories, for example, concepts, constructs or variables, and the relations between them that are presumed to account for a phenomenon. Frameworks offer a structure for supporting or enclosing something else, especially a skeletal support used as the basis for something being constructed. They constitute a set of ideas or facts that provide support for something. Frameworks do not provide explanations; they only describe empirical phenomena by fitting them into a set of categories.

Source: Adapted from Nilsen (2015)

Theories

Perhaps the best-known theory used in implementation science is that of the diffusion of innovations. Conceived by the sociologist Everett Rogers, the theory identifies five factors that have an impact on the pace and rate of adoption of innovations, outlined in Box 3.2.

Box 3.2: Factors influencing diffusion of innovation

- *Relative advantage*: the individual's need to understand whether or not an innovation brings about any advantages and betterment compared to the current means of action;
- *Compatibility*: the consistency between the innovation and the context of the existing needs, values, and experiences of the adopters;
- *Complexity*: the extent to which an innovation is perceived as difficult to understand and use;
- *Trialability*: the chance to try the innovation on a limited and temporary basis rather than on full scale;
- *Observability*: the degree to which an innovation is visible to others. *Source*: Adapted from Rogers (2003, pp. 15–16)

Rogers gave a broad definition of diffusion as the communication of an innovation through different channels over time to individuals of a specific social system. Using data from the study of adoption of hybrid seed corn by Iowa farmers conducted by Ryan and Gross (1943), Rogers created the S-curve model to describe the formation of successful innovation adaptations. The S-curve suggests a normal distribution of innovation diffusion with few 'early adopters' at the beginning of the diffusion process (approximately 13.5%), followed by individuals who adopt the innovation rapidly (34%) or slowly (34%). The curve tails off with a group of 'laggards' (approximately 16%) who gradually utilize the innovation (Rogers, 2003, p. 281).

Besides the key elements of the *innovation* as described above, the classical diffusion model includes the following components. The *adopter* is the individual who adopts an innovation. The adopter's degree of innovativeness is the attribute that has an impact on the process of adoption. A higher degree of innovativeness is expected to contribute to the early adoption of the innovation. Diffusion takes place in a *social system*. Factors embedded in this system include the presence and engagement of local opinion builders, the preparedness of leaders to encourage and support adoption, and the adopter's perception of the push for adoption. The necessary stages of the *individual adoption process* include awareness of an innovation, understanding its value and merit, motivation and decision to adopt the innovation, implementation of the innovation, and finally, securing sustainability of the adoption. A target-oriented diffusion system includes trained change promoters who approach and work with opinion leaders within a social system (Rogers, 2003).

Another widely used theory in implementation science is social learning theory. Developed by Albert Bandura (1986), this theory has been used to explain the role of other providers or organizations in introducing innovative practices to others. Learning is a cognitive process that takes place in a social context and can occur by observing the behavior of others and its consequences (vicarious reinforcement). In this observation, the learner assumes an active role, extracting information and making decisions about the performance of the behavior (observational learning or modeling). Change in behavior and cognition is based on the observation of the behavior of an individual or organization considered successful (the ideal type) or most like the observer (the recognizable or similar type). In this theory, cognition, environment, and behavior all mutually influence each other (reciprocal determinism).

A third theory that has gained prominence in the field of implementation science in recent years is normalization process theory (NPT). NPT Seeks to explain what people do when implementing a new intervention (May and Finch, 2009). It is based on four specific constructs, highlighted in Box 3.3.

Box 3.3: Implementation tasks specified by NPT

1. Coherence or making sense of the intervention, its meaning and use;
2. Cognitive participation or the relational aspects between those implementing the intervention, how they initiate involvement and engage with the intervention;
3. Reflective monitoring of how, individually and collectively, the process of considering and adapting the intervention is conducted;
4. Collective action or the operational work done to implement the intervention.
   Source: Adapted from May and Finch (2009)

Models

Nilsen (2015) distinguishes between two types of implementation models. Process models specify steps (stages, phases) in the process of translating research into practice, including the implementation and use of research. The aim of process models is to describe and/or guide the process of translating research into practice. An action model is a type of process model that provides practical guidance in the planning and execution of implementation endeavours and/or implementation strategies to facilitate implementation.

An example of a process model is the one developed by Grol and Wensing (2004). This model proceeds in ten stages grouped into five categories: 1) *Orientation* includes promoting awareness of innovation and stimulating interest and involvement; 2) *Insight* includes creating understanding and developing insight into one's own routines; 3) *Acceptance* includes developing a positive attitude toward change and creating positive intentions/decision to change; 4) *Change* includes trying out change in practice and confirming the value of change; and 5) *Maintenance* includes integrating the new practice into routines and embedding the new practice in an organization.

A second model used in implementation is the Ottawa Model of Research Use (OMRU) (Logan and Graham, 1998; Graham and Logan, 2004). The OMRU is an example of a group of knowledge translation (KT) models that focuses on research evidence, but has been adapted to incorporate the process of implementing research evidence or EBPs. OMRU also has been described as an interactive planned-action theory and a framework for assessing barriers and facilitators to implementation (Driedger et al, 2010). The model consists of six key elements: the practice environment, potential adopters of the evidence, the evidence-based innovation, research transfer strategies, the evidence adoption, and health-related and other outcomes. The decision to use the innovation may be influenced by how practitioners and policymakers perceive the attributes or characteristics of the EBP. The environment also contains structural and social influences that may foster or impede the uptake of an innovation. According to Driedger and colleagues (2010, pp. 2–3), "the strength of OMRU is its prescriptive feature—assessing, monitoring, and evaluating—throughout the process to ensure that interventions are appropriately tailored to meet the needs of potential users."

OMRU follows a six-step approach to guide the implementation of an innovation (Graham and Logan, 2004), highlighted in Box 3.4.

Box 3.4: Steps to implementation as described by OMRU

1. *Setting the stage*: includes identifying individuals with the authority needed to make changes within organizations, determining available resources that can be used for innovation implementation, and identifying agents of change responsible for implementing the innovation.
2. *Specifying the innovation*: includes clearly articulating what the innovation is and what implementation will involve.
3. *Assessment of the innovation, potential adopters and the environment for implementation barriers and facilitators*: includes conducting a situational assessment and identifying ways to overcome any barriers to implementation, perceptions and attitudes of potential adopters toward the innovation, and gaps between current practice and recommended changes.
4. *Selection and monitoring the knowledge translation strategies*: involves selecting appropriate strategies and interventions to increase awareness of the innovation and understanding of the innovation, and providing skills or training for adopters to be able to carry out the innovation and evaluating the knowledge translation strategies for effectiveness.
5. *Monitoring the adoption of the innovation*: includes determining the extent to which the innovation has spread throughout the organization and how practice has changed and assessing if the knowledge translation strategies applied have been sufficient for effective innovation adoption, or if the knowledge translation strategies need to be changed or additional strategies are required.
6. *Evaluating the outcomes of the innovation*: involves an evaluation of the impact of the innovation on clients/patients, practitioners and systems to determine the effectiveness of the innovation.
    Source: Adapted from NCCMT (2010)

Frameworks

Three of the most commonly used frameworks for understanding implementation in child welfare and child mental health include the National Implementation Research Network (NIRN) implementation framework (Fixsen et al, 2005), the Consolidated Framework for Implementation Research (CFIR) (Damschroder et al, 2009); and the Exploration, Preparation, Implementation, and Sustainment (EPIS) framework (Aarons et al, 2011). These frameworks have been employed in understanding barriers and facilitators to EBP implementation in child welfare and child mental health (Agency for Healthcare Research and Quality, 2014; Bryson et al, 2014; Clara et al, 2017).

The NIRN implementation framework outlines a developmental process that is distinguished by the operation of drivers that move the process along in four stages: exploration, installation, initial implementation, and full implementation. The *exploration* stage is devoted to assessing the feasibility and acceptability of implementing an EBP. This includes an assessment of the elements outlined in Box 3.5:

Box 3.5: Assessment of implementation feasibility and acceptability

- The *needs* of the children and students are considered. How well might the program or practice meet identified needs?
- The *fit* with current initiatives, priorities, structures and supports is looked at, as well as parent/community values.
- *Resource availability* asks what the funding requirements are. Is funding available to implement and sustain the program or practice as intended?
- *Evidence* indicating the outcomes that might be expected if the program or practices are implemented well is required.
- *Readiness for replication* asks to what degree the program or practice is 'education ready'. Has it been successfully implemented in typical educational settings? What assistance will be available for implementation?
- *Capacity to implement* asks about the ability to implement the program or practice as intended and to sustain and improve implementation over time.

Source: NIRN, n.d.

During the *installation* stage, organizations select or hire staff, identify sources for training and coaching, provide initial training for staff, find or establish performance assessment (fidelity) tools, locate office space, assure access to materials and equipment, and other resources that need to be in place before the work can be done effectively (Fixsen et al, 2005). *Initial implementation* is the time when the innovation is being used for the first time. *Full implementation* is reached when 50% or more of the intended practitioners, staff, or team members are using an effective innovation with fidelity and good outcomes. The stages are not conceptualized as not always being linear in character, but more often than not are messy, overlapping, and iterative (Fixsen et al, 2005).

Implementation drivers are considered to be the engine of implementation (Fixsen et al, 2005). Fixsen and colleagues identified three categories of drivers: competency, organization, and leadership supports. Competency drivers include strategies and activities for staff selection, training and coaching. Organizational drivers include conducting a systems intervention, creating a facilitative administration, and developing a decision support data system. Leadership drivers include strategies designed to develop technical and adaptive leadership skills.

The NIRN framework was used by New York City's Administration for Children's Services (ACS), in partnership with and support from Casey Family Programs, to incorporate a range of EBPs into its continuum of preventive family support services. In 2015, ACS provided almost 5,000 families with 11 evidence-based and evidence-informed preventive models of practice, ranging from families with children at low risk of entering foster care to those with very high levels of need (Clara et al, 2017).

The Consolidated Framework for Implementation Research (CFIR) (Damschroder et al, 2009) offers an overarching typology for implementation research and comprises five major domains: the *intervention*, the *outer* and *inner setting* in which it is implemented, the *individuals* involved in implementation, and the *process* by which implementation is accomplished. An illustration of this framework and the components of each domain is provided in Figure 3.1.

Characteristics of the intervention or EBP include where the idea for the EBP came from, the strength and quality of evidence supporting the approach, the relative advantage of implementing the intervention or EBP versus an alternative solution, the ability to adapt the EBP to meet one's own needs, the ability to test an innovative EBP on a small scale and reverse the course of it if warranted, the perceived difficulty of implementing the intervention or EBP, the perceived excellence in how the EBP is bundled, presented and assembled, and the costs associated with implementing the EBP.

Characteristics of the outer setting include the needs and resources of the population being served, the degree to which an organization is networked with other organizations, the pressure exerted by other organizations that are already implementing the EBP or plan to do so, and external policies and incentives that motivate organizations to implement the EBP.

Figure 3.1: Consolidated framework for implementation research domains

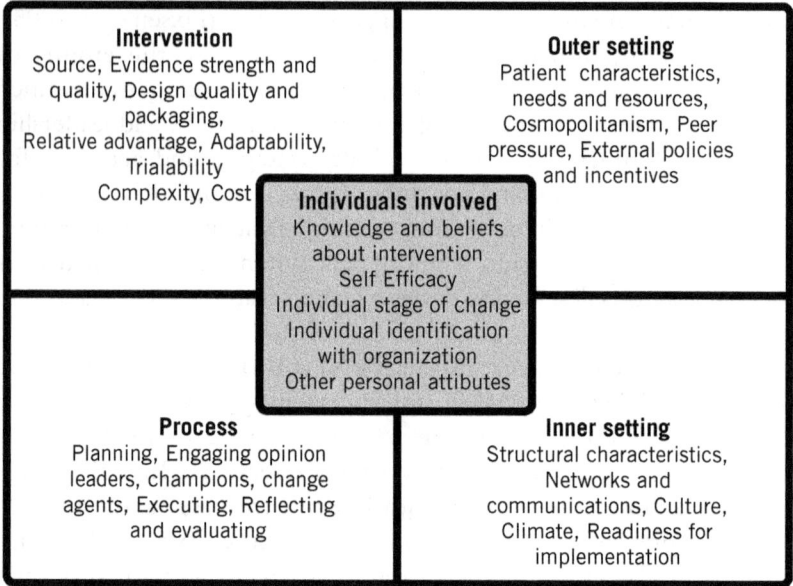

Intervention Source, Evidence strength and quality, Design Quality and packaging, Relative advantage, Adaptability, Trialability Complexity, Cost	**Outer setting** Patient characteristics, needs and resources, Cosmopolitanism, Peer pressure, External policies and incentives
Process Planning, Engaging opinion leaders, champions, change agents, Executing, Reflecting and evaluating	**Inner setting** Structural characteristics, Networks and communications, Culture, Climate, Readiness for implementation

Individuals involved
Knowledge and beliefs about intervention
Self Efficacy
Individual stage of change
Individual identification with organization
Other personal attibutes

Characteristics of the inner setting include structural characteristics (age, maturity, size, social architecture) of organizations responsible for implementing an EBP, the nature and quality of networks and communications between these organizations, the norms, values and guiding principles of these organizations, the capacity for change and shared receptivity of involved individuals to the EBP, the degree to which the current situation is perceived as intolerable or needing change, the degree of tangible fit between meaning and values attached to the EBP by involved individuals, how well they align on values, how they fit with existing workflows and systems, the shared perception of the importance of the EBP within the participating organizations, the organizational incentives and rewards for implementing the EBP, the goals and feedback, learning climate, and readiness for implementation (for example, the engagement of leaders in implementing and sustaining the EBP, the available resources dedicated for implementing and sustaining the EBP, and access to knowledge and information about the EBP).

Characteristics of individuals include knowledge and beliefs about the intervention/EBP, self-efficacy, individual stage of change, and individual identification with the organization.

Characteristics of the process of implementation include the degree to which tasks for implementing and sustaining are developed in advance and the quality of those plans; engaging opinion leaders, formally appointing internal implementation leaders, EBP champions and external change agents in the process of implementing and sustaining the EBP; carrying out or accomplishing the EBP according to plan; and reflecting and evaluating on progress made towards implementation.

The CFIR domains were applied in a systematic review examining dissemination and implementation strategies to improve child and adolescent mental health care with the purpose of identifying potential moderators of strategy effectiveness (Hanson et al, 2016). Specifically, this research aimed to identify the client and contextual variables (for example, characteristics of the child, provider, organization, and EBP) that have an impact on the effectiveness of implementing mental health services for children and adolescents.

A third implementation framework that has gained prominence in recent years is the Exploration, Preparation, Implementation and Sustainment (EPIS) framework developed by Gregory Aarons and colleagues (2011). The EPIS framework also comprises a series of factors believed to be associated with successful implementation, based on the authors' experience and expertise in implementation of EBPs in child welfare and child mental health. Many of the factors are similar to those found in other frameworks and models, specifically an inner context and outer context. Linking the two contexts are the fit between the innovation and the system (outer context) and the innovation and the organization (inner context), characteristics of the innovation, interconnections among collaborating organizations, and the innovation developers. Like the NIRN framework, EPIS describes implementation as a process occurring in stages. Further, while the stages progress in linear fashion, the authors consider the likelihood that experience at a particular stage may necessitate movement back to an earlier stage. However, the importance or weight given to each of the characteristics of the inner and outer contexts may differ, based on the stage in question. The framework also highlights sustainment as the ultimate stage of this process.

An illustration of the use of the EPIS framework in child mental health is provided by a case study conducted by Beidas and colleagues (2016) of the creation and evaluation of a trauma-informed publicly funded behavioral health system for children and adolescents in the City of Philadelphia (the Philadelphia Alliance for Child Trauma Services [PACTS]). Implementation determinants included inner context factors, specifically therapist knowledge and attitudes towards EBPs. Implementation outcomes included the rate of PTSD diagnoses in agencies over time, the number of youth receiving TF–CBT over time, and penetration (that is, the number of youth receiving TF-CBT divided by the number of youth screening positive on trauma screening).

Although theories models and frameworks have been widely used to better understand the challenges or barriers to success of implementation of EBPs, they are not without their limitations. For instance, Nilsen (2015, p. 9) observes:

> Most determinant frameworks provide limited 'how to' support for carrying out implementation endeavours since the determinants may be too generic to provide sufficient detail for guiding users through an implementation process. While the relevance of addressing barriers and enablers to translating research into practice is mentioned in many process models, these models do not identify or systematically structure specific determinants associated with implementation success.

Furthermore, many of the models and frameworks used in implementation science have never been tested or validated due to a lack of available measures to assess their constructs (Tabak et al, 2012). Empirical research is required to confirm the validity of these models and frameworks and assist in their selection for use in specific implementation efforts (Tabak et al, 2018).

Implementation strategies

The second pillar of implementation science is the development and application of several strategies for facilitating the implementation of EBPs. Implementation strategies are methods or techniques used to enhance the adoption, implementation, and sustainabilty of a clinical program, policy or practice (Proctor et al, 2013). Their focus may include the systems environment, organization, group, supervision, or individual providers and/or consumers.

There are three types of strategies: discrete strategies, which are single actions (for example, educational workshops or reminders); multifaceted strategies, which combine two or more discrete actions (for example, training + audit and feedback), and blended strategies, which incorporate multiple strategies that combine two or more discrete actions packaged as a protocolized or branded implementation strategy. Powell and colleagues (2012) identified 71 discrete strategies that were placed into six categories. These strategies are described in Box 3.6.

Box 3.6: Discrete strategies for implementing EBPs

- *Plan* strategies can help stakeholders gather data, select strategies, build buy-in, initiate leadership, and develop the relationships necessary for successful implementation.
- *Educate* strategies can be used to inform a range of stakeholders about the innovation and/or implementation effort.
- *Finance* strategies can be leveraged to incentivize the use of clinical innovations and provide resources for training and ongoing support.
- *Restructure* strategies can facilitate implementation by altering staffing, professional roles, physical structures, equipment, and data systems.
- *Quality management* strategies can be adopted to put data systems and support networks in place to continually evaluate and enhance quality of care, and ensure that clinical innovations are delivered with fidelity.
- *Policy context* strategies can encourage the promotion of clinical innovations through accrediting bodies, licensing boards, and legal systems.

Source: Adapted from Powell et al (2012)

Multifaceted strategies reflect a combination of two or more discrete implementation strategies. The most common form of multifaceted implementation strategy is training plus technical assistance. One example of such a strategy is a study of the effectiveness of intensity of counselor training on student behavioral outcomes (Lochman et al, 2009). In this study, counselors in 57 schools were randomly assigned to one of three conditions: Coping Power (the EBP)-training plus feedback (CP-TF), Coping Power-basic training (CP-BT), or a comparison condition. CP-TF counselors who received the more intensive training and supervision produced significant reductions in children's externalising behavior problems and improvements in children's social and academic skills in comparison to results for target children in both the comparison and the CP-BT conditions.

Another example of a multifaceted strategy is cascading diffusion, designed to gradually reduce the direct role of EBP developers in the training and supervision of front-line providers. A train-the-trainer model (Tobias et al, 2012) is used to build local capacity by training a cohort of local practitioners in the use of an EBP by the intervention developers. Training includes weekly supervision of cohort members and review of audio or videotapes of practitioner performance. The cohort then trains a second cohort and provides weekly supervision and performance/fidelity evaluation. The strategy was employed by Chamberlain and colleagues in the implementation of Keeping Foster Parents Trained and Supported (KEEP), a support and skill-building program for child welfare foster and kinship parents that focuses on preventing placement disruptions and increasing family reunification for children placed in child welfare systems (Chamberlain et al, 2008a), in the child welfare system of San Diego County, California (Chamberlain et al, 2012). An evaluation of the effectiveness of the KEEP intervention showed no decrement in effectiveness of Cohort 2 when developers pulled back and Cohort 1 assumed responsibility for training and supervision (Price et al, 2010).

Blended strategies are similar to multifaceted strategies in that they involve the use of two or more discrete strategies. However, as noted earlier, such strategies differ from multifaceted strategies in that two or more discrete strategies are packaged as a protocolized or branded implementation strategy. One example of a blended strategy used in child welfare and mental health is the Availability, Responsiveness, Continuity (ARC) model, a community- and organization- oriented model that emphasizes the role of the social context in EBP implementation (Glisson, 2002; Glisson and Schoenwald, 2005; Glisson et al, 2006; Glisson and Green, 2006). The core purpose of the model is delivering an EBP effectively and with high quality to clients in a specific social and organizational environment. The model is based on three fundamental assumptions: 1) the implementation of an EBP is as much a social process as it is professional and technical; 2) social and mental health services are delivered in a complex context of organizations and social institutions including service providers, services organizations, family, and community; and 3) effectiveness of service delivery is a function of how well the EBP is mediated by the social environment in which it is delivered.

Typically, this model builds an implementation strategy by studying, understanding, and operationalising organizational and inter-organizational factors in each given implementation context. Drawing on empirical research on how organizations work, it is assumed that meeting the needs of service providers must be a collaborative endeavor which extends to the design of implementation strategies. The culture and climate of service provider organizations are important factors that have an impact on the organization's effectiveness and attitudes; thus, one way to improve performance is by organizational development. When multiple aspects of organizational factors are included in strategy development, organizational performance increases in implementation of EBPs. On an organizational level, the ARC model integrates characteristics of the organizational setting with the EBP.

Glisson and colleagues (2010) conducted an RCT of the use of the ARC strategy to facilitate the implementation of multisystemic therapy (MST) in reducing problem behavior in delinquent youth residing in 14 rural counties in Tennessee, using a 2 x 2 design in which youth were randomized into receiving MST or treatment as usual and counties were randomized into receiving the ARC intervention. A multilevel mixed effects regression analysis of six-month treatment outcomes found that total youth problem behavior in the MST plus ARC condition was at a nonclinical level and significantly lower than in other conditions.

Another commonly used blended implementation strategy is the learning collaborative (LC). A form of quality improvement collaborative (QIC) used in healthcare (Nadeem et al, 2013), this strategy has been widely used to facilitate dissemination and implementation of EBPs and to improve quality of care. One of the best-known illustrations of the learning collaborative approach to implementation is the Institute for Healthcare Improvement's Breakthrough Series Collaborative (IHI, 2003; Ayers et al, 2005; Ebert et al, 2011). The quality improvement (QI) processes of these collaboratives are rooted in industrial process improvement strategies such as the use of ongoing data collection and analysis to identify problems in service delivery and the promotion of continuous learning and improvement (Deming, 1986; Juran, 1964). In a typical LC, individual sites organize staff into multi-disciplinary teams that participate in a series of in-person, phone, distance learning, and independent activities that are led by LC faculty who serve as content and QI experts (Nadeem et al, 2016).

LCs have several core processes reflected in many implementation theories, models and frameworks that are designed to facilitate practitioner and organizational change needed for EBP implementation (for example, Aarons et al, 2011; Damschroder et al, 2009). At the practitioner level, the LC structure provides sites with access to experts in the field, often including treatment developers and QI experts. Participants learn to apply QI methods, such as the plan–do–study–act improvement cycle (Deming, 1986), for the purpose of identifying and addressing implementation barriers and incorporating implementation facilitators. LC teams use these methods to refine new practices within the local setting, identify implementation barriers, field test solutions to identified challenges, and share experiences across sites (Pinto et al, 2011).

> LCs have potential to strengthen social networks and inter-organizational learning (Palinkas et al, 2011a; Nembhard, 2012; Bunger et al, 2016); leverage the influence of key opinion leaders towards improving the implementation climate for innovative practices (Wilson et al, 2004), and foster a public and tangible commitment from leadership (Wilson et al, 2004). (Nadeem et al, 2016, p. 979)

The National Child Traumatic Stress Network has relied on LC to implement evidence-based trauma treatments like TF-CBT described in Chapter Two.

Another set of multifaceted implementation strategies are based on models of knowledge translation (KT), a dynamic and iterative process that includes the synthesis, dissemination, exchange, and ethically sound application of knowledge, and knowledge transfer and exchange (KTE), an interactive interchange of knowledge between research users and researcher producers (Keifer et al, 2005). For instance, knowledge mobilization (KMb) includes a range of activities that help move available knowledge (often from formal research) into active use. It involves efforts to bridge the gap between research, policy and practice in order to improve outcomes in various organizations or sectors. KMb involves knowledge sharing between research producers (for example, university researchers) and research users (including professionals or others whose work can benefit from research findings), often with the help of third parties or intermediaries (Research Impact, 2014). Strategies include relationship building among knowledge creators and users involving brokers (individuals or intermediary organizations that support knowledge brokering) and the co-production of knowledge (Nutley et al, 2007).

More recently, interventions have been developed to prepare leaders to support EBP implementation. One such example is the leadership and organizational change for implementation (LOCI) intervention (Aarons et al, 2017). This intervention is framed within the EPIS framework described earlier (Aarons et al, 2011). LOCI includes leadership training for workgroup leaders, ongoing implementation leadership coaching, 360° assessment, and strategic planning with top and middle management regarding how they can support workgroup leaders in developing a positive EBP implementation climate. LOCI takes an active approach to improving leadership and congruent organizational strategies that lead to improved transformational and transactional leadership, implementation leadership, and subsequent implementation and psychological safety climate. These, in turn, should lead to changes in provider attitudes toward EBP, implementation citizenship behaviors, and to better EBP fidelity and implementation process (Aarons et al, 2017).

Measures of implementation process and outcomes

The third pillar of implementation science is the assessment of the process and outcomes of implementation efforts. There have been several attempts to develop metrics for accessing implementation process and outcomes (Chamberlain et al, 2011; Weiner et al, 2017). One of the best known of these efforts is the Stages of Implementation Completion (SIC) scale. The SIC is an eight-stage assessment tool of implementation processes and milestones, with sub-activities within each stage (Chamberlain et al, 2011). The stages range from engagement with the developers to development of practitioner and organizational competency. The SIC spans three phases of implementation: pre-implementation (stages 1–3), implementation (stages 4–7), and sustainability (stage 8). As an observational measure, the SIC is flexible in assessing implementation activities conducted by a number of different individuals involved in the process, including the county system leaders involved in the decision of whether or not to adopt an EBP, agency leaders and practitioners, and clients receiving services. Implementation progress is assessed on the basis of furthest stage completed (that is, stage score), and the percentage of activities completed within a phase calculated (that is, proportion score). An earlier study (Saldana et al, 2012) found that SIC scores predicted variations in implementation behavior for sites attempting to adopt the TFCO model. Sites also were accurately identified (that is, face validity) through agglomerative hierarchical cluster analyses (Wang et al, 2010).

Proctor and colleagues (2011) identified a set of implementation outcomes (acceptability, adoption, appropriateness, costs, feasibility, fidelity, penetration, and sustainability) for conceptualizing and evaluating successful implementation. Distinguished from service and client outcomes, implementation outcomes have three important functions. "First, they serve as indicators of the implementation success. Second, they are proximal indicators of implementation processes. And third, they are key intermediate outcomes (Rosen and Proctor,

1981) in relation to service system or clinical outcomes in treatment effectiveness and quality of care research" (Proctor et al, 2011, p. 65).

The RE-AIM model, developed by Russell E. Glasgow and his colleagues (1999), is often used to monitor the success of intervention effectiveness, dissemination, and implementation in real-life settings. The acronym RE-AIM stands for Reach, Efficacy/Effectiveness, Adoption, Implementation, and Maintenance. A description of these outcomes is provided in Box 3.7. Originally, RE-AIM was developed out of the needs observed in healthcare delivery service organizations, but it has evolved as a model of translation and implementation of innovations in diverse settings of service delivery (Glasgow et al, 1999). Garmy and colleagues (2015) used RE-AIM to evaluate the implementation of a school-based, cognitive-behavioral program targeting the prevention of adolescent depressive symptoms.

Box 3.7: RE-AIM outcomes

- *Reach*: the absolute number, proportion, and representativeness of individuals who are willing to participate in an intervention. Reach also emphasizes availability of information on the characteristics of the setting (organization, agency, and culture) where the intervention is implemented, as well as the staff who deliver the intervention.
- *Efficacy/Effectiveness*: the intended and negative outcomes, as well as effects on quality of life and economic impact.
- *Adoption:* where and for whom this program works, and under what specific conditions, including characteristics of the intervention setting and the staff who deliver the intervention, the presence of specific mediators, and other contextual factors essential to understanding success.
- *Implementation:* the individual practitioner and organizational use of intervention strategies, as well as the intervention program fidelity, including the intervention protocol, delivery consistency across program components, staff, over time, duration, and costs.
- *Maintenance*: on the individual level, the long-term effectiveness of an intervention is usually measured six months or more after the most recent intervention input; on the organizational level, whether a successful intervention is institutionalized so as to become a routine practice.

Source: Adapted from Glasgow et al (1999)

Implementation methods

The fourth pillar or set of tools of implementation science is characterized by methodological innovation. One form of methodological innovation is the design and application of innovative designs that are alternatives to the traditional randomized controlled trial (RCT). Several authors (Palinkas and Soydan, 2012; Brown et al, 2017; Landsverk et al, 2018), have identified circumstances that may preclude the use of the RCT design, including the ethics of providing service to one group and denying the same service to another group of clients, the expense and logistics involved in conducting such research, and the unwillingness of participants or organizations to accept randomization. According to Glasgow and colleagues (2005), nonrandomized designs may be desired when external validity is very important and the intervention takes many forms and levels of quality, the diversity of the population requires multiple adaptations, or the intervention is part of a complex, multilevel approach requiring adaptations "In many clinical and community settings, and especially in studies with underserved populations and low resource settings, randomization may not be feasible or acceptable" (Glasgow et al, 2005, p. 554). In such circumstances, alternatives to the randomized design such as step-wedge, interrupted time series, multiple baseline across settings, or regression-discontinuity designs may be advisable.

Landsverk and colleagues (2011, p .60) recommended the use of designs that "mimic the element of choice by consumers and providers in community service settings targeted for implementation of evidence-based practices." They cite as examples a set of randomized designs that are considerably more complex than traditional RCTs but also more sensitive to issues of external validity. These include a randomized encouragement trial that randomizes consumers to encouragement strategies for the targeted treatment and facilitates their preferences and choices under naturalistic clinical practice settings (West et al, 2008); the Sequential Multiple Assignment Randomized Trial clinical trial design that experimentally examines strategy choices, accommodates patient and provider preferences for treatment while using adaptive randomization strategies, and allows multiple comparison options (Ten Have et al, 2003); and the randomized fractional factorial design, which screens more efficiently and tests multiple treatment components with less cost (Collins et al, 2005). A list of available designs for implementation research is provided in Box 3.8 below. Examples of such innovation in child welfare and child mental health include the use of an adaptive rollout randomized design in evaluating the effectiveness of community development teams, a form of learning collaborative (Brown et al, 2014).

Box 3.8: Research designs in implementation science

- Within-site designs
  - o Post design of an implementation strategy to adopt a novel clinical/ preventive intervention
  - o Pre-post design of an implementation strategy of an existing clinical/preventive intervention
- Between-site designs
  - o New implementation strategy versus usual practice implementation designs
    - − Cluster randomized designs
    - − Randomized encouragement implementation designs
  - o Head-to-head randomized implementation trial design
- Roll out randomized implementation trials
    - - Dynamic wait-list
    - - Stepped wedge
  - o Designs for a suite of evidence-based clinical/preventive interventions
  - o Factorial designs for implementation
    - − Multiphase optimization strategy (MOST)
    - − Sequential multiple assignment randomized implementation trial (SMART)
  - o Doubly randomized, two-level nested or split plot designs for testing two nested implementation factors
- Within and between site comparison designs
  - o Pairwise enrollment rollout design

Sources: Brown et al, 2017; Landsverk et al, 2018

Hybrid designs are intended to efficiently and simultaneously evaluate the effectiveness and implementation of the EBP. There are three types of hybrid design (Curran et al, 2012). Type I designs are primarily focused on evaluating the effectiveness of the EBP in a real-world setting; secondary priority is given to assessing the barriers and facilitators of implementing the EBP under evaluation. Type II designs give equal priority to an evaluation of EBP effectiveness and implementation. This may involve a more detailed examination of the process of implementation or the outcomes of using a specific strategy to facilitate implementation. Type III designs are primarily focused on the evaluation of an implementation strategy, but may also evaluate the effectiveness of the EBP as a secondary priority, especially when EBP outcomes may be somehow linked to implementation outcomes.

Another method commonly used in implementation research is the mixed method design. Mixed methods is a methodology that focuses on collecting, analysing, and mixing both quantitative and qualitative data in a single study or multi-phased study. Its central premise is that the use of quantitative and qualitative approaches in combination provides a better understanding of research problems than either approach alone (Creswell and Plano Clark, 2011). Mixed methods have come to play a critical role in implementation science. This role has emerged from both necessity and opportunity. Similar to the use of hybrid designs described earlier, mixed methods are often used to simultaneously answer confirmatory and exploratory research questions, and therefore verify and generate theory in the same study (Teddlie and Tashakkori, 2003). As implementation science is a relatively 'new' discipline, generating theory has been accorded the highest priority (Proctor et al, 2009). Some of the theories, frameworks and models that have been developed explicitly call for the use of both quantitative and qualitative methods due to the complexity of the subject matter, the importance of understanding both general principles and specific context, and the need to acquire depth as well as breadth of understanding of dissemination and implementation (D&I) (Demakis et al, 2000; Damschroder et al, 2009).

In implementation science, mixed methods are most commonly used to identify barriers and facilitators to successful implementation, but may also be used as a tool for developing strategies and conceptual models of implementation and sustainment, monitoring implementation process, and enhancing the likelihood of successful implementation and sustainment. Qualitative methods are generally used inductively to examine the context and process of implementation with depth of understanding, while quantitative methods are commonly used deductively to examine the content and outcomes of implementation with breadth of understanding (Palinkas et al, 2011b; Palinkas, 2014).

Examples of the use of mixed methods in understanding implementation of EBPs in child welfare and child mental health include analysis of qualitative data obtained from semi-structured interviews and a focus group with child welfare, mental health and juvenile justice systems leaders to inform the development of the quantitative Structured Interview for Evidence Use (SIEU) (Palinkas et al, 2016) and Cultural Exchange Inventory (CEI) (Palinkas et al,

2017b). Aarons and Palinkas (Aarons and Palinkas, 2007; Palinkas and Aarons, 2009), simultaneously collected qualitative data through annual interviews and focus groups and quantitative data through semi-annual web-based surveys to assess the process of implementation of SafeCare®, an in-home parent training program designed to prevent child maltreatment, increase positive parent–child interaction, improve how parents care for their children's health, and enhance home safety and parent supervision (Lutzker, 1990). Zazzali and colleagues (2008) connected qualitative data collected from semi-structured interviews with 15 program administrators to the development of a conceptual model of implementation of Functional Family Therapy (Alexander et al, 2013) that could then be tested using quantitative methods. Bachmann and colleagues (2009) merged qualitative data collected from semi-structured interviews with quantitative data collected from two surveys to describe and compare the experience of integrating children's services in 35 children's trusts in England.

Implementation research has also increasingly utilized methods associated with systems science (Brown et al, 2017). Social network analysis is one such method for understanding, monitoring, influencing or evaluating the implementation process when programs, policies, practices, or principles are scaled up or adapted to different settings (Valente et al, 2015). Social network analysis has been used to examine the influence of social networks to scale up the use of an EBP in public child service systems (Palinkas et al, 2011a; Palinkas et al, 2014), which is described in detail in Chapter Five. Davis and colleagues (2012) used social network analysis to measure change in child and adolescent and adult mental health service system integration over time.

Another systems science method increasingly being used in implementation science is agent-based modeling. Used to carry out simulations of different implementation strategies, this procedure focuses on interactions among diverse agents, captured in probabilistic rules that produce 'emergent behavior' (Epstein, 2007). System dynamics methods have been used to predict the behavior of complex systems based on stocks and flows, allowing complex system level behaviors to be modeled using differential equations. These methods have been applied to examine successful and unsuccessful implementation in diverse organizations (Brown et al, 2017).

Summary

- EBP implementation is often confronted by numerous challenges, including limited availability of time and resources to learn about and use them in routine practice, lack of access to information about EBPs, lack of feedback and incentives for their use, design of efficacy and effectiveness trials, lack of control and disruption of therapeutic process, and limited organizational capacity.
- Implementation science relies on four pillars or sets of tools to address these challenges: theories, models and frameworks; strategies; measures of implementation process and outcomes; and innovative methods.
- Identification of implementation barriers and facilitators and selection of appropriate strategies for implementation usually rely on a host of theories, models and frameworks, including the Diffusion of Innovation Theory (Rogers, 2003), models that describe the process of translating research into practice, and frameworks listing potential predictors of successful implementation.
- Implementation strategies are methods or techniques used to enhance the adoption, implementation, and sustainability of a clinical program, policy or practice.
- Implementation outcomes serve as indicators of implementation success, proximal indicators of implementation processes, and key intermediate outcomes in relation to service system or clinical outcomes in treatment effectiveness and quality of care research.
- Implementation research is commonly distinguished by their use of mixed qualitative and quantitative methods, focus on EBP effectiveness and implementation in hybrid designs, innovative experimental designs that deviate from the classical RCT, and methods grounded in systems science.

4

EBP implementation in child welfare and child mental health

> There is a type of foster care that would like to contract through our county, to open up in this county, and it's evidence-based practice that comes out of Oregon. And the Department of Children's Services likes it, but in talking with other providers and looking at their materials, their costs for training are extraordinary and their fidelity requirements are extraordinary, and consequently, even if I had a grant to pay for it, I'd be less likely to support it than some models. (Mental health services director)

As noted in the last chapter, there are numerous theories, models and frameworks used in implementation science to understand the features of an intervention, an organization and its external environment believed to be associated with implementation outcomes, and to identify strategies designed to facilitate successful implementation (Nilsen, 2015). With all of these theories, models and frameworks to guide the selection of strategies for implementation, why is there a need for yet another theory, model or framework? The answer to this question lies in the emphasis that this model places on the transactions that occur in both social relations and cultural systems and the roles they play in implementation.

In this chapter, we introduce four major studies where the four pillars of implementation science were applied to identify barriers and facilitators to EBP implementation, evaluate strategies designed to overcome barriers and maximize facilitators, and employ innovative methods for examining the process and outcomes of EBP implementation. The lessons learned from each of these studies serve to build upon existing implementation theories, models and frameworks to highlight the roles of social networks, use of research evidence (URE), local models of implementation and evidence, research–practice–policy partnerships (RPPP), and cultural exchanges among implementation stakeholders in implementation processes and outcomes.

The social context of EBP implementation

Social interactions among various stakeholders have been a prominent feature of existing implementation theories, models and frameworks. For instance, Rogers (2003) highlights the role of social networks and the importance of the social system in his diffusion of innovations theory. Greenhalgh and colleagues (2004) hypothesize that organizations that are well connected to other comparable organizations in networks are more susceptible to the network impact in terms of adopting innovations, and that the role of inter-organizational support becomes more important when the implementation of an innovation is more complex. The CFIR framework includes the nature and quality of networks and communications between organizations as a feature of the inner setting (Damschroder et al, 2009). The EPIS framework also considers the influence of social networks in linking features of the inner and outer settings (Aarons et al, 2011). The Availability, Responsiveness, Continuity (ARC) model emphasizes the role of the social context in the implementation of evidence-based interventions (Glisson and Schoenwald, 2005; Glisson et al, 2008a; 2008b), and is based on the assumption that the implementation of an EBP is as much a social process as it is professional and technical. Three of the ten specific strategies embedded in the ARC model focus specifically on social relations (Glisson, 2002) (Box 4.1):

Box 4.1: Social relational components of the ARC model

1. With the assistance of a change agent, *teams are built* to bring together community leaders and service providers who can approach issues together in order to ease the delivery of the evidence-based intervention.
2. A project change agent *develops a network* of service providers, organizational representatives, and community leaders to address concerns of the end users.

3. Change agents *develop personal relationships* with community leaders to promote communication, information sharing, and problem solving. *Source*: Adapted from Glisson (2002)

The model introduced in this book expands this emphasis by focusing on the influence of the transactions that occur in relationships between organizations and the relationships embedded in RPPP. While networks linking individuals are considered key to changes in individual behaviour, networks linking organizations represented by these individuals are as important if not more so in examining the adoption, implementation and sustainment of new EBPs. A key component of these networks are the relationships between treatment developers and academic researchers as well as practitioners and policymakers. These relationships are often formalized in partnerships, but partnerships are not created equally, nor do they evolve in the same way. Rather, they exist to satisfy what community activists refer to as "mutual self-interest" (Eichler, 2007). As self-interests may vary as a function of different partners, settings and activities, there may be more than one model of a successful research–practice–policy partnership.

Along with many other implementation theories, models and frameworks, the ARC model also acknowledges the role of organizational culture in implementation and sustainment (Glisson, 2002). Rogers (2003) used the term *compatibility* to refer to the consistency between the innovation and the context of the existing needs, values, and experiences of the adopters as one of five factors that affect the pace and rate of adoption of innovations. The CFIR framework identifies the norms, values and guiding principles of organizations as a component of the inner setting of implementation (Damschroder et al, 2009). Organizational culture can be defined as the implicit norms, values, shared behavioural expectations, and assumptions of a work unit that guide behaviours (Cooke and Rousseau, 1988). Organizational culture can affect how readily new EBPs will be considered and adopted in practice (Hemmelgarn et al, 2001; Simpson, 2002). In human services, organizational culture influences case manager attitudes, perceptions, and behaviours (Glisson and James, 2002). Aarons and Sawitzky (2006) found that a constructive organizational culture of programs providing mental health services for youth and families was associated with positive attitudes of providers toward adoption of EBPs. Manuel and colleagues (2009) found a lack of agency culture encouraging and supporting EBP implementation to be a significant barrier to implementing the Bringing Evidence to Social

Work Training (BEST) intervention. Glisson and colleagues (Glisson et al, 2008b) found organizational culture to be a significant independent predictor of new program sustainability. The model introduced in this book expands on this emphasis by focusing on culture as a system of shared understandings that constitute a model of as well as a model for two specific behaviours related to implementation, the URE and the integration of global and local models of implementation and evidence in the decisions exercised by organization leaders as to whether or not to adopt evidence-based and other innovative practices.

While many existing implementation theories, models and frameworks include a focus on cultural norms and values, the model introduced in this book is unique in several respects. First, it highlights two specific elements of organizational cultures engaged in implementation, the URE and the integration of global and local models of implementation and evidence when assessing the costs and benefits of EBPs and their implementation. Second, it places the social relations that are critical to the task of implementation within the context of shared understandings that constitute cultural systems. As described by one county mental health services director, "it takes relationships. I mean, you know, I think it is really years of forming relationships and having a philosophy that collaborative initiatives are important." These shared understandings constitute models of as well as models for implementation. Third, this model treats organizational cultures as more than influences on implementation success or failure, but as products of the implementation experience itself. By exchanging knowledge, attitudes and practices relating to implementation, various participants in the implementation process and the organizations they represent begin to experience a transformation in their own cultural systems.

Origins of a new model

The new model originated from research conducted in several studies of dissemination and implementation, but four in particular will be highlighted in this book.

The California–Ohio Study

The California–Ohio (CAL–OH) Study was a clinical trial of the effectiveness of implementation strategy, community development teams (CDTs) (Saldana and Chamberlain, 2012) to scale up Treatment Foster Care Oregon (TFCO) (Chamberlain et al, 2007), described earlier in Chapter Two, in public youth-serving systems (child welfare, child mental health, juvenile justice) in California and Ohio (Chamberlain et al, 2008b; Wang et al, 2010; Brown et al, 2014). Funded by the National Institute on Mental Health, the CAL–OH study targeted 40 California counties that had not already adopted TFCO. They were matched to form three nearly equivalent groups. The matched groups were then randomly assigned to three sequential cohorts in a wait-list design with staggered start-up timelines (at months 6, 18, or 30). Within each cohort, counties were randomly assigned to CDT or standard implementation conditions, thereby generating six replicate groups of counties, with three assigned to CDT. The trial was expanded to include 11 Ohio counties to the participating California counties from March 2009 through November 2010. Follow-up ran from approximately March 2007 to April 2012 in California, and from June 2009 to May 2012 in Ohio.

The CDT is a multifaceted intervention developed by the California Institute of Mental Health (CIMH), now called the California Institute for Behavioral Health Solutions, a statewide training and technical assistance center, dedicated to dissemination and implementation of EBPs for treatment of mental health problems (Saldana and Chamberlain, 2012). CIMH serves as an intermediary, an organization that translates and packages research for use by legislators, agency staff, and nonprofit and private service providers (Tseng, 2012). Along with other individuals and organizations who serve as intermediaries, CIMH also brokers relationships between researchers and practitioners/policymakers. Although it plays an important role in the dissemination of information on EBPs and programs, it actively engages with researchers, practitioners and policymakers to facilitate the implementation and scale-up of these practices and programs throughout California.

The CDT model consists of seven core processes (needs–benefits analysis, planning, monitoring and support, fidelity focus, technical investigation and problem solving, procedural skills development, and peer-to-peer exchange and support) that are designed to facilitate the successful adoption, implementation and sustainability of a new practice. These processes are accomplished through seven distinct activities: development team meetings, development team administrator conference calls, prompted listserv, site-specific correspondence and conference calls, fidelity and outcomes protocols and monitoring, CDT practice developer conference calls, and titrated technical assistance. CDTs utilize some of the same components as quality improvement collaborative (QIC) or learning collaborative (LC) models of implementation (Nadeem et al, 2013), particularly providing structured opportunities for collaboration and problem solving across sites.

Counties randomized to the individualized implementation (IND) strategy received the usual technical assistance and implementation support as is typically provided to teams who are adopting a new TFCO program. This included three readiness calls with a TFCO purveyor and a face-to-face stakeholder meeting where the county stakeholders meet to ask questions, work through implementation procedures, and develop a concrete plan for start-up. This was followed by a five-day all staff training for administrators, supervisors, therapists, and skills trainers, a two-day foster parent training, training in using the TFCO fidelity monitoring system, program start up (placement of youth in TFCO foster homes), and ongoing consultation and support in implementing the model through weekly viewing of video recordings of foster parent meetings and consultation calls to maintain fidelity to the model.

Counties randomized to the CDT condition received all of these activities as well as technical assistance from two CDT consultants who were trained and experienced in offering support for the implementation of the TFCO model. This support was offered in six peer-to-peer meetings and in monthly conference calls with program administrators. Meetings were attended by representatives from five to seven counties randomized to the CDT condition and were structured to help problem-solve and share information about implementation issues, including discussion of key barriers experienced by counties in California or Ohio that were unique to the state landscapes, and resource sharing. CDT facilitators either were the developers of the CDT model or trained by the CDT developers (Brown et al, 2014).

As part of the CAL–OH Study, two smaller studies funded by the William T. Grant Foundation examined the associations between individual and organizational social networks, URE, cultural exchanges among implementation participants, and implementation of TFCO. Using both quantitative and qualitative data, this study sought to understand the role that social networks play in EBP implementation. Our aims were to accomplish the following: 1) describe the structure and operation of information and advice networks of public youth-serving systems; 2) determine the influence of these networks in the implementation of TFCO; and 3) determine whether the CDT implementation strategy had any influence on the structure and operation of these networks (Palinkas et al, 2011a; Palinkas et al, 2013b).

To address the inconsistency of findings and lack of information related to the role of inter-organizational collaboration in EBP implementation, we examined the experiences of collaboration in EBP implementation of agency directors and senior administrators of county child welfare, mental health and juvenile justice agencies. Our objective was to identify the determinants and processes of successful collaborations. Specifically, we were interested in the following: 1) what factors led to the creation and sustainment of effective inter-organizational collaborations for the purpose of EBP implementation; 2) what factors contributed to unsuccessful collaborations or served as barriers to successful collaborations; and 3) how did such collaborations function to implement new EBPs (Palinkas et al, 2014).

Participants for the examination of social networks and inter-organizational collaborations were members of the agencies that comprised the first cohort of counties (n = 13) of the CAL–OH Study. Of the 45 administrators from all 13 counties invited to participate, 38 representing 12 counties agreed to do so, yielding a response rate of 84 percent. Each participant completed a semistructured interview conducted between July and September 2008, with the number of interviews per county ranging from two to six. Thirty of the 38 participants also completed a web-based survey asking them to provide general demographic information (that is, gender, age, and number of years in occupation, current position, and time with agency) and identify up to ten individuals on whom they relied on for advice about whether and how to use EBPs for meeting the mental health needs of youth served by their agency. Data on network ties from the web-based survey were supplemented by additional data provided in participants' qualitative interviews (Rice et al, 2014).

To determine whether a decision to adopt or not adopt, implement and sustain a particular EBP is based on the quality and quantity of evidence supporting its effectiveness, its relevance to the population served, from where and how the evidence was obtained, and how the evidence is used to make or support such a decision, we examined the URE among systems leaders participating in the CAL–OH Study. The study had two specific aims: 1) to determine whether URE was independently associated with stage of implementation and proportion of activities completed at the pre-implementation, implementation and sustainment phases; and 2) to determine whether URE was significantly associated with the CDT implementation strategy used to scale up the EBP (Palinkas et al, 2017c).

Participants of the URE study were 151 of the 221 (67.9 percent response rate) available child-serving system leaders, who were participating in the RCT at the time this study was conducted (2010–12). Participants had an average age of 49 years, and were predominately non-Hispanic white (84.4%), female (69.4%), and living in California (61.6%), with a Master's degree or higher (62.6%). A little over one-third of the participants (35%) were child welfare system directors; the remaining participants were leaders of mental health (24%), juvenile justice (18%), and other social services (23%).

URE was assessed using the Structured Interview of Evidence Use (SIEU), a 45-item instrument designed to measure the extent of engagement in the total URE (Total) and use in three subscales: acquisition of research evidence (Input), evaluation of that evidence for reliability, validity and relevance to one's own clients (Process), and application of that evidence in deciding whether or not to adopt an evidence-based or other innovative practice (Output) (Palinkas et al, 2016). Respondents indicate level of agreement with a series of statements using a Likert scale ranging from 1 (not at all) to 5 (all the time) for the 17 items contained in the Input subscale, and a similar five-point Likert scale ranging from 1 (not important) to 5 (very important) for the 16 items contained in the Process and the 12 items contained in the Output subscale. Palinkas and colleagues (2016) report high internal reliability of the total SIEU (Cronbach's $\alpha = 0.88$) and all three primary subscales (input = 0.80; process = 0.86; output = 0.80).

Finally, we examined the influence of three forms of cultural exchange that occur when EBP is implemented in service systems that rely on research evidence to make decisions whether or not and how to implement evidence-based programs, practices, and interventions: 1) exchange between treatment developers and providers; 2) exchange between providers and organizations representing different systems of care (for example, healthcare, schools, child welfare, juvenile justice agencies); and 3) exchanges between each of these stakeholders and intermediary organizations tasked with disseminating EBPs. Our aim was to determine whether these forms of cultural exchange were associated with stage of implementation and proportion of activities completed at the pre-implementation, implementation and sustainment phases, as well as engagement with the CDT implementation strategy (Palinkas et al, 2017b).

Participants in the cultural exchange study included 105 of the 221 (47.5% response rate) CAL–OH Study participants. The mean age was 48 years (range = 26–67) and the majority was female (68.9%) and Caucasian (80.6%). Most attained master's degrees or higher (62.2%), and most (69.3%) were agency directors. Participants were employed in the state of Ohio (56.1%) or California (43.9%), and worked either in child welfare (29.5%), mental health (19.0%), juvenile justice (12.4%), departments of health and/or social services (28.6%), or community-based organizations (10.5%).

The Cultural Exchange Inventory (CEI) (Palinkas et al, 2017b) was used to measure the extent of interactions between systems leaders, the TFCO treatment developer, and representatives of the two intermediary organizations and the impact of these interactions on knowledge, attitudes and practices. The CEI is a 15-item instrument, seven items assessing the interactions themselves (exchange process) and eight items assessing changes in knowledge, attitudes and behaviors resulting from the interactions (exchange outcomes). The CEI includes questions concerning the extent he/she has contributed to these activities and the extent to which his/her agency has changed as a result of the cultural exchanges. All items were measured on a seven-point scale ranging from 1 (not at all) to 7 (a great deal). Internal consistencies (Cronbach's alpha) for the total scale and the two subscales were high, ranging from 0.95 to 0.99 (Palinkas et al, 2017b).

In all three of these studies, the Stages of Implementation Completion (SIC) scale (Chamberlain et al, 2011), described in Chapter Three, was used to assess progress made in implementing TFCO. The network study used "furthest stage reached" as the primary outcome, while the URE and cultural exchange studies also used "proportion of activities completed" in the pre-implementation (Stages 1–3), implementation (Stages 4–7) and sustainment (Stage 8) phase.

IDEAS: the New York State model of innovation adoption

The Community Technical Assistance Center (CTAC) (www.ctacny. com) is a training, consultation, and educational center for clinical and business needs that strengthen practitioners' professional development and clinics' abilities to meet the financial and regulatory challenges of healthcare reforms. Funded by the New York State Office of Mental Health (OMH) in 2011, CTAC provides technical assistance to 346 outpatient mental health clinics that are licensed to serve children, adolescents, and their families in New York State. CTAC also offers statewide training and collects data on clinics' attendance of its offerings.

CTAC trainings are delivered in three ways—webinar, in-person training, and learning collaborative; these represent varying levels of training intensity and clinic commitment. The trainings were developed on the basis of OMH feedback and clinics' expressed needs. Hour-long webinars are the least intensive. In-person training requires full-day participation. Learning collaboratives are the most time intensive because they require ongoing participation in group learning sessions and consultations over a 6- to 18-month period. Participation in all CTAC offerings is voluntary.

To better understand the key factors involved in deciding whether or not to adopt an evidence-based or other innovative practice, a qualitative study was conducted by investigators who were affiliated with the Center for Implementation-Dissemination of Evidence-Based Practices among States, known as the IDEAS Center, an Advanced Center funded by the National Institute of Mental Health. The aim of the study was to construct an agency leadership model of implementation by exploring the following: 1) the most salient or important barriers and facilitators to innovation and adoption of EBPs for children and adolescents as determined by executive directors and program directors of mental health clinics in New York State; and 2) how these barriers and facilitators operate in the process of weighing the costs and benefits of implementation (Palinkas et al, 2017a).

The study included 75 agency CEOs, vice presidents and program directors representing a 10 percent random stratified sample of the 346 clinics (n = 34) licensed by the New York State Office of Mental Health (OMH) to treat youth in New York State. These 34 clinics were randomly selected based on their level of adoption of EBPs in New York State, as operationalized in Chor et al (2014). These levels were: Non-adopters, that is, clinics that did not participate in any CTAC training (n = 11); Low adopters, that is, clinics that participated in webinars only (n = 5); Medium adopters, that is, clinics that participated in an in-person training (n = 6); High adopters, that is, clinics that participated in one learning collaborative (n = 6); and Super adopters, that is, clinics that participated in two or more learning collaboratives (n = 6).

RPPP in child welfare and child mental health

From 2012 to 2014, the William T. Grant Foundation, in collaboration with the Forum for Youth Investment, convened a learning community aimed at strengthening research–practice partnerships in education. The learning community, which met twice annually for two years, involved partnerships of researchers and school district leaders from across the nation.

As part of this effort, the Foundation commissioned a group of scholars to prepare a position paper detailing research–practice partnerships in education (Coburn et al, 2013). Upon receipt of this report, the Foundation commissioned Palinkas and colleagues (2015) to prepare a similar position paper, but one focused on such partnerships in child welfare and child mental health.

We examined three different models for successful RPPP representing a continuum of approaches to the generation and dissemination of knowledge with policy and practice relevance. All three models involve some degree of research and some degree of technical assistance, some degree of knowledge generation and knowledge dissemination. Where they differ is in regards to the amount of attention given to either research or technical assistance and to either knowledge generation or dissemination. They also differ with respect to the research or policy/practice background of the partnership's leadership. Model 1 represents a long-term partnership between researchers affiliated with a nationally recognized research center and practitioners and policymakers affiliated with local youth-serving public service systems. Led by a prominent researcher, the primary function of this partnership is to conduct research and generate knowledge. Model 2 represents a short-term partnership between researchers with practice experience and policymakers and practitioners affiliated with one of the largest child welfare systems in the United States. Led by the service system leaders, the primary function of this partnership is to provide technical assistance and disseminate knowledge related to evidence-based interventions. Model 3 represents a combination of the first two models such that both research and technical assistance, knowledge generation and dissemination are undertaken in equal measure under the leadership of an individual with research, policy and practice experience who acts as a 'culture broker'. Each model is illustrated by a case study of a particular partnership dedicated to child welfare and child mental health. Information used to develop these case studies was based on individual semi-structured interviews with 12 'key informants' who assumed the role of researcher, practitioner, or policymaker in these partnerships. Interviews were recorded and transcribed for analysis. A 'template approach' (Crabtree and Miller, 1992) was used to identify 'common elements' of successful partnerships.

MacArthur Research Network Clinic Treatment Project

The Clinic Treatment Project (CTP) was carried out by the Research Network on Youth Mental Health, funded by the John D. and

Catherine T. MacArthur Foundation. The CTP focused on children aged 8–13 years who had been referred for treatment of problems involving disruptive conduct, depression, anxiety, or any combination of these. Ten clinical service organizations in Honolulu, Hawaii and Boston, Massachusetts, 84 therapists, and 174 youth participated in the project. Youth participants were treated with the usual treatment procedures in their settings or with three selected EBPs: cognitive-behavioral therapy (CBT) for anxiety (Kendall, 1990), CBT for depression (Weisz et al, 1997), and behavioral parent training (BPT) for conduct problems (Barkley, 1997). These evidence-based treatments were tested in two forms: standard manual treatment (standard), using full treatment manuals, in the manner they have been tested in previous research trials; and modular treatment (modular) in which therapists learn all the component practices of the evidence-based treatments but individualize the use of the components for each child, guided by a clinical algorithm (Chorpita et al, 2005) and measurement feedback on practices and clinical progress (Chorpita et al, 2008). Therapists in the modular condition used the Modular Approach to Therapy with Children with Anxiety, Depression, or Conduct Problems (MATCH) (Chorpita and Weisz, 2005), a collection of modules that correspond to treatment procedures included in the standard treatment manuals. MATCH prioritizes a focus on the initial problem area identified, using a default sequence of modules outlined in a protocol flowchart. If interference arises (for example, a comorbid condition or stressor impedes the use of the default sequence), the sequence is altered, with other modules used systematically to address the interference. For example, if treatment begins with a focus on depression, but disruptive behavior interferes, the therapist may use modules from the disruptive behavior section of the protocol to help parents manage that behavior, returning to depression treatment when the interference is resolved.

Therapists who consented to participate were randomly assigned to one of the three conditions: standard manualized treatment (SMT), modular manualized treatment (MMT), or usual care (UC). Therapists were assigned to condition using blocked randomization stratified by therapist educational level (doctoral versus masters). Youth who met study criteria were randomized to treatment delivered by one of these three groups of therapists (Weisz et al, 2012). Therapists randomized to standard or modular conditions were trained together in the specific treatment procedures, but were given different reference materials (that is, MATCH vs. the standard manual for that workshop), and were separated to talk specifically about issues unique to their study condition (for example, MATCH therapists would discuss common structured adaptations and use of the flowcharts, whereas the standard group would discuss strategies to maintain fidelity of the planned sequence of sessions in the face of challenges). Both groups of therapists then received weekly case consultation from project supervisors familiar with the protocols to assist the therapists in applying the treatment procedures in their study caseload. Usual care therapists received no instructions or feedback about their practice. UC sessions were audiotaped, and a coded sample of audiotapes revealed that only 8 percent of the content of the UC sessions involved procedures that were represented in either the MATCH or standard protocols (Weisz et al, 2012).

Mixed effects regression analyses showed significantly superior outcome trajectories for modular treatment relative to usual care on weekly measures of a standardized Brief Problem Checklist and a patient-generated Top Problems Assessment, and youth receiving modular treatment had significantly fewer diagnoses than usual care youth at post-treatment (Weisz et al, 2012). In contrast, none of these outcomes showed significant differences between standard treatment and usual care. Follow-up tests also showed significantly better outcomes for modular treatment than standard treatment on the weekly trajectory measures. In general, the modular approach outperformed usual care and the standard approach on the clinical outcome measures, and the standard approach did not outperform usual care. Additional details on the RCT protocol and study results are available in Weisz and colleagues (2012).

As part of the CTP, a qualitative study was conducted to identify factors that facilitated or hindered the successful implementation of the SMT and the MMT interventions. An ethnographic study focused on the interface between clinicians and clinical supervisors and the treatment and services delivered. It also focused on the interactions between clinicians and researchers (Palinkas et al, 2008). A follow-up study examined therapists' continued use of the evidence-based treatments with nonstudy clients upon conclusion of the clinical trial. Our aim was to examine therapists' reported patterns of use of these treatments for nonstudy clients, reasons for continued use, and reasons for treatment adaptation or modification (Palinkas et al, 2013a). A third study examined the dynamics of interactions and exchanges between EBP developers and trainers and organizations and providers that deliver the EBP. Our objective was to examine both the process and outcomes of these interactions with respect to EBP implementation and to identify requirements for interactions that facilitate the implementation of EBP (Palinkas et al, 2009).

Participants in this study were seven clinic directors, 47 therapists, four trainers and six supervisors involved in the implementation of SMT and MMT in Boston and Honolulu. Most of the clinicians (80%) had master's degrees; the remainder had doctorates in clinical psychology. Of the professional disciplines represented, most were trained in social work, followed by clinical psychology, mental health counseling, and marriage and family therapy.

Components of the new model

Research on these four projects, in addition to others that will be introduced over the course of this book, led to the identification of five major components of EBP that reflect the integration of social and cultural influences on EBP implementation and sustainment. These include the role of inter-organizational social networks and RPPP, URE, the integration of global and local models of implementation stakeholders, and the cultural exchanges that occur in RPPP. A summary of these research initiatives and their linkages to the model is provided in Table 4.1. Some of these components have links to existing theories—for example, social network theory is tied to both the diffusion of innovations and social learning theory, while shared understandings and cultural exchange have their origins in culture theory and transactional models of social change. The common thread to all five components is that they rely on the construction and maintenance of social relationships and shared understandings. They also involve a series of transactions of knowledge, attitudes and practices that lead to a transformation of the organizational cultures of stakeholders involved in implementation efforts.

Table 4.1: Major research initiatives informing the transactional model of implementation

Study	Title	Setting	Participants	EPIS implementation stage	Topic	Chapter
CAL–OH	The California–Ohio Study	California, Ohio	15 leaders of county-level child welfare, child mental health and juvenile justice systems	Exploration Preparation Implementation Sustainment	Social Networks Inter-organizational collaboration Use of research Evidence Cultural exchange	5 5 6 9
RPPP	Research–practice–policy partnerships in child welfare and child mental health	California, New York	12 researchers, practitioners and policymakers	Exploration Preparation Implementation	Research–practice–policy partnerships	8
IDEAS	New York State adoption study	New York	75 CEOs and directors of child mental health clinics	Exploration	Use of research evidence Local models of EBP implementation	6 7
CTP	MacArthur Research Network Clinical Treatment Project	Hawaii, Massachusetts	7 clinic directors, 47 therapists, 4 trainers and 6 supervisors	Implementation Sustainment	Cultural exchange	9

73

Summary

- Social interactions among various stakeholders are a prominent feature of existing implementation theories, models and frameworks, as well as implementation strategies like the Availability, Responsiveness and Continuity (ARC) model.
- The model introduced in this book expands this emphasis by focusing on the influence of the transactions that occur in relationships between organizations and the relationships embedded in RPPP.
- The model is based on findings obtained from studies of the use of community development teams for scaling up the implementation of an EBP for at risk youth in foster care placements in California and Ohio; adoption of innovative and evidence-based programs and practices in state-supported mental health clinics in New York State; successful RPPP in child welfare and child mental health; and a randomized clinical trial of standard versus modular manualized treatments for depression, anxiety, and conduct disorders in 8–13 year old clients of school-based and community mental health clinics in Boston and Honolulu.
- This model highlights the URE and the integration of global and local models of implementation and evidence when assessing the costs and benefits of EBPs and their implementation; places the social relations that are critical to the task of implementation within the context of shared understandings that constitute cultural systems; and treats organizational cultures as more than influences on implementation success or failure, but as products of the implementation experience itself.

5

Social networks and EBP implementation

I go monthly to the Children's System of Care meeting in Sacramento. And that's where other people in similar administrative positions to myself who are responsible for children's mental health services, we chew on these kinds of things. We discuss these kinds of things. And, you know, we have presentations, and so forth. So that is my peer group. And that, uhm, certainly provides a lot of information to me in making decisions. (Mental health services director)

In this chapter, we examine in detail the role of social networks in implementation process and outcomes. Beginning with a review of the importance of such networks in current implementation theories, models and frameworks, we focus on the Exploration, Preparation, Implementation and Sustainment (EPIS) framework developed by Aarons and colleagues (2011), and the Consolidated Framework for Implementation Research (CFIR) developed by Damschroder and colleagues (2009). The chapter then summarizes research on the influence of social networks and inter-organizational collaborations in implementing Treatment Foster Care Oregon (TFCO) (Chamberlain et al, 2007), an EBP designed to meet the behavioral health needs of youth in foster care, in California and Ohio. This research also demonstrates how community development teams, a continuous quality improvement strategy developed by the California Institute of Mental Health, can be used to build and sustain such networks.

Interpersonal contacts and implementation

Interpersonal contacts within and between organizations and communities are among the most important influences on the adoption of new behaviors. Interpersonal relations were given a prominent role in diffusion theory in explaining how new ideas and cultural practices expand within and between communities (Green et al, 2009). The importance of interpersonal contact and the social networks that provide such contacts in the diffusion of new ideas and practices has been repeatedly demonstrated by empirical research, including the pioneering study of Ryan and Gross (1943), which emphasized the importance of social factors in understanding farmers' adoption of new patterns of behavior. Rogers (2003) also emphasized the importance of social networks for both the diffusion and adoption of innovations. These contacts may influence the behavior of individual providers or the behavior of entire organizations.

Interpersonal contacts may occur through champions or opinion leaders. Champions within peer networks or organizations play an important role in managing organizational agenda setting, change, and evaluation of changes that occur in the process of implementing new programs and practices (Valente, 2010). Studies and meta-analyses have also shown that both the influence of trusted others in one's personal network and having access and exposure to external information are important influences on rates of adoption of innovative practices, including tobacco prevention programs, contraceptive use and family planning, HIV prevention, and clinical practice guidelines (Valente et al, 2003; Valente, 2006; Valente et al, 2007). Intervention effects may vary as a function of the recipients' social networks (Valente et al, 2007; Shin et al, 2014). For instance, children with friends who are physically inactive gain more from an obesity prevention program than those with physically active friends (Shin et al, 2014). Peer-led suicide prevention programs have differential effects based on the extent to which a youth is peripheral or isolated from her or his peer group (Wyman et al, 2010). Interventions implemented by community-identified leaders are more effective than those by non-leaders (Valente, 2010). Interventions delivered by people from the community of the beneficiaries of the program are more effective than when delivered by outside agencies that are less connected to the target population (Valente, 2012).

There are a number of social processes that are necessary in getting EBPs adopted, implemented, and sustained. Four that relate directly to social networks and program effects are: 1) partnerships between researchers, community, policymakers, and practitioners that support implementation; 2) intervention agents (that is, those who deliver the program); 3) implementation agents and intermediaries (that is, those who support the delivery of the program), and 4) organizations that influence the social context of how people receive the program (Valente et al, 2015).

Inter-organizational collaboration

One of the central features of social networks from the perspective of EBP implementation is the coordination and collaboration of network members. Numerous models and frameworks exist for understanding the complex array of factors responsible for successful implementation of EBPs in organizational settings (Greenhalgh et al, 2004; Aarons et al, 2011). Although inter-organizational networks are included in many of these models as part of the 'outer context' of implementation (Greenhalgh et al, 2004; Aarons et al, 2011), an understanding of the role of collaboration between organizations throughout the process of implementation has been somewhat limited. Furthermore, most EBP implementation studies that do focus on inter-organizational collaboration fail to consider the wider context within which collaboration occurs, including factors such as involvement of external stakeholders, socio-political processes, and the roles of relationships and leadership (Horwath and Morrison, 2007). Increasingly, this context is characterized by government mandates and fiscal realities that require collaboration in the form of integrative multidisciplinary practice in the delivery of children's services (Ehrle et al, 2004). In a sociopolitical climate in which organizations face increasing budget restrictions and are challenged to do more with less, collaboration across agencies and organizations appears to be a critical element to successful EBP implementation. In turn, an understanding of effective collaboration seems to be at the crux of many EBPs developed to improve outcomes in child-serving systems.

Collaboration can be viewed as involving several activities, including an exchange of information, sharing of resources, and enhancement of each other's capacity for mutual benefit and a common purpose by sharing risks, responsibilities and rewards (Himmelman, 2001). Collaboration is considered to be essential to the delivery of a complex array of health and social services (Jones et al, 2004). Several studies have pointed to improved access to services and improved outcomes associated with inter-organizational collaboration (Cottrell et al, 2000; Bai et al, 2009).

Factors that specifically have been found to contribute to successful interagency collaboration between child welfare and other agencies include shared goals, a high level of trust, mutual responsibility, open lines of communication, and strong leadership (Johnson et al, 2003; Weinberg et al, 2009). Barriers to building effective collaborations include deeply ingrained mistrust and continued lack of other systems' values, goals, and perspectives, different organizational priorities, confusion over how services should be funded and who has jurisdiction over youth, and difficulty in tracking cases across organizations (Green et al, 2008).

Social networks and inter-organizational collaboration in existing implementation frameworks.

Two of the more widely used frameworks in implementation research at present are the EPIS framework developed by Aarons and colleagues (2011) and the CFIR framework developed by Damschroder and colleagues (2009). Both frameworks highlight the important of individual and organizational networks as characteristics of the inner (that is, individual provider and organizational) and outer (that is, external environment) setting or context in which implementation occurs. The EPIS framework includes individual provider social networks as a characteristic of the inner context in the exploration stage, inter-organizational networks as part of the outer context in the preparation implementation stage, and social network support as an organization-level characteristic of the inner context in the sustainment stage. The CFIR includes the degree to which an organization is networked with other organizations as part of the outer setting of implementation and the nature and quality of networks and communications between these organizations responsible for implementing the program as part of the inner setting. However, neither the EPIS nor the CFIR frameworks provide any specifics on how organizations are linked to one another and how they collaborate to facilitate EBP implementation.

Strategies for building successful implementation networks and collaborations

Valente (2012) described four strategies that capitalize on network data to develop planned change programs such as implementation of EBPs: 1) identifying individuals (called nodes within the network) who are selected on the basis of some network property such as opinion leaders or bridging individuals; 2) segmentation, in which the intervention is directed toward groups of people; 3) induction, in which novel interactions between people (links to the network) are activated; and 4) alteration, interventions that change the network. One of the most frequently used network intervention tactics has been the recruitment and training of peer identified opinion leaders to implement behavior change programs (Valente and Pumpuang, 2007; Valente, 2012). Other strategies with a similar aim include the Institute for Healthcare Innovation's Breakthrough Series collaborative (IHI, 2003), the community development team (CDT) strategy (Saldana and Chamberlain, 2012) described in Chapter Four, and plan strategies that develop relationships, build a coalition, develop resource-sharing agreements, obtain formal commitments, and develop academic partnerships (Proctor et al, 2013). Valente and colleagues (2015) recommended that the following activities be conducted during the exploration stage of implementation (Box 5.1).

Box 5.1: Steps to identifying and developing an implementation network

- Determine if there is a network.
- Determine if there are individuals, groups, or organizations that are isolated or marginally connected to existing networks.
- Use the network information to identify individuals or groups that can and should be solicited to help identify community needs, barriers to change, and positive motivations for change.
- Determine if there are subgroups in the network that should become inter-connected or that need to be addressed separately.

Source: Adapted from Valente et al (2015)

Structure and function of influence networks

Analysis of interviews conducted with child welfare, child mental health and juvenile justice systems leaders participating in the CAL-OH study revealed that networks of information and advice are developed and maintained according to their position in an agency (for example, directors, program managers), responsibility (probation, mental health, child welfare), geography (within a county, neighboring counties), and friendship ties (co-workers, classmates). These networks expose leaders to information about EBPs and opportunities to adopt EBPs and influence decisions to adopt EBPs. This information comes from others within the same county, including supervisors or employees within the same agency, counterparts in other agencies, community-based providers, and community advocates.

Information on EBPs was available from network members within and outside of a system's leader administrative jurisdiction (that is, county). Within counties, participants said that they drew on advice from individuals in their own agency, outside agencies, community-based organizations, and community advocacy organizations. Network members located outside the county included professional organizations; intermediaries; nonprofit foundations; universities; and consultants. Peers from other counties were also an important source of information and advice. For instance, one mental health services director stated: "There's a...always checking with Orange County. LA, although quite big, they do some very progressive things as well. Uhm, and so you know which counties are kind of doing some leading edge, and, not just leading edge, but that also have uh, the evaluation component of it." However, this occurred more in small rural counties than in large urban counties. Among the forums for the exchange of information and advice about EBPs were regularly scheduled meetings within the county, region, and state; initiatives that involved contact of systems leaders by CIMH; agency staff; and other county agencies and community-based organizations. Systems leaders also obtained information and advice on EBPs from counterparts in counties widely regarded for serving as 'models' for innovation and EBP implementation (Palinkas et al, 2011a).

Study participants described a wide range of advice seeking in qualitative interviews, which included both whether to implement TFCO or any other EBP in particular in their county and how to best implement such an EBP. Several participants discussed advice seeking in relation to the cost and feasibility of implementing a particular program; this included instances of where they had decided not to implement a specific program because they had been informed by their counterparts in other counties or directors of community-based organizations within their own county that the cost of implementation would be prohibitive. Others discussed advice seeking related to approaching appropriate community partners for collaboration.

These information and advice networks appear to have played an important role in the implementation of TFCO among the first cohort of counties participating in the CAL-OH study. For those who had agreed to participate or were considering participation at the time they were interviewed, information about TFCO and the CAL-OH study was obtained from presentations given by CIMH representatives at state or regional meetings, direct contact by CIMH with county agency directors, direct contact by other agency directors within the county, or staff within the agency. Only one of the seven systems leaders interviewed from the three counties that had either decided not to participate in the first cohort of the CAL-OH study or had not advanced beyond Stage One had received any information about TFCO or the CAL-OH study (Palinkas et al, 2011a).

> It came to my attention two different ways. I started hearing some discussion about it at the small county association meetings, which is a break off of the full body county Mental Health Directors Association. And I heard it from one or two of my peers. I cannot exactly remember how that went up, and that was…that was probably nine months ago. My timeline might be a little fuzzy, but the newest program manager brought it to my attention. And I think she found it on the CIMH website, if I'm not mistaken. (Mental health services director)

> I first heard about this project on the internet. And I did some research on it because I was curious about it. (Child welfare services director)

Representations of the influence networks for exchanging information related to EBPs in general are found in Figure 5.1. Light grey nodes represent individuals who reported being in implementation stages 0–1, dark grey nodes represent stages 2–6, and black nodes represent stages 7–8. White nodes depict individuals about whom insufficient information was obtained to ascertain implementation stage or about whom implementation stage is not relevant, such as individuals who work for CIMH or other non-county-affiliated organizations. A simple visual inspection of the network diagram reveals that many of the nodes in this network are connected to others in similar implementation stages.

Figure 5.1: EBP advice networks by implementation stage

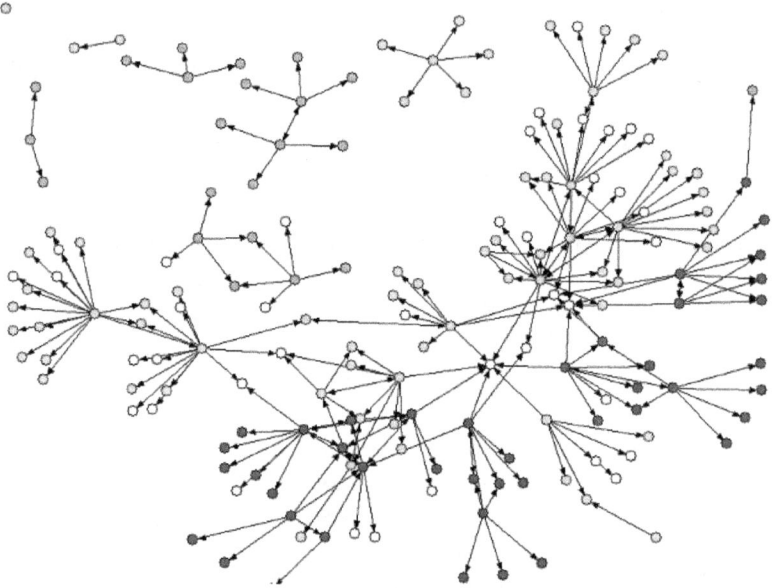

Legend: Light grey nodes represent individuals who reported being in SIC stage 0-1, dark grey nodes in stage 2-6, and black nodes in stages 7-8. White nodes depict individuals about whom insufficient information was obtained to ascertain implementation stage, or about whom implementation stage is not relevant, such as individuals who work for the California Institute of Mental Health (CIMH).
Source: Adapted from Palinkas et al (2011a)

A total of 176 individuals with 233 ties comprised this network. There were eight 'disconnected' components or sub-networks. One of these components contained 81 percent of the overall network, while the remaining seven components ranged in size from one to nine individuals. Individuals from ten of the 12 counties were represented in the largest component, and three counties were each represented in two or more components.

The principle of homophily (that is, likeness between individuals in a network based on a specified criteria) was well supported for both county and implementation stage among members of the original sample. On average, 81 percent of network ties were among individuals who came from the same county, and 83 percent of network ties were among individuals who were classified in the same implementation stage as the respondent. Interestingly, only 38 percent of network ties were among individuals who came from the same county agency as the respondent. Taken together, these results indicate that individuals often rely on others from within their own county for advice on EBPs, although not necessarily individuals from within their agency, and from individuals outside their county. This latter observation was supported by the fact that seven counties had links to one individual who works for the CIMH and was known throughout the state as someone on whom agency directors can rely for information about EBPs (Palinkas et al, 2011a).

Implementation stage was also associated with position in the overall advice network. County-level and network-position specific variables were important independent correlates of implementation stage. Individuals in large counties, relative to small, and individuals in urban counties, relative to rural, reported a higher implementation stage. Increasing in-degree centrality was positively associated with implementation stage at the two-year follow-up, while out-degree centrality was not. These latter results indicate that, adjusting for county-level attributes, being nominated more frequently by others in the network was positively associated with the implementation stage two years later, while the number of nominations an individual provided was not associated with implementation stage.

Collaboration and EBP implementation

In addition to identifying the potential predictors of the implementation stage and supplementing the construction of social networks, the qualitative analysis of the semistructured interviews identified features of these networks that were critical to the process of EBP implementation. Perhaps the most salient of these features was the role of collaboration within and between counties. Within counties, single agencies often lacked resources to implement EBPs independently. As explained by one child welfare services director, "We're a small county with very few resources. And I mean, I tell you that, you know, trying new things, uhm, it's real hard to that because of the lack of funding, and the county has always had a policy of partners not applying for too many grants." In small, rural counties where agencies have limited resources to implement EBPs on their own, agency directors cited a desire to participate in the CAL-OH study in clusters with neighboring counties (Palinkas et al, 2011a).

Poor history of collaboration was often cited as a reason for failure to implement EBPs. The reasons for the lack of collaboration identified by study participants included the following: lack of funding to support a collaboration, different priorities and mandates of the collaborating agencies, different organizational cultures of the collaborating agencies and the lack of understanding of these cultures, and differences in personality and the strained relationships caused by these differences.

Finally, criteria for effective collaborations among agencies in public youth-serving agencies included individuals who can play key roles in the collaborative process, especially agency directors and administrators with knowledge or experience working for another agency who can serve as a collaboration broker or facilitator. For example, one mental health department program director cited her varied experience working for multiple agencies as beneficial to understanding complex system interactions, stating, "I fortunately have had the experience of being a probation officer, a social service worker, and a mental health clinician." Having good systems partners was also cited as an important requirement for successful collaboration: "And that's where I think, uhm, you know, it's the relationships you build with your system partners, so that you can, you can pretty much get to the issue right away with, without all the niceties around, how's your day" (child welfare services director).

Lessons learned

The structure and operation of social networks—specifically, higher in-degree centrality of network members, as well as network context, reflected in the size of county and whether it was predominately urban or rural—are central to implementation of EBPs. Further, social networks influence the implementation process through two mechanisms, development and operation of successful collaborations and acquisition of information and support related to EBPs.

The majority of network ties occurred within the same county and same implementation network stage. This is understandable given that both randomization and use of the SIC measurement in the CAL-OH study occurred at the county level (Chamberlain et al, 2008b). However, only a little over one-third of network ties existed among individuals in the same agency. This could be accounted for, in part, by the CAL-OH study requirements that at least two of the three agencies in a county had to agree to participate, one of which had to be the mental health agency, in order to enroll in the study (Chamberlain et al, 2008b). The results also supported the importance of collaboration between agencies. This was reflected in the number of ties among individuals representing different agencies in the same county and the qualitative data highlighting the importance of collaboration for EBP implementation, especially in resource-poor rural counties, even when participation of more than one agency is not a requirement for implementation of a specific EBP.

This research also helps us to understand the context in which these networks influence the implementation of EBPs and how differences in context, like the size of a county or the structure of personal networks, can influence whether or not EBPs are adopted by public youth-serving agencies. Characteristics of the county and in-degree centrality are associated with EBP implementation stage. Larger, urban counties were classified in a higher implementation stage than their smaller, rural counterparts. A similar association between county size and days to consent to participate in the CAL-OH study in all three California cohorts was reported by Wang and colleagues (2010). Analysis of qualitative interviews with systems leaders found that small, rural counties often lack the resources to implement innovative practices on their own due to a limited supply of qualified staff, funding, and available clients. The two counties that declined to participate in the first cohort of the CAL-OH study were small, rural counties possessing networks that were also small and lacking ties to other networks that had decided to participate in the study and were proceeding with TFCO implementation. These findings highlight the importance of networks involving ties to counties with resources or the pooling of resources via existing networks. These networks also exposed agency directors and senior administrators to information about and opportunities to implement EBPs, which, in turn, influenced decisions about whether or not to implement these practices.

We also found, however, that TFCO implementation stage at the two-year follow-up was associated with position in the overall advice networks at baseline. Higher-status individuals, measured by in-degree centrality, were more likely to work in counties that achieved a higher stage of implementation two years later. These individuals were nominated by others as a source of information and advice about EBPs and innovative programs in general. The central position of these individuals in influence networks makes sense since systems leaders would be inclined to seek information and advice from someone who had experience and was successful in implementing such practices.

Not all opinion leaders need have a high degree of centrality; in some cases, opinion leaders are persons who bridge different social networks, and their position as a bridging tie facilitates their success in bringing new practices from one network to another (Burt, 1999). There are several nodes in this network whose structural position could allow for such bridging between sub-networks. Further, although our results point to an association between state of CDT implementation and in-degree centrality but not out-degree centrality, it is possible that these two forms of status operate differently at different stages of implementation, with the former being more important in the earlier stages and the latter being more important in subsequent stages.

The study results also provide an indication of how influence networks operate to implement EBPs. There were numerous instances of exchange of information within agencies, within counties, and across counties. This exchange usually occurred through regularly scheduled meetings or conferences, through a search for information concerning the EBP by the systems leader, or through dissemination efforts of intermediary organizations like CIMH. Influence networks also operated to implement EBPs by sharing resources, which include funding, staffing, or consumers. This sharing was easier in large counties because agencies in these counties possessed more resources than similar agencies in small counties. However, the existence of subgroups or cliques may preclude sharing due to competition for the same resources. In smaller, rural counties, on the other hand, resources are often shared between agencies in the same counties or with agencies in neighboring counties because the individual agency frequently lacks the capital, staffing, or consumer demand necessary to initiate or sustain implementation efforts.

Implementation was also associated with greater connectivity across counties. Counties who declined to participate or did not advance beyond Stage One had no ties or links outside the county. In contrast, counties that had achieved Stage Six or higher were all linked to CIMH, a primary source of information on EBPs in the state. Most of the network links to CIMH were with county mental health agency leaders and with county Chief Probation Officers, which can also be explained by the fact that the key CIMH 'node' was a former county chief probation officer.

One of the conclusions to be drawn from this research is that implementation strategies should be designed to either build influence networks or capitalize on existing networks. The CDT approach tested in the parent study was designed to build social networks that offer support to network members in implementing EBPs. For instance, networks provide access to opportunities to observe firsthand the implementation and effectiveness of EBPs in systems that are regarded as models or early adopters. Strategies for implementation should strive to create partnerships between agencies within counties that serve the same target population and build influence networks across counties, thereby enabling systems leaders in agencies based in small rural counties or possessing small influence networks to acquire more information and resources from leaders in agencies based in large urban counties.

Inter-organizational collaboration

Analyses of interview transcripts revealed three sets of characteristics related to collaboration in implementing EBPs and other innovative programs: 1) characteristics of the collaboration process; 2) characteristics of the external environment in which the collaborations took place; and 3) characteristics of the organizations and their members participating in the collaboration. The characteristics of collaboration process are determined, at least in part, by the characteristics of the external environment and participating organizations and individuals. Each of the three sets of characteristics, in turn, influences the structure of influence networks of implementation collaborators, which, in turn, influences the outcome of implementation efforts (that is, stage of implementation) (Palinkas et al, 2011a). These relationships are illustrated in Figure 5.2.

Characteristics of the collaboration

Accounts of previous experiences with EBP implementation and current efforts to implement TFCO revealed four distinct characteristics of collaboration process that were relevant to EBP implementation: focus, formality, frequency, and function (Box 5.2).

Figure 5.2: Model of inter-organizational collaborations

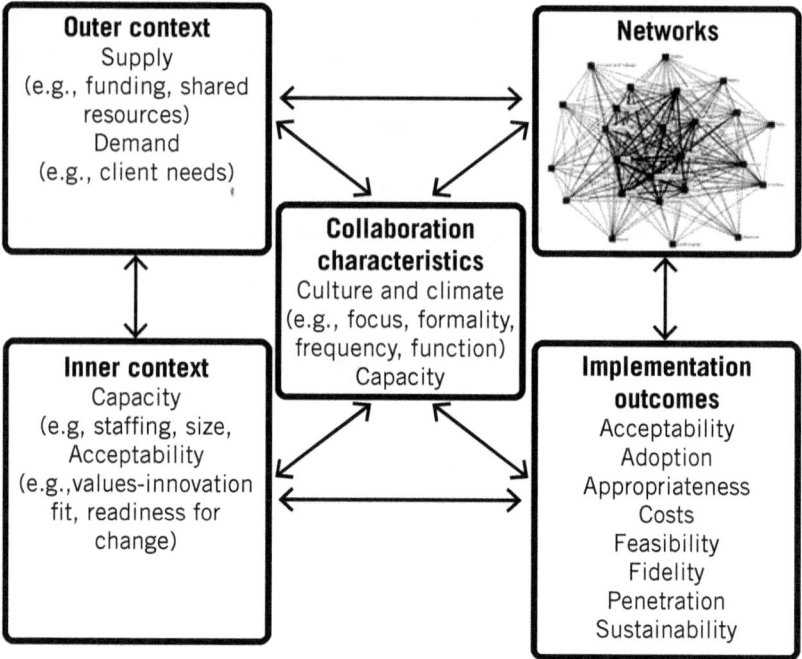

Box 5.2: Characteristics of the collaboration

- *Focus*: Collaboration focus referred to whether the intention was to implement a broad array of innovative programs or practices (broad focus) or a very specific practice (narrow focus).
- *Formality*: Collaborative activities also ranged along a continuum of formality, from simple and informal communications to more formalized meetings such as participation in statewide professional associations; or regional and county-wide planning councils or consortiums which were often formed and structured by policies or mandates.
- *Frequency*: Collaboration occurred along a continuum of frequency, from infrequent or ad hoc efforts to respond to specific initiatives related to EBP implementation to frequent or continuous efforts to identify and implement innovative programs for the sake of improving service quality.
- *Functions*: Collaborations across counties and across agencies within the same county occurred for the purpose of information exchange and pooling of resources in the short term and to alter services delivery

and enhance capacity to prevent or treat problem behaviors in at risk youth in the long run.
Source: Adapted from Palinkas et al (2014)

Characteristics of the external environment

Characteristics of inter-organizational implementation collaborations were associated with certain features of the external environments in which these collaborations occur. These included the extent to which funding is available to introduce and sustain the EBP, the size of the county, the existence of clients in need of the services provided by each agency, and local, state, or federal mandates that dictated the specific form of collaboration (Box 5.3).

Box 5.3: Characteristics of the external environment

- *Availability of funding*: "I suspect in many counties, the money brings people to the table" (child welfare services director). "We look at... who are the possible partners for those types of projects. So if we don't have the internal resources, you know, are there other ways to get those resources? You know, by collaborating with somebody else, for instance" (child welfare services director).
- *County size*: "I have the advantage in a small county of having established relationships with the folks that we so desperately need to partner with. And it's a phone call. And it's a taking them out to lunch. And we've launched two projects that way. Over a lunch...But you can't do that in a large county, it just doesn't work. It does for us" (mental health services director).
- *Shared clients*: "Families who come into our systems, via Mental Health, Probation, Child Welfare, even our Drug and Alcohol Services, uhm, you know, pick any of those doors, and it's the same family" (child welfare services director).
- *Government mandates*: Mandates served as both facilitators and barriers to collaboration. "You know, everybody will always still sort of have their mandates or their place that they have to sort of say, 'This is all I can do'" (child welfare services director).
Source: Adapted from Palinkas et al (2014)

The pressure to collaborate in the face of limited funds is especially great during times of budget shortfalls such as the one experienced by the state of California at the time the study was conducted. According to one child welfare services director, "it's forced us to collaborate more, to share our resources." This pressure is especially intense in small, rural counties who collaborate with neighboring counties in order to maximize the use of limited funds. One example of such collaboration was the decision of two small rural counties to jointly pay for someone to train the staff of both counties in a particular EBP and share the cost because of limited resources. Nevertheless, the acquisition of such resources usually implied some form of reciprocity. According to one mental health agency director: "we'll put some staff here and we'll put some money in here, and you put some money in there…So, you know, you give something, you get something."

Characteristics of the participating organizations

The third set of characteristics that distinguished implementation collaborations pertained to the organizations represented in the collaborations. These characteristics included features of the ideology or organizational culture and features of the members of these organizations. The first set of features included a common language, common recognition of the problem to be addressed, common goals and values, a buy-in and commitment to innovation and change, and policies and procedures designed to ensure transparency and accountability. The second set of features included the existence of interpersonal relationships and social ties, presence of an individual who could serve as a broker or advocate for the EBP, leadership that was supportive of the implementation, and participants possessing qualities of honesty, credibility, trust and respect for others (Box 5.4).

Box 5.4: Characteristics of participating organizations

- *Common language:* "we had to learn some different language, talking about milieus and this and that. But, any time our staff were involved in any type of collaborative with our Children's Mental Health, we always have combined training, so that we can come up, come up with a common language, so that the various, uh, schools of thoughts, or disciplines, understood one another, as opposed to… 'We call our people "probationary", they call theirs "clients"', you know, and things like that" (chief probation officer).

- *Common recognition of the problem:* "I think there has to be agreement as to what the issues are. That [if] we're all going to bring people together, we all have to recognize that there's, there is a problem... and that it, it mutually affects all of us, in one way or the other" (chief probation officer).

- *Common goals and values:* "We share a common belief...that we really do want to see our kids succeed. And we really do want to have better communities and families. We want to make sure that not only are we providing services, we help [families] become self-sustainable. So, I think we all share those beliefs" (chief probation officer)

- *Commitment.* "If you're going to get groups together to collaborate, well you have to have the will and the commitment to do this job" (child welfare services director).

- *Accountability.* "We want a collaborative where everybody's involved. Everybody has accountability. And everybody has contributions" (child welfare services director).

- *Interpersonal relationships and social ties.* "We have a new partner now...who is the executive director that came out of Drug and Alcohol. She's been a friend of mine for years. So, all of these people, well, I would say I have, you know, personal alliances and commitments to. I'm there to support them when they need me. They're there to support me. We have the same philosophy, whenever we want to try something new" (mental health services director).

- *Collaboration broker and/or facilitator.* Examples of collaboration brokers included California Institute of Mental Health consultants or an influential county opinion leader. In other instances, this key person served as the collaboration facilitator, who coordinated the necessary meetings and had experience with facilitating the collaboration's group work processes.

- *Supportive leadership.* "The agency directors have to set the tone for collaboration, working together" (chief probation officer).

- *Honesty, credibility, trust, and respect:* "You know, when you think about any relationship, you're hoping that there is honesty and there's trust. So, those are critical to collaborating and establishing any relationship" (chief probation officer).

Source: Adapted from Palinkas et al (2014)

Collaboration characteristics and influence networks

As evidenced by many of the examples and illustrations provided earlier, each of the three sets of characteristics is linked to one another in important ways. Thus, characteristics of the external environment such as availability of funding and existence of common clients was associated with more exchanges of information and resources to change patterns of services delivery and improve outcomes for at risk youth. Size of county and existence of state mandates could lead to increased or decreased exchanges depending on whether there was sufficient information or resources to exchange or whether the mandate required or prevented the exchanges from occurring. All of the characteristics of organizations and individual members of these organizations were similarly associated with increased exchanges of information and resources. Frequency of exchanges also appeared to be associated with a broader focus, less formality, and greater frequency of interactions.

All three sets of characteristics, in turn, appear to be associated with characteristics of influence networks. For instance, with respect to characteristics of the collaboration, smaller but more connected (as measured by level of in-degree centrality) networks appeared to be associated with the collaboration processes of a broader focus, less formality, and greater frequency of interaction. The external environmental characteristics of available funding and state mandates were associated with large networks in some instances and small networks in other instances. Smaller counties were associated with smaller networks, while existence of common clients was associated with larger networks. The organizational characteristics of a common language, recognition of the problem, goals and values, commitment, and accountability and the individual characteristics of interpersonal ties, brokering or advocacy, supportive leadership, and personal qualities of honesty, trust, and respect were all associated with larger and more connected networks.

Lessons learned

Collaboration between organizations is a critical factor in the development and maintenance of these influence networks. In contrast with some studies that found that inter-organizational collaborations had little or no effect on program outcomes (Chuang and Wells, 2010) or may even hinder achievement of successful outcomes (Glisson and Hemmelgarn, 1998), we found no instance of where such collaborations hindered the acceptance, adoption or routine use of new EBPs, and several instances of where such implementation could not have been achieved in the absence of the identified characteristics of inter-organizational collaboration. Consistent with the definition of collaboration provided by Himmelman (2001), the collaborations described by these systems leaders were for the purpose of exchanging information, sharing resources, altering behavior, and enhancing capacity to serve at risk youth. They also reflected different degrees of focus, formality and frequency that ranged from statewide entities that met once a quarter to county-wide consortiums that met once a week to individual systems leaders who may have limited interactions for the purpose of obtaining or providing specific information or a specific resource.

This study also found that the success of efforts to create such collaborations and the extent to which these collaborations were successful in developing and maintaining the influence networks instrumental in implementing EBPs were dependent on a set of characteristics of the collaboration's external environment and of the participating organizations and individuals. These latter two sets of characteristics constitute the 'outer context' and 'inner context' of inter-organizational collaboration (Greenhalgh et al, 2004; Damschroder et al, 2009; Aarons et al, 2011). The outer context includes the availability of funds and clients necessary to introduce and sustain the EBP, size and proximity of collaborating entities and their administrative jurisdictions, state and local mandates requiring collaboration between agencies, and responsibility for the same group of clients or consumers of provided services. The inner context includes the characteristics of the organizations, including a common language, recognition of problems, goals and values, commitment and accountability, and their individual members, including interpersonal relations and social ties, willingness to serve as a broker or EBP advocate, willingness to exercise supportive leadership, and reputation for honesty, trust, and respect. Our results suggested that these characteristics were, for the most part, associated with increased levels of exchange of information and resources and with larger and more connected networks. However, we also found instances in which the same characteristic (for example, county size, availability of funding, existence of state mandates) was associated with more or less exchange or with larger or smaller networks. Further research is required to account for these differences across different collaborations operating in different contexts.

As with the networks themselves, the implementation model of Greenhalgh and colleagues (2004) also places inter-organizational norms and values within the outer context of implementation. In contrast, the inner context of the model of inter-organizational collaboration introduced here includes two sets of characteristics that represent an "organizational culture of collaboration." Organizational cultures represent "'the way things are done around here,' as well as the way things are understood, judged, and valued" (Davies et al, 2000, p. 112). As with cultural systems in general, organizational cultures comprise sets of shared understandings, arranged in hierarchical order, that serve as models of as well as models for behavior (Palinkas et al, 2005), in this case, the behavior that drives the process of collaboration (that is, focus, formality, frequency, and function) and creates and sustains influence networks. An organizational culture of collaboration is shaped by the existence of a common language, common recognition of the problem to be addressed, common goals and values, a buy-in and commitment to innovation and change, and policies and procedures designed to ensure transparency and accountability. It is also shaped by external factors like the availability or lack of availability of funding, state and local mandates and a common client base, as well as internal factors like the presence of individuals who serve as 'brokers', supportive leadership, and social networks that link organizations and their members. The collaboration is the product of the intra- and extra-organizational cultures; in turn, the collaboration also influences the development and evolution of these cultures. Thus, while organizational cultures at both levels may influence the outcomes of implementation efforts (Greenhalgh et al, 2004; Damschroder et al, 2009; Aarons et al, 2011), their ability to exert such an influence is mediated by the collaboration processes and the structure of the influence networks that are created and sustained by these processes.

Influence of network promoting strategies in building networks

As a strategy designed to build and maintain social networks among systems leaders, we were also interested in determining whether the CDT intervention accomplished its goal. Of the 176 network members of the first cohort of CAL-OH counties, a total of 45 percent (n = 80) were in the CDT group, 33 percent (n = 57) were in the control group, and 22 percent (n = 39) could not be classified since they were affiliated with a non-county organization (for example, CIMH) (Palinkas et al, 2013b). Figures 5.3 and 5.4 depict the CDT and control condition networks, respectively (including those non-county actors who may have been nominated). It is evident by visual comparison of these two networks that the CDT network is more interconnected than the network involving the control group, which is fragmented into several disconnected components. Although the CDT network (105 nodes) and the control network (98 nodes) were roughly the same size, the CDT network had more links than the control network (114 vs. 77). Not including isolates, the CDT condition had fewer components (1) compared to the control group (5), indicating a more cohesive structure. Likewise, raw out-degree centrality was higher in the CDT group (mean = 1.09, SD = 2.75) than the control group (mean = 0.78, SD = 2.51), indicating greater communication among actors. Reflecting the greater number of discrete components in the standard condition, average distance between any two nodes was slightly higher among the CDT group (1.75) than the control group (1.37), and average betweenness centrality was significantly greater in the CDT condition (mean = 5.544, SD = 14.883) compared to the control condition (mean = 0.741, SD = 2.970) (p = 0.019). Since there was only one component in the CDT group, most nodes eventually connect. Both betweenness and average node distance

Figure 5.3: Network of CDT condition with actors from non-county organizations

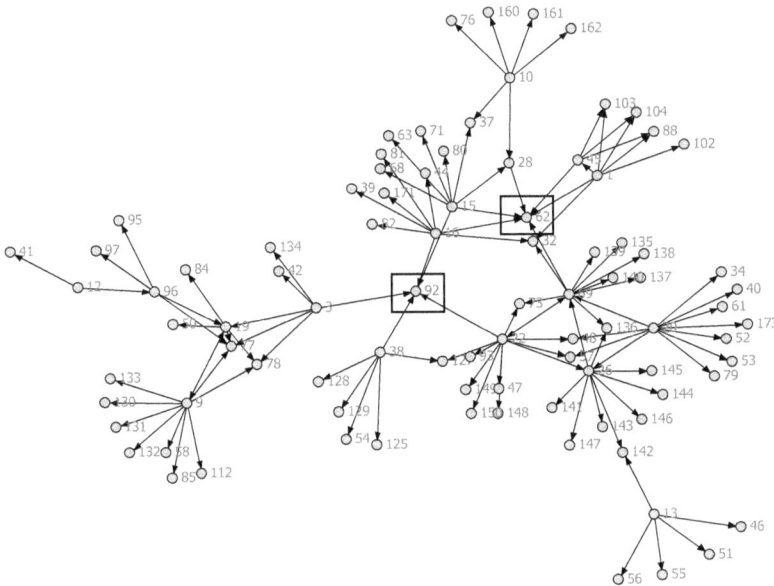

Note: Nodes 62 and 92 are CiMH representatives.
Source: Adapted from Palinkas et al (2013b)

Figure 5.4: Networks of control condition with actors from non-county organizations

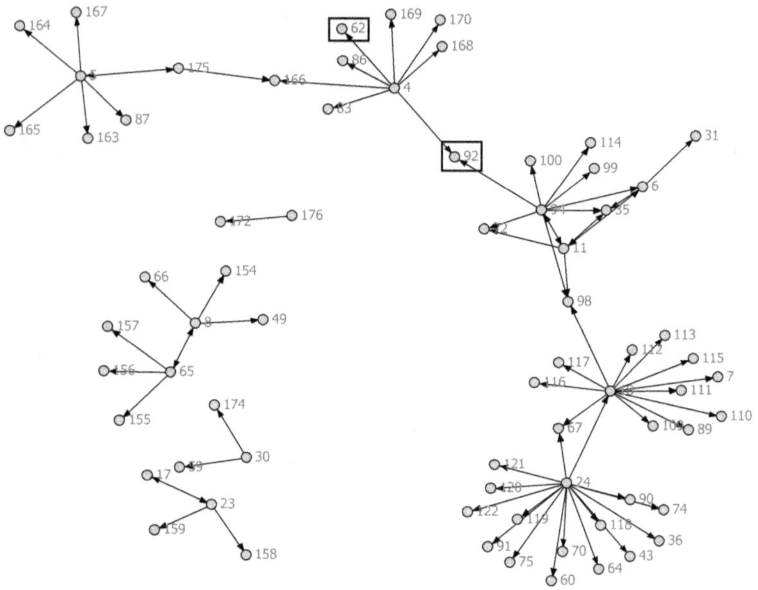

Note: Nodes 62 and 92 are CiMH representatives.
Source: Adapted from Palinkas et al (2013b)

are greater in that network, reflecting this 'larger reach' of the CDT network. When the two representatives of CIMH were excluded, the number of components in the CDT condition increased from one to two, indicating the importance of CIMH in forming bridges, and the number of links decreased to 103; however, the other network metrics were essentially unchanged (Palinkas et al, 2013b).

Lessons learned

The network of the counties in the CDT condition had fewer components (one versus five), exhibited greater size and density, and significantly greater betweenness centrality than the network in the control condition. These results confirm, as we had hypothesized, that there was more cohesion and connectivity among members of the CDT condition than among members in the control condition. This result is consistent with one of the six core processes of the CDT model, which is the use of peer-to-peer exchange and support to promote engagement, commitment, and learning by a group of sites, and encourage cross-fertilization of ideas (Saldana and Chamberlain,

2012). As the CDT counties had participated in two CDT meetings prior to data collection, these results suggest that the intervention was successful in creating or strengthening network steps among counties engaged in the shared goal of implementing TFCO. Furthermore, as noted earlier, network size and centrality were found to be significant independent predictors of implementation stage. Inasmuch as one of the aims of the CDT intervention is to foster the development of influence networks for the purpose of facilitating EBP implementation, and that such networks are associated with the pace of implementation, it becomes particularly important to take into consideration in both design and analysis the roles of influence networks that are not directly involved in the RCT but which nevertheless may influence the study outcomes.

Summary

- Social networking is central to implementation of EBPs through two mechanisms: development and operation of successful collaborations and acquisition of information and support related to EBPs.
- Networks of information and advice are developed and maintained according to position in agency, responsibility, geography, and friendship ties.
- Implementation progress is associated with size of service area, degree of urbanization, and numbers of individuals who are a source of information and advice for other network members.
- The success of efforts to create collaborations between and among different organizations and the extent to which these collaborations are successful in developing and maintaining the influence networks instrumental in implementing EBPs are dependent on characteristics of the collaboration's external environment and of the participating organizations and individuals.
- Implementation strategies should be designed to either build influence networks or mobilize existing networks.

6

Use of research evidence and EBP implementation

Family Functional Therapy is the evidence-based program that we had some data from the California Institute of Mental Health and also some websites that look like it was being implemented in Los Angeles County, and we had some contact with them and CIMH and we looked at the research and it looked very promising. So, we made a decision. We were pretty happy with it, the Family Functional Therapy, to move forward with this, so that's what we did. And it hasn't disappointed us…My assistant chief talked to [a CIMH staff member] pretty extensively about that and we had some discussion and several meetings with our providers here and our community-based organization. We looked at a lot of data in the Washington State Institute of Public Policy and, again, some of the websites on evidence-based programming and what works. So we reviewed a lot of literature and I can't remember all the places that we looked, they had not only analysis, but meta-analyses, that showed that if you do it with fidelity, any of these programs would work well. (Chief probation officer)

As we observed in the last chapter, social networks play an important role in the flow of information to and from network members. Much of this information occurs in the form of research evidence that is used to support the choice of an EBP by a service system as well as to provide guidance on how the EBP should be implemented. In this chapter, we examine in closer detail the process of acquiring, evaluating, and applying research evidence in EBP implementation.

We draw on the experience of using research evidence to implement TFCO among county-level child welfare, child mental health and juvenile justice systems in California and Ohio and adopting EBPs and other innovative practices in New York State-supported child mental health clinics. The experience of implementation in California and Ohio enables us to examine the extent to which EBP implementation is associated with the source of evidence, how practitioners evaluate the evidence obtained, how they apply it, or ignore it, when deciding whether or not to implement, and whether this use of research evidence (URE) is associated with the implementation stage from engagement to sustainment. The experience in New York enables us to examine the source of available information and the impetus for its acquisition that marks the distinction between adopting and non-adopting organizations.

Use of research evidence

One of the greatest challenges facing health system management, policy and decision-making is the timely and appropriate URE (World Health Organization, 2006; Ellen et al, 2013). The relatively limited use of EBPs in systems of care that serve children and adolescents is but one illustration of a larger phenomenon of the underutilization of evidence emanating from significant worldwide investments in biomedical and health research. Failure to optimally use research evidence leads to inefficiencies, reduced quantity and quality of life for citizens, and lost productivity (Grol, 2001). This failure has been attributed to the lack of timely and effective communication of this evidence and the limited skills and capacity of practitioners and policymakers to find and use evidence (Lavis et al, 2006).

As described in Chapter Three, there are numerous theories, models and frameworks that are employed in implementation science in general and the identification of barriers to and facilitators of EBP implementation in service sectors that cater to children and adolescents in particular. Some of these theories, models and frameworks focus on, or make reference to, the interactions that occur between intervention developers and consumers (for example, Rogers, 2003). Still other models focus on the transfer of research evidence from knowledge producers to knowledge consumers or from EBP developers to potential users (Landry et al, 2001; Lavis et al, 2003; Landry et al, 2003). In fact, the definition of the field of implementation research itself makes references to methods to promote the systematic uptake of research findings (Eccles and Mittman, 2006). As Green and colleagues (2009, p. 153) argue, "knowledge utilisation, in particular, may hold potential to help break the frustrating impasse that seems to have characterised the more traditional ways of conceptualising and pursuing the dissemination and implementation of research to and in practice and policy."

For the most part, however, these models do not highlight how the research findings are used by consumers and how such use is associated with the likelihood of EBP implementation and sustainment. An exception to this is the EPIS framework (Aarons et al, 2011). The framework specifically mentions the role of research evidence use in EBP implementation, noting that public service sector organizations generally do not have strong absorptive capacity for gathering and weighing research evidence. Absorptive capacity refers to an organization's preexisting knowledge/skills, ability to use new knowledge, specialization and mechanisms to support knowledge sharing.

There are several models that focus on URE in policy and practice in general. Nutley and colleagues (2007), for instance, identified four factors associated with the outcome of using research evidence: 1) the nature of the research to be applied, 2) the personal characteristics of both researchers and potential research users, 3) the links between research and its users, and 4) the context for the use of research. Honig and Coburn (2008) emphasized process (searching for evidence, incorporating or not incorporating it in decision making), and predictors (features of the evidence, working knowledge, social capital, organization, normative influence, political dynamics, and state and federal policies) of evidence use. According to their Evidence-Based Decision Making (EBDM) model, URE is predicted by the nature of the evidence itself, leader/administrator social capital, organizational characteristics, normative influences, political dynamics, and state and federal policies. An instrumental view of URE suggests that knowledge might be utilized to legitimize a point of view, to conceptually enlighten policy decisions, to warn about potential or existing problems, or to manipulate knowledge strategically for power or profit (Green et al, 2009).

Among the best-known models of evidence use are the variations that fall under the rubric of knowledge transfer and exchange (KTE) (Lomas, 2000; Lavis et al, 2002; Lavis et al, 2006; Mitton et al, 2007). These models take as their foundation Caplan's 'two-communities' theory (1979), which posits that the utilization of research by policy analysts and decision makers is poor because the assumptions and cultural practices of the two groups differ greatly, so effort is required to bridge the research–policy interface. A common approach to addressing these challenges is regular and direct contact between those who produce knowledge and those who use it (Lomas, 2000). Direct interactions between knowledge producers and consumers have improved user perception of research's value (Kothari et al, 2005) and correlate significantly with URE by practitioners and policymakers (Ouimet et al, 2010). Another approach to addressing these challenges is the tailoring of presentations to meet users' needs. Such tailoring requires the researcher to understand the needs and to speak the language of practice or policy (Haynes et al, 2011). A third approach to addressing these challenges is knowledge brokerage. "Knowledge brokerage refers to efforts to make research and policymaking more accessible to each other with various mechanisms of knowledge sharing and transfer" (Hukkinen, 2016, p. 321). Knowledge brokers include individuals and organizations that serve as intermediaries between knowledge producers and consumers and engage in a variety of activities, including dissemination, matchmaking, consulting, engaging, collaborating, and capacity-building (Meyer, 2010). Although the evidence for the effectiveness of knowledge brokerage in transferring evidence into policy or practice is somewhat equivocal (Knight and Lightowler, 2010; Phipps and Morton, 2013), there is some evidence that knowledge brokerage can improve comprehension of the evidence and increase the intention to use it (Kothari et al, 2011).

Based on these models, a number of knowledge transfer strategies have been developed to translate research into practice (Couturier et al, 2014; Gill et al, 2014; Myers et al, 2017). For instance, the six-step Ottawa Model for Knowledge Transfer includes a thorough assessment of the evidence-based innovation itself (development process and innovation attributes), potential adopters (their awareness, attitudes, knowledge/skill, concerns, and current practice), and the practice environment (patients, culture/social, structural, economic, and uncontrolled events) (Graham et al, 2006). "Based on the assessment, specific implementation intervention strategies and monitoring adoption procedures are developed and implemented, and outcomes of patients, practitioners, and the health care system are then collected and evaluated" (Myers et al, 2017, p. 70).

URE and implementation of TFCO

In the CAL-OH study, we examined URE by leaders of county-level child welfare, specialty mental health and juvenile justice systems to determine whether such use was independently associated with stage of implementation and proportion of activities completed at the pre-implementation, implementation and sustainment phases; and whether URE was significantly associated with the knowledge brokerage implementation strategy used to scale up the EBP. URE was assessed using the Structured Interview for Evidence Use (Palinkas et al, 2016), a 45-item instrument that assesses acquisition of research evidence (Input), evaluation of the evidence for reliability, validity and relevance to one's own clients (Process), and application of that evidence in deciding whether or not to adopt an evidence-based or other innovative practice (Output) (Box 6.1). To assess progress toward implementation and sustainment of TFCO, we used the Stages of Implementation Completion (SIC) scale (Saldana and Chamberlain, 2012), described in Chapter Three. In addition to using the score for the furthest stage completed (that is, stage score), we examined the percentage of activities completed within the pre-implementation, implementation and sustainment phase (that is, proportion score).

Box 6.1: Dimensions of URE

- Acquisition of evidence (Input)
  - o From local networks (for example, consultant, government agencies, colleagues in other agencies or counties, one's own agency): "Bay area counties meet monthly. And we're always asking each other, you know, 'What's going on?'" (Mental health services director)
  - o From outside experts (for example, conference presentations, intervention developers: "We're always out there trolling conferences to see what's working and what's not working and then we find out whether it's something we can do and then we find out if there's somebody available who can help us implement it." (Mental health services director)
  - o From widely accessible (global) documents (for example, internet, journal articles, manuals; intermediary organizations): "You know, one of the things that I do periodically, is that if I have a problem, with a particular area, diagnosis, group of people, what have you, that we're treating, I go in the internet and I just start surfing the

net about treatment and what people are doing and I start looking at that." (Mental health services director)

- Evaluation of evidence (Process)
    - o Self-evaluation of validity and reliability of evidence (for example, based on theory, credibility of developers, information from more than one source, strengths and weaknesses listed): "I guess what I'll look at is this program and how's its been demonstrated to be effective. Has it been tested in the field for a long time? Can it be administered with fidelity? Is it hard to administer with fidelity?" (Chief probation officer)
    - o Self-evaluation of relevance of evidence to local needs and circumstances (for example, client needs, costs, time required for training, comparability of study population with client population): "Because we see a lot of these models and they come from out of state, such as Oregon or the east coast. And our populations here are so different from those other states. So it's helpful for me to talk to the children's coordinators in those other counties because their populations are much more similar to ours. The product that is created in Oregon doesn't necessarily persuade me that it's going to be relevant to our county, but if I talk to Riverside and they've already implemented that project successfully, that's more persuasive to me." (Mental health services director)
    - o Reliance on others to assess validity, reliability and relevance of evidence: "Well that's kind of the job of my psychologist and my data folks, but I'm comfortable given that in the level of training and the success that we've had historically it would be their job to conduct some analysis of the research to determine if there were any concerns relative to the design or implementation of the studies upon which the product is built. And once we're satisfied that the analysis is trustworthy, then we would feel comfortable moving forward." (Child welfare services director)
- Application of evidence (Output)
    - o Apply the evidence (for example, to support decision already made, eliminate ineffective programs, compare multiple program strengths and weaknesses): "I think sometimes we end up using it [research evidence] to justify to ourselves that we have made the right choice. I think that when you're contracting with an entity to provide services to children, that you're looking for every detail that tells you that you're making the right choice." (Chief probation officer)
    - o Ignore the evidence (for example, EBP is considered too expensive, too inflexible, not feasible, or doesn't match staff skill level):

"Again, we just look at it realistically. Is it something we can implement? Do I have the capacity to implement? Can I implement it in an evidence-based way? Can I afford to do it? And would my partners do it? I wanted my partners to implement MFT; they didn't want to do MFT, so we're doing Wraparound. Now they're trying to study Wraparound; they're trying to get more evidence behind it. We know it's met a lot of our outcomes that are good outcomes. So, I don't know if I would go so far as to ignore, but yeah, there are other considerations on whether I am going to use the research or not." (Chief probation officer)

- Total engagement in URE
  Source: Adapted from Palinkas et al (2016)

In the CAL-OH study, the most frequently used sources of evidence by systems leaders were the internet, contacts with other systems leaders who have implemented the program or practice, and attendance at conferences and workshops (Palinkas et al, 2016). Self assessments of the relevance of the evidence to their own service sectors and communities received the highest mean scores for processing the evidence, followed by self-assessments of the validity and reliability of the evidence and reliance on others such as intermediaries to assess validity, reliability, and relevance. The most frequent application of evidence was to support a decision on adopting a specific program or practice, followed by determining whether that program or practice could result in harm to clients and evaluating the information provided by experts and community members.

> CIMH came down last year and they talked to us about ART (Aggression Replacement Training), and they talked to us about several different family therapies that we could use with kids that have had antisocial behavior problems, and so we looked at it. It has to be an evidence-based practice, but it has to be something that we can locate people who can help us, contact with them, and they can help us implement a model. (Mental health services director)

This study found that URE was associated with certain demographic characteristics (Palinkas et al, 2017c). Among leaders of all systems, men were more engaged than women in evaluating the validity, reliability and relevance of the research evidence. Men also exhibited a significantly higher level of total engagement in URE. Directors with a master's or doctoral degree were more engaged than directors with a bachelor's degree or less in accessing research evidence and in total engagement in URE. Compared to other systems leaders, child welfare system leaders were significantly less engaged in applying the evidence in making a decision to adopt an innovative practice. In multivariate analyses, male gender was an independent predictor of evaluation of the evidence, while being in a service system other than child welfare was an independent predictor of application of evidence.

Influences on type of research evidence use

We also found differences in level of engagement in different forms of URE (Palinkas et al, 2017c). For instance, child-serving systems leaders were more engaged in evaluating the validity, reliability and relevance of the evidence than they were in accessing or applying the evidence. They were more engaged in applying the evidence than in accessing it. In accessing the research evidence, they were more likely to rely on external experts than on local networks or documents like articles in peer-reviewed publications or internet searches. They were also more likely to use documents than to rely on local networks. In evaluating the research evidence, leaders were more engaged in assessing relevance of the evidence to their clients than in relying on others to assess validity, reliability and relevance or in conducting their own assessment of the validity and reliability of the evidence. They were also more likely to conduct their own assessment of the validity and reliability of the evidence than rely on others to do so. However, they were also more likely to ignore the evidence than they were in applying it when making a decision.

Self-assessment of research evidence for validity and reliability was significantly associated with all three subcategories of evidence accessing (documents, experts and local networks) and using the evidence for decision-making. Reliance on others to assess validity, reliability and relevance was significantly associated with use of local networks to acquire research evidence. Self-assessment of relevance of research evidence was significantly associated with accessing evidence from outside experts and local networks and its use in decision-making. In turn, using the evidence in decision-making was significantly associated with accessing evidence through documents, experts, and local networks.

Influence of other types of evidence used in making decisions

Analysis of the data collected from individual semi-structured interviews and a child welfare system leaders focus group indicated that three other types of evidence are typically used when considering whether to seek, evaluate and apply research evidence in making decisions: 1) evidence of resources necessary and available for making URE (supply), 2) evidence of the need for research evidence, usually obtained from local conditions of client and service needs (demand), and 3) personalized evidence gained from experience (consistency with practice experience or observation). Each type is examined in Box 6.2.

Box 6.2: Other types of evidence used in EBP implementation

- Resources for using research evidence
  - *Availability of funding to support the practice*: "If I can't afford it, then there is no point of going further" (Chief probation officer). This is especially important given the time and loss of revenue associated with EBP training.
  - *Access to and exchange of information*: "We use other counties in terms of 'You know, we've got something cool going on here'...And that it's been able to demonstrate its success rate. You know, it's been able to show how they implemented it, how operational... and in fact you see the outcome measures really start to take root." (Child welfare services director)
  - *Collaborations with other agencies and counties*: "And in collaboration, besides just meeting with people, we all are sharing a lot of data. So, I have access not just to my own department's data, I have access to child welfare data, I have access to probation data and I can get access to the public school's information. And since we are all living in the same community, it's hugely important that we share that information. It helps each of us make better judgments on behalf of the kids." (Behavioral health services director)
- Need for research evidence
  - *Client needs*: "We get a lot of these kids that are not successful in foster placements and they end up in group home placements which cost the county a lot of money and they end up in other systems. So, I think that the main thing we're looking at is approaches that are going to allow us to be more successful with

these children and to avoid them ending up in more restricted types of placements." (Mental health services director)

o *Lack of such evidence*: "One of the problems that you're facing, going through this evidence-based stuff is you can't get good data on how it actually works and you're talking to the people who are selling you the instrument and they may or may not...I mean, they obviously have a vested interest." (Chief probation officer)

- Consistency with practice experience

o *Clinical practice experience*: "You know, social workers are seeing tangible changes right in front of them. They're participating in TDM's [Team Decision Making] and they're seeing the difference at that moment." (Child welfare services director)

o *Observation of the program being implemented elsewhere*: "We were able to go to Ohio and see the Team Decision Making meetings. And that experience was so valuable because you actually got to ask all those questions that you had about how to engage your staff, how to get finance, all that stuff that you are thinking about, 'How am I going to do this?' You can ask these people and they can help walk you through that and you can actually see it in action. Reading about it is fine, but it doesn't really help you see whether it would fit with your circumstance unless you can see it and ask those questions that you need to ask. And I think that's why we rely on each other so much because it's all we really have." (Child welfare services director)

Source: Adapted from Palinkas et al (2017c)

URE as a predictor of TFCO implementation

In the CAL-OH study, URE in general (SIEU total score) was significantly correlated with furthest stage reached, proportion of activities completed in stages 4–7 (Implementation) and stage 8 (Sustainment). Acquisition of research evidence (Input) was significantly associated with proportion of activities completed in stages 4–7 and stage 8, and marginally associated with furthest stage reached. When controlling for county, state, year of observation, and experimental condition, URE in general (SIEU total) and acquisition of research evidence (Input) were significantly associated with furthest stage of implementation of TFCO and with the proportion of activities completed in the implementation and sustainment phases. Evaluation of research evidence (Process) was marginally associated with proportion of activities completed in the pre-implementation and implementation phases. Community Development Team participation was significantly associated with acquisition of research evidence (Input) and marginally associated with engagement in URE in general (SIEU total) (Palinkas et al, 2017c).

In this study, leaders of child welfare agencies were significantly more likely than leaders of other service systems to ignore the research evidence. Possible explanations for this difference include differences in organizational characteristics such as size or resources, or differences in normative influences or organizational culture (Honig and Coburn, 2008; Aarons et al, 2011). However, these differences do not explain the absence of system-based differences in other forms of URE, including accessing and evaluating the research evidence.

Instead, the key to understanding this one particular difference may lie in the outer context. As noted in the qualitative interviews and focus group, if there is no funding to support a program, there is no point to accessing, evaluating or applying the evidence. The absence of differences in URE between systems in California and Ohio may be attributed to the fact that both states were experiencing one of the worst recessions in modern times while the study was taking place; consequently, funding for social services was more limited than usual (Brown et al, 2014). However, mental health and juvenile justice service systems in California benefited from additional funding available for implementing EBPs through the Mental Health Services Act and the Mentally Ill Offender Crime Reduction (MIOCR) Grant Program, respectively. Programs such as these were not available to child welfare systems at the time.

Systems leaders also exhibited significant differences by type of use. They were most engaged in evaluating the evidence and least engaged in accessing it. Information gathered from the qualitative interviews and focus group suggest that systems leaders are often overwhelmed with the amount of evidence available and they have limited time available to search for the evidence on their own, suggesting that their systems may have had low absorptive capacity (Aarons et al, 2011) or organizational resources (Honig and Coburn, 2008), intra-organizational characteristics of the inner context of URE and EBP implementation. They are also most engaged in use of external experts and least engaged in using local networks to acquire the evidence, suggesting a preference for access based on the nature of the evidence gained from each source (Honig and Coburn, 2008). However, consistent with the EPIS and EBDM models (Honig and Coburn, 2008; Aarons et al, 2011), several of the participants in the qualitative interviews and focus group mentioned reliance on local networks to acquire information about an innovative practice. Moreover, accessing local networks for research evidence was significantly associated with reliance on others to evaluate the validity, reliability and relevance of that evidence, suggesting a model of URE as a cultural system comprising shared but distributed understandings (D'Andrade, 1984). However, their preference was to use their social capital to visit settings where the innovation had been successfully implemented, followed by obtaining information at professional conferences and association meetings. This suggests the possibility that local networks (a characteristic of the inner context, compare Aarons et al, 2011) may be where systems leaders hear about a specific practice and the opinions of their peers regarding that practice, but that evidence supporting the use of that practice that is based on research usually comes from social ties to external experts (a characteristics of the outer context) such as practice developers, people who have implemented the innovation, or people whom they encountered at conferences and workshops.

With respect to evaluating the research evidence, systems leaders were most engaged in assessing the evidence for its relevance to their own clients and least engaged in relying on people they know and trust to evaluate the evidence. The importance placed on the suitability of a particular innovation for one's own clients has been documented in previous research on barriers and facilitators to EBP implementation (Palinkas et al, 2013a). Evidence gained from studies with one population or locale are often perceived as being of limited value when considering their use with another population such as underrepresented minorities (Kumpfer et al, 2002) or youth with co-occurring problems (Weisz et al, 2012).

Analysis of the influence of non-research based evidence also revealed the influence of inner and outer context on URE and EBP implementation. Availability of funding, a characteristic of the outer context (Aarons et al, 2011), was also uncovered during the qualitative interviews and focus group as an example of the use of evidence that may be based on personal knowledge rather than systematic research. Availability of funds, costs associated with staff training, additional time in delivering the service, and potential work overload are often cited as barriers to implementation of innovative practices in child welfare and child mental health (Aarons and Palinkas, 2007; Palinkas and Aarons, 2009; Palinkas et al, 2017a). Similarly, the availability of an inter-organizational network or collaboration where evidence may be accessed and exchanged, a characteristic of the outer context of URE and implementation (Honig and Coburn, 2008; Aarons et al, 2011), is another important resource that determines whether or not research evidence is used (Palinkas et al, 2011a; 2013b; 2014).

With respect to the demand for research evidence, systems leaders first and foremost point to the needs of their clients and communities, another characteristic of the outer context of URE and EBP implementation. In the absence of such a need, there is little incentive to seek, evaluate and apply research evidence. The absence of research evidence serves as another impetus for seeking, evaluation, and application. However, systems leaders also face pressure, often from sources in the outer context (for example, state mandates, other systems) to adopt innovative practices lacking research evidence to support its effectiveness. Hence, there may be competing demands that either encourage or discourage the processes of accessing, evaluating and applying research evidence in making a decision whether or not to innovate, revealing a political dimension to URE as outlined in the EBDM model (Honig and Coburn, 2008).

Finally, participants expressed confidence in 'global' research evidence (that is, evidence based on randomized controlled trials intended to have external validity and generalizability), that resonated with their own 'local' evidence, that is, evidence based on clinical experience, the observation of positive outcomes in youth served using EBPs, and the findings of one's own research conducted in locations where such practices had been successfully implemented. This personalized local evidence highlights the tension between advocacy and adoption of EBP and practice-based evidence (Soydan and Palinkas, 2014), mentioned in Chapter One. In this instance, systems leaders appear to rely on local evidence of supply and demand and personal experience to validate (Lindblom and Cohen, 1979) and contextualize (Honig and Coburn, 2008) the use of global research evidence. Moreover, the use of practice-based evidence that is based largely on face validity has important implications for how research evidence should be generated and disseminated for maximum effect (Soydan and Palinkas, 2014).

Previous studies have identified numerous challenges faced by policymakers and practitioners when using research evidence to make or support decisions, including the following: limited skills and abilities of public officials to access and understand research evidence, absence of forums that expose decision makers to research data or infrastructure to ensure accessibility of evidence, budgeting constraints and limited timeframes that impinge on policy decisions, lack of perceived relevance and the timeliness of academic research findings, absence of a supportive organizational context that promotes URE, and the dynamics and configuration of formal research partnerships between academic researchers and government and non-government agencies (Landry et al, 2001; Landry et al, 2003; Lavis et al, 2003; Orr and Bennett, 2012; Buckley et al, 2013). Despite these challenges, URE by systems leaders in this study was associated with the implementation and sustainment of a specific EBP. URE in general and acquisition of research evidence were also found to be significantly associated with stage of implementation completion of TFCO and with the proportion of activities completed in the implementation and sustainment phases. There also is some evidence to suggest that evaluation of research evidence for its validity, reliability and relevance to the county was associated with proportion of activities completed in the pre-implementation and implementation phases, although the associations failed to reach statistical significance.

Although most URE models contain elements that reflect distinct theoretical orientations (that is, human information processing, distributed cognition, diffusion of innovations, decision making theory) and organizational settings (for example, healthcare, education), most if not all acknowledge two essential considerations to understanding when research will be used and in what ways (Nutley et al, 2007). The first consideration is the context of research use. As noted by Davies and colleagues (2008, p. 190), "research use is a highly contingent process. Whether and how new information gets assimilated is contingent on local priorities, cultures and systems of meaning. What makes sense in one setting can make a different sense in another." As noted above, URE must be placed in context that requires information or evidence that is not based in research, but rather in the availability of resources to enable URE, the demand for such evidence or lack thereof, and on the local evidence that is obtained from personal experience and observation. Context also includes the existence of an organizational culture and climate that supports URE, technical infrastructure and ability to access research evidence when and where it is needed, and enabling of staff to participate in training programs designed to develop skills to acquire, assess, adapt and apply the evidence (Ellen et al, 2013).

The second consideration is that 'interpersonal and social interactions often are seen as key to accessing and interpreting such research knowledge, whether among policy or practice colleagues, research intermediaries or more directly with researchers themselves' (Davies et al, 2008, p. 189). However, evidence in support of the importance of such networks and interactions in the CAL-OH study was somewhat mixed. On the one hand, a previous study found no evidence that the CDT implementation strategy achieved higher overall implementation compared to that for IND using either a composite score or assessments of how many stages were completed, how fast they were achieved, whether a county achieved placement of any child, or whether a county achieved full competency (Brown et al, 2014). On the other hand, we found in the study described in this chapter that participation in CDTs was significantly associated with total engagement in URE in general and acquisition of research evidence in particular. A post-hoc analysis of treatment condition and Input subscales revealed a significant association between CDT participation and use of local networks to acquire research evidence, which suggests that the network-building function of the CDT did result in greater acquisition of research evidence. In both conditions, acquisition of evidence supporting the EBP (in this case, TFCO) occurred primarily through the treatment developer. However, the networks developed by participating in the CDTs provided access to evidence supporting other types of EBPs, as well as evidence supporting strategies for obtaining financial support for and sustaining TFCO. Further, as noted in Chapter Five, by exposing leaders to information about EBPs and opportunities to adopt EBPs, networks also influence decisions to adopt, implement, and sustain EBPs.

URE and adoption of innovative practices in state mental health systems

In the New York State Adoption Study, we examined the association between URE and EBP implementation by interviewing mental health clinic chief executive officers and program directors to determine whether there were any differences in sources of information by level of engagement in adopting new and innovative programs and practices. Two themes emerged from the analyses of these data. The first theme pertained to differences in the variety of sources of information. Sources of information among the 21 directors of clinics that failed to respond to any efforts to participate in CTAC efforts to introduce new practices (that is, non-adopters) included emails (33.3%), professional associations (19%), staff trainings (19%), or an identified staff member (14.3%). For the most part, these directors relied on a single source of information. Although emails were the most common source of information, leaders of non-adopter agencies often had difficulty recounting the source of the emails or their content:

> I get some of those (CTAC) e-mails, but I don't open them. I just don't get the time to open it. So if it's not something that I'm familiar with, or that someone has recommended or that's kind of a requirement, I haven't really had the time to open them. There's just too much information being sent every day and too many trainings and too many things. So, I've heard the term but, honestly, I couldn't even tell you what it is. (Clinic Program Director)

Among leaders of super-high adopter clinics (those who had participated in two learning collaboratives), emails were also a commonly used source of information (30.4%). However, in contrast to the non-adopters, these leaders also acquired information through multiple sources, including professional associations (35%), staff clinicians (35%), conferences and meetings (30.4%), specific individuals and colleagues (31.2%), self (25%), and consultants (25%).

> Often it's conferences. It's our own conversation with colleagues. It's obviously being on, everyone's on every list serve it seems. So I get 150 emails a day and half of those are from, whether it's advocacy groups or associations that are encouraging things, whether it's from the federal government talking about a promising practice. So I'd say we get them from a lot of different places, as well as from the leadership in our own county who are saying, you know, we're interested in this model or that model. So I'd say a lot of different places. Conferences, I try to at least go to one major conference a year just to try to keep up with the field and what's going on. (Agency director)

A second theme that emerged from these data was related to the impetus for acquiring research evidence. In non-adopter clinics, clinic leaders frequently commented on influences that were external to the clinic: "And some of it is initiated from external sources, where a regulatory agency might be encouraging adoption of a particular evidence-based model or encouraging a reduction in length of stay that forces us to think about shorter term treatment models" (Clinic director). Information reflecting a requirement is more likely to be accessed and evaluated than other sources of information by non-adopter clinics. In contrast, leaders of super-high adopting clinics were more likely to identify influences internal to the organization itself. As one agency CEO observed:

We've been pretty proactive, and so we have done some literature reviews. There's a lot of activity in the child welfare arena around EBPs and QI initiatives. And so it's a combination of proactive literature searching. We have found two models that we're going to use...are using, and one that we are using and one that we are setting out to implement. Actually, three models, agency-wide, that we found through research. And then there's a number of models that the Administration for Children's Services has promoted, a couple of which we are in the process of adopting. So some combination of proactive searching and seeing opportunities that come up from public funders.

Compared to super/high adopters, non-adopter clinics were more passive recipients of information than active seekers of information. Their URE was more reactive than proactive in nature. They were also less likely to obtain information at conferences and meetings or from specific individuals. Furthermore, the accessing of information on innovative and EBPs in non-adopter clinics appears to be related to external demands (that is, mandates) than to internal demands (that is, clinician interest). Although both clinic directors and staff are important drivers of seeking research evidence, the impetus to seek information on innovative and EBPs is more bottom-up (staff) than it is top-down (leadership) in high and super-adopter clinics than in non-adopter clinics. Furthermore, both non-adopter and high-super adopter clinics appear to rely on personal networks for source of information, but the networks of the high-super clinics seem more extensive than the networks of the non-adopter clinics.

Although these comparisons are based on a small sample of agency directors in one state, both themes suggest that agencies that seek out information on innovative and EBPs are more likely to adopt such practices than agencies that may be exposed to such information from a more limited number of sources but do not actively engage in seeking out this information. While most models of URE point to characteristics of potential consumers of research (that is, practitioners and policymakers), the links between research and its users, and the context for URE as predictors of URE (Lomas, 2000; Landry et al, 2001; Lavis et al, 2003; Nutley et al, 2007; Ouimet et al, 2010), access to research evidence is itself based on relationships and values. In this case, the relationships are those involving the producers of research evidence (that is, researchers), those disseminating the evidence (that is, funding agencies, intermediary organizations), and those consuming the evidence (that is, practitioners and policymakers). The values are embedded in assessments of the need for and utility of the research evidence made by each of the stakeholders in the implementation process.

Strategies for promoting URE

Implementation strategies designed to educate stakeholders are one potential means for facilitating the URE. These strategies include education through peers such as informing a local opinion leader, creating learning collaboratives, shadowing other clinicians, and informing and influencing stakeholders through the use of mass media and increasing demand for EBPS (Proctor et al, 2013). As described earlier in this chapter, there are also several strategies for facilitating URE based on models of KTE (Lavis et al, 2006). A report prepared by Casey Family Programs identifies six research utilization strategies that are specifically relevant to child welfare systems (Box 6.5).

Box 6.5: Strategies for facilitating URE in child welfare

1. Develop trusting relationships by connecting with intermediaries and establishing mutually beneficial relationships.
2. Open productive communication through exchange of ideas, creating opportunities for consensus building, and ensuring more effective and informed decision-making.
3. Engage stakeholders and advocates by nurturing use of champions or change agents, building awareness through community mobilization, and identification and use of social networks.
4. Make research accessible by reporting findings using accessible language, presenting data in a way that is interesting and easy to understand, presenting data at a frequency/exposure rate that is helpful for retention and utilization, and converting research findings into specific directions for practice.
5. Increase stakeholder investment by using research study co-creation approaches to ensure that study design allows for findings that can be readily applied to policy, planning, management, or practice, using participatory methods of dissemination to ensure data are meaningful, and integrating research evidence with other types of knowledge.
6. Help to ensure sustained use of research by building leadership and staff capacity to apply new research evidence to designing and

implementing practice, collecting and use data on the fidelity to the model or practice and using diffusion-innovation processes to help with adoption and utilization.

Source: Adapted from Roberts et al (2017)

Successful use of the strategies requires significant investment by an organization. These strategies are not necessarily linear, nor are they mutually exclusive.

Nevertheless, we must introduce a note of caution here; just because people think that the evidence is good doesn't necessarily mean that it is. As noted earlier in this chapter, systems leaders in California and Ohio were more likely to rely on their own assessments of the validity and reliability of the evidence than to rely on others they know and trust, including intermediaries. As Nutley and colleagues (2007) observe, policymakers and practitioners are much more likely to pay attention to research that is seen as high quality and to ignore research when they have doubts about its methodological adequacy. However, the standards used by these consumers of evidence to evaluate its quality may not be the same as those used to produce the evidence. For instance, policymakers and practitioners in social services may rely more on qualitative observational studies than to systematic reviews and experimental studies to make decisions (Nutley et al, 2007). Consequently, even if they report relying on the evidence to make decisions or to support existing decisions, as was found in the CAL-OH study (Palinkas et al, 2016), the quality of that evidence is subject to several different influences, including the procedures and rigour employed in collecting and analyzing the evidence and the social and organizational context in which the evidence is interpreted and utilized. Use of evidence alone will not guarantee that a particular program or practice is likely to be successfully implemented or produce successful outcomes in a specific setting or instance; the quality of the evidence must also be considered.

Summary

- The most frequently used sources of evidence by systems leaders are the internet, contacts with other systems leaders who have implemented the program or practice, and attendance at conferences and workshops.

- Systems leaders are most likely to conduct self-assessments of the relevance of the evidence to their own service sectors and communities followed by self-assessments of the validity and reliability of the evidence and reliance on others such as intermediaries to assess validity, reliability, and relevance.
- The most frequent application of evidence by systems leaders is to support a decision on adopting a specific program or practice, followed by determining whether that program or practice could result in harm to clients and evaluating the information provided by experts and community members.
- URE in general and acquisition of research evidence in particular are associated with stage of EBP implementation.
- Three other types of evidence are typically used when considering whether to seek, evaluate and apply research evidence in making decisions: 1) evidence of resources necessary and available for making URE (supply), 2) evidence of the need for research evidence, usually obtained from local conditions of client and service needs (demand), and 3) personalized evidence gained from experience (consistency with practice experience or observation).
- Organizations most engaged in adopting innovative and EBPs are more likely than are the least engaged organizations to utilize several different sources of information rather than a single source and be motivated to do so by their own staff.
- Support for implementation and sustainment should include assistance in making the evidence for the effectiveness of an EBP or innovative program accessible to policymakers and practitioners and in evaluating the evidence to assure its validity, reliability and relevance to the populations served by these individuals and the organizations they represent.
- Support should also include providing resources necessary to facilitate the application of evidence in decision-making.

7

Local models of EBP implementation

I'd say MST, Multi-Systemic Therapy by Scott Henggeler. Well promoted, good evidence-based practice, but their approach is very expensive, and in a civil service county environment…You know, some of the larger counties have been able to implement that, perhaps with the grant. We ended up choosing alternate, less expensive approaches that might serve a similar target population. So we use the public domain Intensive Case Management model based on the New York model to help treat many of our court wards at risk of group home placement. We might have done MST, but rather chose a less expensive model. (Mental health services director)

As we observed in the last chapter, the evidence used to support an EBP can come from a variety of sources. One often thinks of EBPs as being supported by rigorous scientific methods using data that is more often than not collected from populations and communities that are external to the community considering implementation. An agency in the United Kingdom considering the adoption and implementation of multisystemic therapy (MST) (Henggeler et al, 1998), for instance, may be asked to place their faith in the evidence-base of this EBP that was generated from a randomized controlled trial (RCT) conducted in the United States or Australia. To the degree that MST works in the U.K. in much the same manner that it does in the United States, the EBP and the evidence base for the EBP can be viewed as being global in nature. Global evidence is *external* (that is, originates outside of an agency or jurisdiction), scientifically *rigorous* (for example, RCTs), and *generalizable* or transferable from one setting to another. Global evidence is the foundation for EBP.

In the last chapter, however, we also identified other sources of 'evidence' used in the evaluation of whether or not to implement a particular EBP. This evidence relies heavily on characteristics of the local context in which the implementation occurs (that is, the supply of resources to support evidence use and the EBP itself, and the demand for the EBP and supporting evidence), as well as clinical experience of those responsible for implementing the EBP. These forms of evidence are considered to be local in nature. Local evidence is *internal* (that is, originates within an agency or jurisdiction and may include administrative data), *personal* (that is, based on either involvement in data collection and analysis or familiarity with population studied, and *specific* to the population and its needs. Local evidence is the foundation for practice-based evidence (Dodd and Epstein, 2012).

In this chapter, we examine the difference between global and local models of EBP implementation and the principles underlying the decision-making process related to EBP implementation. It summarizes the findings of a study of perceptions of barriers and facilitators to adopting evidence-based and innovative practices in child mental health services organizations in New York State. This study illustrates a decision-making model that is anchored by concerns related to the costs associated with, capacity for, and acceptability of the EBPs and their adoption. This study also illustrates the importance of certain principles of behavioral economics such as orientation to the present rather than the future (temporal discounting), having greater concern about losing something one possesses than about gaining something one has not yet experienced (loss aversion), and use of heuristics or rules of thumb to make complex decisions rather than going through all possible choices.

Global and local theories, models and frameworks

In much the same way that evidence supporting the implementation of an EBP can be viewed as being global or local, the theories, models, and frameworks used to explain and support implementation efforts can be characterized as global or local in nature. As illustrated in Chapters Two and Three, there has been a proliferation of theories, models and frameworks that link different sets of potential predictors with implementation processes and outcomes. These include characteristics of the innovative program, practice or policy, the organizations and individuals tasked with implementing the innovation, and the external environment in which such implementation occurs. All of these characteristics may serve as implementation barriers, facilitators or both. The development of strategies to facilitate EBP implementation has relied on these theories, models or frameworks to identify the barriers that must be overcome and the facilitators that can assist in this task.

Although there seems to be general consensus as to the potential of such theories, models and frameworks for facilitating implementation of evidence-based and other innovative practices, some have questioned their value for understanding and guiding implementation and pointed to their limitations for connecting implementation theory with practice (Oxman et al, 2005; Bhattacharyya et al, 2006). For instance, frameworks and models in general provide checklists of potential determinants of successful implementation but do not prioritize them or indicate which are most important or predictive of implementation outcomes and which are least predictive (Nilsen, 2015). Further, as Proctor and colleagues (2011, p. 72) observe, "the success of efforts to implement evidence-based treatment may rest on their congruence with the preferences and priorities of those who shape, deliver, and participate in care. Implementation outcomes may be differentially salient to various stakeholders, just as the salience of clinical outcomes varies across stakeholders."

Related to the lack of information on stakeholder preferences and priorities for implementation is a limited understanding of the principles and processes of deciding whether or not to adopt, implement and sustain a new and innovative practice. Panzano and Roth (2006) found that the propensity to adopt an innovative mental health practice was negatively related to the perceived risk of adopting the practice and positively related to expected capacity to manage risk and an organization's past propensity to take risks.

Finally, perceptions of barriers and facilitators to adoption of EBPs and other innovations have been associated with the characteristics of the organization itself and the extent to which it adopts such innovations. Perceived costs and benefits and the assessment of risk associated with adopting an innovation have been linked to perceptions of the attributes of the innovation itself (for example, how much it costs to train staff, the amount of time required to use the EBP with fidelity, what outcomes are associated with use of the EBP) (Rogers, 2003), which, in turn, have been linked to the decision to adopt or not adopt an innovation (Panzano and Roth, 2006; Seffrin et al, 2009). These attributes (that is, the barriers and facilitators) vary from one organization to the next (Damanpour, 1991; Frambach and

Schillewaert, 2002; Panzano and Roth, 2006), which may account for the variation among organizations in implementation of EBPs. An earlier study by Seffrin and colleagues (2009) found that the proportion of facilitators to the sum of facilitator and barrier comments made by project informants were higher for innovative mental health projects that moved forward with implementation than those that did not. By contrast, a case study comparing two sites' implementation of a measurement feedback system found a higher proportion of barriers to facilitators in the higher implementing clinic; however, this clinic also reported better organizational and leadership supports to overcome the identified barriers (Gleacher et al, 2016). In both studies, the assessment of barriers and facilitators was primarily limited to *a priori* content topics based on the existing global literature of adoption and diffusion of EBPs and did not consider the potential influence of local practitioner/policymaker models.

Findings from the New York State adoption study

One approach to understanding how local models of research evidence and EBP implementation are constructed and operate is by examining how providers evaluate the barriers and facilitators and associated costs and benefits of the EBP and its implementation. The New York State adoption study, described in Chapter Four, identified a number of barriers and facilitators associated with the adoption of evidence-based and innovative practices in child mental health clinics. A list of these barriers and facilitators is presented in Figures 7.1 and 7.2, respectively. The highest percentage of participants (86.7%) mentioned cost as a

Figure 7.1: Barriers to adoption of innovative and evidence-based practices in state-supported mental health clinics

Costs	Capacity	Acceptability
• Financial – costs • Financial – loss of staff • Lost productivity • Time for training • Organizational impacts • EBP requirements	• Financial – reimbursement • Organizational • Lack of staff • Leadership • Environmental constraints • Lack of technical support	• Staff buy-in • Client fit and buy-in • Organizational fit and buy-in

Figure 7.2: Facilitators of adoption of innovative and evidence-based practices in state-supported mental health clinics

Costs	Capacity	Acceptability
• Free/low cost • Little impact on organization	• Available training • Money/financial support • Leadership support • Evidence of positive outcomes • Available trained staff • Organizational capacity and resources • EBP flexibility • Available supervision • Regulatory mandate	• Staff motivation to change • Client need • Supportive organizational culture and fit

barrier, followed by limited capacity (55.9%) and lack of acceptability (52.9%). With respect to facilitators, the highest percentage (82.3%) of participants identified available capacity, followed by acceptability (41.2%) and benefits or limited costs (24.0%).

Costs and benefits of adoption

Analysis of the qualitative data collected as part of this study revealed three central themes of barriers and facilitators to implementing EBPs. The first theme focused on issues of cost and included additional time required to train staff, direct costs, reduced productivity, staff turnover, resource requirements for use of the EBP, and lack of evidence of the innovation's benefits. Parallel to the theme of costs as a barrier were benefits and reduced costs as a facilitator. This theme included available time, evidence of positive outcomes associated with the innovation, flexibility in use of the innovation, little impact on the organization, and availability of the innovation for free or at low cost.

The cost of implementing a new program or practice was the most frequently cited barrier. As one clinic chief executive officer explained, "the first thing I look at is how much is this gonna cost us if we try to implement it" (Palinkas et al, 2017a, p. 3). The most frequently cited cost was associated with the training of staff. Such training involves two types of costs, the cost of the training itself and the lost revenues that occur when staff members are not seeing clients while they are getting trained. Training costs include the expense of paying for someone skilled in the practice to train one's staff, purchasing of treatment manuals and/or other instructional aids, and perhaps travel expenses of staff who are sent elsewhere for training. What is most important, is that training results in lost productivity and revenue when therapists engaged in training activities are unavailable to perform billable services. This, in turn, results in reduced productivity of the clinic as a whole.

In addition to lost revenues and productivity, participants cited other costs associated with the impact of adoption on the organization as a whole. A number of participants cited the additional paperwork associated with the adoption of a new practice. Others cited the additional workload that would affect staff morale because it would make it more difficult "to be able to stay current, to read, to take a deep breath, to look at things" (Agency CEO).

Lack of evidence of positive outcomes is another barrier because it calls into question the benefits of adopting the innovation. Participants questioned the rationale for implementing new practices when there was insufficient evidence that clinical outcomes would be markedly better than those associated with existing practices. There was a general reluctance to switch to another treatment modality unless they were convinced that clients would do equally well if not better than they were at present.

Another cost associated with training is potential staff turnover. As explained by one program director:

> You're investing in a staff member for, let's say a year in a training program and then they take think that experience is great, and they go to another place...People don't see how much it costs to the agency, unfortunately. Or the clinician doesn't see. It's a great opportunity for them, but it's a great opportunity for them to market themselves.

Related to the cost of training staff are the costs involved in supervising staff to use the practice with fidelity.

> Because now if you have any new model, somebody has to oversee it and supervise it. And that again, becomes a money and time factor of who's going to have the time to now supervise this model and make sure it's being done effectively. And what does that take in terms of a supervisor's time and the money for them to be doing that versus something else that they need to be doing. (Program director)

In contrast, flexibility in adapting the innovation to the practice was considered a facilitator to adoption.

Practicing an EBP with fidelity also incurred another cost in terms of time required to do so. As observed by one agency vice president:

> And I think also the other challenge that makes it difficult is that some of these evidence…these innovations require a certain amount of time. And it doesn't fall within the business plan that we have. So for example, the CPT requires forty-five minutes. That means that for the clinicians that are implementing this model, we don't have that flexibility of scheduling their patients in those thirty-minute slots to increase productivity. So productivity, oftentimes, is compromised because of the extent of time that you have to provide under this model.'

Capacity for adoption

The second theme focused on issues of clinic capacity to implement the EBPs. Barriers included lack of trained staff, lack of organizational capacity and resources, environmental constraints, lack of financial reimbursement for implementing the innovation, limited access to training, lack of technical support, and lack of support from leadership. Facilitators related to capacity for adoption included available training, funding or financial support and incentives, trained staff, leadership that was supportive of the adoption, organizational resources, and supervision, a regulatory mandate, the presence of an innovation champion, more information about the innovation, and access to an interagency network.

While the additional costs associated with training and supervising staff and an increased workload and time devoted to using the innovation with fidelity may be viewed as a disincentive to adoption, there is the additional risk of not being adequately reimbursed for incurring these costs. The program director and vice president at one clinic cited a specific practice, Dialectical Behavior Therapy, as an illustration of where a fee per session model might not work and where the clinic would be unable to get compensated for the type of supervision that is required to remain with the fidelity of the model.

Even if one were to obtain reimbursement for training and supervision, the limited access to useful resources is also an important barrier to adoption. Participants noted the paucity of high quality training opportunities and the absence of supervision as a follow-up to training as barriers to adopting innovations.

Lack of trained staff is another important barrier. This includes the lack of staff qualified to use the innovation, the lack of staff available to be trained, and the lack of support staff. This was especially true in non-adopter clinics where the lack of financial resources to hire additional staff meant that existing staff would have to take on additional responsibilities if a new EBP were adopted and implemented.

Another barrier to adoption relates to constraints on capacity imposed on a clinic by its external environment. Often mentioned by participants was the challenge of providing mental health services to school age clients during school hours. Another environmental constraint is the absence of a regulatory policy governing implementation. This constraint is also associated with the limited capacity to obtain reimbursement for using the innovation, as in the instance of managed care companies not wishing to approve compensation for evidence-based models for group therapy. However, regulations that mandate services may also be seen as a facilitator in that they eliminate the need to make a decision because the decision has been made for them

Related to the lack of fit is a lack of support from the clinic's leadership. As noted by one program director, "barriers are definitely if the executive team doesn't agree with what we're trying to do or doesn't feel that it is the appropriate initiative to expend a lot of time and energy on" (Palinkas et al, 2017a, p. 5).

The presence of a champion for the innovative program or practice within the clinic was also cited as a facilitator that enhanced a clinic's capacity to adopt an innovation. While innovation champions could be senior administrators or supervisors, they may also be frontline staff. Such champions were seen as fellow staff who would be able to communicate enthusiasm to the other staff and help support them through the implementation.

Another facilitator related to capacity is the ability to provide financial incentives to staff. This was especially an issue in non-adopting clinics that lack the fiscal stability and revenues to reward staff for using EBPs, despite the fact that use of such services might produce long-term financial benefits to the state (reduced recidivism due to improved clinical outcomes). Lacking such incentives, directors were concerned that staff would lack motivation to get trained in an EBP or to use the EBP with fidelity.

Other distinct facilitators reflecting the capacity to adopt included prior experience with adopting other innovations, the existence of a quality improvement unit within the clinic, being in a supportive academic environment, and having more information about the innovation itself.

Acceptability of adoption

The third theme focused on the acceptability of the EBPs from the perspective of the staff responsible for using them, the clinic as a whole, and the clients or consumers who are the presumed beneficiaries of the EBPs. Barriers to acceptability of an EBP included staff resistance to change, lack of fit with the client and client's needs and preferences, and lack of fit of the innovation with the organization (Box 7.1).

Box 7.1 Barriers to adoption acceptability

Staff resistance: "When you're working with evidence-based practice that are different from what people are used to doing, you certainly have to overcome staff resistance." (Clinic vice president)

Lack of fit with the client and the client's needs and preferences: "It's also the patient resistance to change and the lack of cooperation from the parents." (Program director)

Lack of fit of the innovation with the organization: "And obviously, yeah, anything that would go against the clinic's mission, clearly, you know that we're not going to touch." (Clinic CEO)
Source: Adapted from Palinkas et al (2017a)

Facilitators related to acceptability of the innovation included staff motivation to change current practices, evidence of positive outcomes in addressing client need and preferences, and the existence of a supportive leadership and organizational culture. For instance, related to evidence of positive outcomes was the manner in which the information related to the innovation was presented or 'framed'. As explained by one program director:

What motivates? Well, just how it's presented to me, how I present it to the staff meetings. Is it presented to the managers the same way, basically saying this is the new program, for instance, that we're going to be using and how this will be effective for clients. So I like to see examples how it may help another program. Or I like to see numbers and see how effective it is…So once I see those numbers, then I'm driving to make sure that it's in my program. (Palinkas et al, 2017a, p. 5).

The only facilitator related to acceptability that was not the opposite of staff buy-in, organizational fit and client need and buy-in was the observation that other agencies were also adopting the innovation. As expressed by one clinic CEO, "So if the health system's doing it, then obviously it's easy for us to do. If other hospitals are doing it and we want to compete with other hospitals, or sometimes we need to show that we're doing it too" (Palinkas et al, 2017a, p. 5).

Weighing costs and benefits

Although participants were asked to identify barriers and facilitators separately, it was evident in several instances that both factored into some form of assessment or calculation of the benefits relative to the costs. There were several references to being motivated by EBPs as being 'cost effective' and the need to determine whether the clinical value of the program or even the efficiency value is an investment that a clinic could afford to do. Benefits were viewed both in terms of improved outcomes for the individual client as well as improved productivity or revenues for the clinic as a whole. In some instances, this assessment is made with the recognition that the benefits are not immediate, but are likely to occur at some point in the future. In other instances, the benefits are not entirely clear, as when clinics experienced a loss of revenue when their staff were being trained in an EBP.

Two particular patterns were observed in the assessment of costs and benefits, however. The first pattern was a focus almost entirely on the costs of adoption with an expressed desire to avoid these costs with little or no attention given to benefits. In many instances, the costs are perceived to clearly outweigh the benefits. For instance, one program director expressed an unwillingness to adopt EBPs that were not user friendly, were hard to fit into clinic operations, did not seem to fit with the population being served, were very time consuming, required a lot of other documentation, did not appear to be effective, and "just don't make sense." In another instance, unless the innovative practice is short-term, it may not be cost-effective because "the longer you're working with a family the more questions and challenges there are around the effectiveness of our work" (Clinic CEO) (Palinkas et al, 2017a, p. 6).

The second pattern was the reliance on untested assumptions in assessing costs and benefits. For instance, references to staff resistance to change in general were often based on personal experience and did not appear to rely on 'data' based on the specific instance (that is, a particular innovation).

> You know, like certain…I know, within myself and sense that maybe with colleagues, there's a certain resistance to change. And I think sometimes it comes from more seasoned clinicians, even though they have the experience and in some ways they have so much to give. Changing, you know, innovating, it gets a little more difficult if you've been doing something one way for twenty-five years. It's hard to make change. (Program director)

A local behavioral economic model of implementation

Our analyses of the perceived barriers and facilitators of innovation adoption revealed a local clinic leadership model of implementation based on assessments of the cost and potential benefits of adoption, the organization's capacity to adopt, and the acceptability of adoption to the client, providers, and the organization itself. The cost of adopting was the most frequently cited barrier, followed by the organization's capacity to adopt and the acceptability/fit of the innovation to clients, staff and the organization. In contrast, the available capacity for adoption was the most frequently cited facilitator of adoption, followed by acceptability and limited costs and potential benefits.

In many respects, the clinic leadership model prioritizes the salient factors in existing global models and frameworks of adoption and implementation developed by researchers. For instance, if we take the CFIR (Damschroder et al, 2009) as an illustration, all of the barriers and facilitators identified by study participants reflect characteristics of innovation (for example, costs associated with implementing the program, need for and availability of training and supervision evidence of positive outcomes, flexibility, adaptability, and perceived excellence in how the program is presented), the external environment or outer setting/context (availability of funds, client needs, regulatory mandates, pressure from other agencies), the inner setting/context (organizational structure, availability of trained staff, fit with organizational culture, leadership support, financial incentives for implementation), characteristics of individuals (staff fit and buy-in), or implementation process (presence of program champions). Costs, capacity (fidelity) and acceptability also represent three of eight implementation outcomes in the model proposed by Proctor and colleagues (2011). Elements of the CFIR and other implementation frameworks that are not especially salient in the clinic leadership model include the role of inter-organizational networks, ability to test a program on a small scale, client advocacy, planning, and evaluation or fidelity monitoring.

The model also exhibits five of the six characteristics of the innovation as described in Roger's Diffusion of Innovations theory (2003). Relative advantage is represented in the benefit of improved clinical outcomes. Compatibility is represented in the barriers and facilitators related to organizational fit and leadership support and staff buy-in and motivation to change. Complexity is represented in EBP requirements and flexibility. Observability is represented as improved clinical outcomes and client acceptability. Trialability was not represented in participant comments.

The local clinic leadership model of innovation adoption revealed in this study, however, illustrates several principles of behavioral economics (Simon, 1955; Kahneman and Tversky, 1979; Bickel et al, 1995; Kahneman, 2011; Rice, 2013) that are not found in most implementation theories, models or frameworks. In contrast to traditional economic theory which assumes that individuals make rational decisions in order to maximize the utility or personal benefits derived from their choices, behavioral economics recognizes the systematic biases inherent in decision making and the notion of "bounded rationality" (Simon, 1955), and posits that utility is a subjective concept representing the individual's personal satisfaction with the decision (Kahneman, 2011). The principles of behavioral economics are summarized as follows (Box 7.2):

Box 7.2: Principles of behavioral economics

1. People tend to be overly oriented to the present rather than the future (temporal discounting); they are more concerned about losing something they have than about gaining something they have not yet experienced (loss aversion); and they are very sensitive to monitory incentives, especially those that are most tangible.

2. People are cognitively limited, using heuristics or rules of thumb to make complex decisions rather than going through all possible choices; they exhibit decision fatigue, which accounts for a preference for less rather than more choice; and they are influenced by how choices are framed (framing).
3. People's preferences are influenced greatly by the environment and can be manipulated, especially through advertising.

Source: Adapted from Rice (2013)

In this study, clinic leaders do appear to compare the costs and benefits of adoption in accordance with principles of classical economic theory and models of comparative effectiveness research (Garber and Meltzer, 2009). Benefits include improved outcomes that address the needs of clients and expanded service capacity. However, consistent with the principle of loss aversion, the leaders also tend to focus more on the costs than they do on the benefits of innovation adoption. Costs were identified by the largest percentage of study participants (85.2% versus 14.9% who perceived positive outcomes as a benefit). They also expressed concern over loss of staff that received additional training and reduced staff morale. Avoiding these costs was a predominant concern of many of the program directors interviewed:

> I think that certainly the disconnect between policy and financial policy, on innovative practices not being supported, is one barrier. I think cost of training. And by cost, meaning the cost of whoever the trainers are and then the cost of lost productivity, lost revenue by virtue of those needing to be trained, have to be away from what their current position is in order to get the training. (Agency director)

> Yeah, sure. Because it could be a great model, but if it costs too much to train everybody then we can't even do it then we don't...you know, it's not something we're ever going to bother with. (Program director)

> I mean, the cost of...First, there's the actual cost of buying some of these programs is quite expensive. And then the cost in implementing them and training is very, very high. Not the opportunity cost in relationship to time, but the actual financial cost. (Clinic director)

Examples of the use of heuristics included the untested assumption that staff would resist adoption in general or that it would require too much time to implement the innovative practice.

> And sometimes it's hard to get people to change ways or change roles. Or requiring more training and skills. Some staff have been in the field many years and have no idea about recovery evidence-based treatments [to promote recovery]. So I think there's even staff resistance that goes into play. (Program director)

> Then you have staff resistance as well. You know, people often feel like evidence-based practice is like a dirty thing sometimes. Especially among psychologists. I mean, not here, but just the other psychologists I know, manualised treatment, garbage. (Program director)

In these instances, there was no evidence that leaders had polled their staff to determine how receptive they would be to a particular innovation and no evidence of a willingness to experiment (that is, adopt the innovation on a trial basis).

Consistent with the principle of temporal discounting, some clinic administrators expressed concern over whether the long-term benefits in clinic efficiency and client outcomes were worth the short-term costs associated with lost productivity during training.

> Because as soon as you're sending someone to a training, they're not doing billable services. So you have to ask yourself whether the chance that you will get better outcomes somewhere down the road is worth the risk of going out of business because you're losing money now. (Program director)

> So that's a prerequisite to even do any of this stuff. And that costs a lot of money, and already I'm in deficit and I'm going to be in deficit even if I meet my goals. So, my fiscal goals, I'll still be in deficit. So I don't know we're going to do that. So that's one thing that bothers me. But aside from that, even if I got that it's just another thing. It's really another thing and it's just so involved and it's just... Right now we're just involved on reporting out on the SED [serious emotional disorder] kids. And that's enough.

[Chuckles] But I don't see it going anywhere. Like what am I doing with it? It's just an activity. It doesn't have any meaning for me and everything else I do has meaning. (Program director)

Consistent with the principle of framing, some clinic administrators claimed to be motivated to adopt based on how the innovation is presented to them and how they, in turn, present it to their staff.

And I think that's sort of the salesmanship of kind of framing things…from different peoples' perspectives and trying to create some agreement that way. And I think that, generally…I think we've been pretty successful in that. I think it's much more…You know, the challenges come. And like, well, how will that work? How will we implement it? And how will it be sustainable, and you know those sort of things? So I think, you know, we've generally been pretty successful in being able to get people on the same page. I think it's in the implementation sometimes that those challenges come back up. (Agency director)

Consistent with the principle of incentives, participants made reference to the importance of incentivizing use of the innovation by both clients and practitioners.

So we're part of the 1199 Union. And I can't incentivize a mental health clinic without incentivising the part of the 1199 Union. And I can't incentivize a mental health clinic without incentivizing the entire organization who's an 1199. So what we've talked about, clinician reaches one hundred percent productivity, they are full time staff in the union, salary, benefits, they reach a hundred percent and then they go over a hundred percent. They're fabulous, they have a great week. We would like to incentivize that and say for every session you go over we can either reimburse you at a fee for service rate, we can give you a gift card for twenty-five dollars, you know, something. And we're struggling right now in trying to kind of incentivize that drive, or strive to do more than what is needed. (Agency director)

I mean, I know that this is probably not an option, but if there was any way that we could receive some sort of deficit funding or some sort of financial incentive specifically attached to an innovation. (Program director)

Consistent with the principle of decision fatigue and preference for limited choices, participants expressed a preference for mandates as a facilitator because it eliminated the need to make a decision.

Well, the easy choice, I mean, it's multi-factorial. But the easy one is it's a regulation and you have to. You know, so if OMH promulgates something it's not elective. You have to do it. I mean, you can drag your heels but eventually they will cite you if you don't. So that's the easy one. The other drivers are, has the health system decided that it wants to do it? We're part of a health system. So if the health system on a macro level has decided this is what you're going to do for all patients. Again, there's no choice, this is what you do. (Agency director)

Yeah, the most obvious [facilitator] is if there's a regulatory change. I have no choice. I mean, I get to go to my boss and say, we have no choice we have to do this in order to be compliant. (Agency CEO)

I think the other thing is, I think there's a little bit of model fatigue that happens. As an organization that's always looking at new ways of doing things, I think that frontline staff often don't get attached to any one way of doing things because they know it's going to change. And so they're just, oh, here's another model. Here's another important thing to do. And so what can happen I think with staff is they just, well, I do what I do and this thing will go away too, so I'll just keep doing things the way I do things. So I think there's a little fatigue related to that, and so we've got to be selective about what kinds of things that we take on. Some things we don't have choices about, so we have to do. (Agency Director)

Reliance on mandates by the New York State Office of Mental Health to motivate adoption is also consistent with the principle of preferences being influenced by the environment that can be manipulated, along with other agencies' adoption of innovation as motivation to adopt.

For individuals making the decision to innovate, however, the determinants of successful implementation can be reduced to answers to three simple questions: 1) What will it cost me to innovate? 2) Do I have the capacity to innovate? 3) Am I motivated to innovate? As the results indicate, the same information may be used to answer more than one question. Thus, having a supportive leadership reflects both a capacity for innovation and a desire to do so from an organizational perspective. Evidence of positive outcomes associated with the innovation may be viewed as a benefit contrasted with the costs as well as a motivation by staff, clients and organizations for adopting the innovation.

What is more important is that the clinic leadership model presented here suggests that the barriers and facilitators are prioritized such that decision makers give greater weight to costs than to capacity or acceptability when evaluating barriers, but give greater weight to capacity than to costs and acceptability when evaluating facilitators. The most important costs from the perspective of clinic decision makers are temporal and monetary. The lack of trained staff is the most significant or salient barrier related to capacity. The reluctance of staff to adopt new practices is the most significant or salient barrier related to acceptability. Availability of time to innovate and evidence of positive outcomes associated with the innovation are the most important facilitators. Access to training activities and materials and availability of financial support and incentives are the most important capacity facilitators. Organizational fit and leadership support are the most important acceptance facilitators. Thus, while existing implementation frameworks, theories and models may help to guide implementation practice by identifying potential barriers and facilitators that might be important to address when undertaking an implementation endeavor, they are more like checklists of factors relevant to various aspects of implementation (Nilsen, 2015). Local decision-making models such as the ones used by clinic leaders in mental health clinics in New York State are potentially useful in identifying the most important factors within a specific context or setting and devoting limited resources and strategies to addressing these factors.

Variations by engagement in adoption activities suggests that what is perceived to be a barrier or facilitator may reflect the characteristics of the entire organization and where it happens to be in the process of implementation. One interpretation of the observed associations found between certain facilitators and degree of engagement is that they reflect differences in the willingness and capacity of the organization itself to adopt the innovation. As noted by Seffrin and colleagues (2009, p. 261), "it is reasonable to expect that the specific mix of factors seen as hindering (that is, barriers) and supporting (that is, facilitators) the adoption and implementation of a given innovation may vary by organisations." In turn, these differences may have an impact on beliefs (for example, capacity to manage risk) that affect the perceived risk of adopting the innovation and/or the risk of proceeding with implementation (Panzano and Roth, 2006). Another interpretation is that what constitutes a facilitator or barrier is not uniform across all phases of adoption or implementation. In either instance, "differences in organisational context reflected in views about barriers and facilitators may partly explain the decision to adopt innovations" (Seffrin et al, 2009, p. 261). However, in this study, there were some significant differences in perceptions of facilitators but no significant differences observed in perceptions of barriers by adopter status (Palinkas et al, 2017a), suggesting that facilitators may be more relevant than barriers to understanding the willingness and ability to innovate.

Finally, the data from this study seem to suggest key factors that researchers should pay attention to and test in quantitative models. In an earlier study with the entire cohort of mental health clinics in New York State from which this sample was drawn, Olin and colleagues (2015) found clinic size, efficiency and outsourcing were significantly associated with participation in business trainings and proportion of youth clients and full-time clinical staff were associated with participation in clinical trainings. The present study enriches those findings by highlighting the potential importance of local/contextual factors not available in state administrative data sets. This knowledge should be used in combination with state administrative data to help states develop targeted strategies for promoting innovation adoption and implementation.

Summary

The findings from this study illustrate a clinic leadership model of innovation adoption reflecting certain principles of behavioral economics. There appears to be a high level of consensus or shared understandings as to perceived costs and benefits, capacity to adopt, and acceptability of the innovation. Furthermore, the findings point to areas where current models can be enhanced or modified, particularly with respect to the prioritization of barriers and facilitators, as well as to the need to take local stakeholders into consideration when developing strategies to facilitate implementation of evidence-based and innovative practices for children and adolescents.

- The decision to adopt an innovative or EBP by clinic leaders is based largely on assessments of the cost and potential benefits of adoption, the organization's capacity to adopt, and the acceptability of adoption to the client, providers, and the organization itself.
- This clinic leadership model also illustrates certain principles of behavioral economics, including temporal discounting, loss aversion, sensitivity to monetary incentives, use of heuristics, decision fatigue, and susceptibility to advertising or behavior of competitors.
- The clinic leadership model is a 'local' model of evidence and EBP implementation in that the determination of costs and benefits, clinical capacity for adoption, and the acceptability or desirability of adoption in is based on a specific set of contextual factors such as clinic size and fiscal health and state policies and mandates, as well as the values and personal experiences of those responsible for deciding whether or not to adopt an EBP.
- Successful implementation may require the integration of these local models with the more global models of implementation science.
- Such integration is likely to occur when researchers responsible for developing and evaluating the EBPs and practitioners and policymakers responsible for using them to deliver services engage in some form or transaction or exchange where preferences and priorities related to EBPs and their implementation are generally if not entirely satisfied.
- Such a transaction might best occur in a partnership involving researchers, policymakers, and practitioners.

8

Research–practice–policy partnerships

> It serves us because we understand the system better and make better policy decisions, and it helps them because they get to showcase their skills and publish things and get more grants and stuff. So it is a mutually beneficial process. I think what has happened with all of the systems change over the last year or two years is that the relationship has gone from mutually beneficial to symbiotic and absolutely positively critical for doing the work that we do. And the level of reliance is just skyrocketed exponentially and the partnership is more like closely intertwined than what it was previously…So people that you can rely on, that you can trust, that get it, that can be responsive to your needs real quickly and that can help you carry on the vision that you need to achieve in a short period of time, of having them as our partnership has been extremely beneficial, more so now than ever. (Policymaker, New York State)

In Chapter Five, the role of social influence networks in implementing EBPs was highlighted. These networks included staff members of one's own organization as well as peers working in other organizations in the same jurisdiction (that is, county) or in other jurisdictions. In the case of the CAL-OH study, the networks also included researchers who developed the EBP (TFCO) and the implementation strategy (CDT) and who assessed the effectiveness of the implementation strategy in scaling up the EBP. However, the specific role of these researchers was not addressed in the CAL-OH study, but rather was viewed implicitly.

In Chapters Six and Seven, two different models of evidence and implementation were introduced: a global model that is external to most settings, scientifically rigorous and generalizable across different settings; and a local model that is internal and originates within an agency or jurisdiction, based on personal experience, and specific to the needs of an organization and the community it serves. Global models typically represent the cultural understandings of researchers, while local models typically represent the shared understandings or cultural systems of practitioners and policymakers. However, there is little understanding of how these two models operate in tandem when researchers and practitioners/policymakers work together to implement an EBP.

Despite their different roles, researchers, practitioners, and policymakers are united by their efforts to meet the needs of the communities they serve. This work, however, is often carried out independently. For instance, researchers may assume responsibility for generating the knowledge to identify the most effective services, while practitioners and policymakers may assume responsibility for delivering these services. However, the responsibilities themselves are not independent, but rather are fundamentally linked to one another. This linkage is embodied in the processes of translational research and the translation of research into practice (Palinkas and Soydan, 2012).

Research–practice–policy partnerships (RPPPs), which conduct research that is valid, reliable, and relevant to the needs of policymakers and practitioners, represent an important strategy for narrowing the gap between research and practice described in Chapter One. Although many if not most efforts to implement an evidence-based policy, program or practice occur without a research component, such partnerships are critical to the effective translation of research into practice. It is a process that often assumes a cyclical character (Aarons et al, 2011) and relies on close communication between researchers and community-based service agencies. One way they facilitate the implementation process is by integrating the global and local models of evidence and implementation described in Chapters Six and Seven. They also have potential for striking a balance between fidelity and adaptation and between internal and external validity. But partnerships between these two groups are not always easy to maintain. Differences in organizational cultures of stakeholders, a lack of trust and long-term commitment, unclear roles, insufficient and unequal distribution of resources, and inadequate exercise of scientific rigor all present challenges along the way (Palinkas and Soydan, 2012).

The aim of this chapter is to describe the structure and operation of RPPPs for health and social services, with a particular focus on disseminating and implementing EBPs. The chapter presents three models of effective partnerships in child welfare and child mental health, illustrates these models through case studies, and highlights key elements of successful partnerships.

Models of successful RPPPs in child welfare and child mental health

RPPPs are carried out in many different ways, ranging from investigator-initiated research with minimal community input to joint decision-making on all aspects of research with active community direction and interpretation of the results (Hatch et al, 1993; Chamberlain et al, 2012). In this section, we introduce three models for successful RPPPs. All three models involve some degree of research, technical assistance, knowledge generation, and knowledge dissemination. Where they differ is in the amount of attention given to each component, and in the background of the partnership's leadership, be it research, policy, or practice.

Box 8.1: Three models of successful partnerships

- **Model 1** represents a long-term partnership between researchers affiliated with a nationally recognized research center and practitioners and policymakers affiliated with local child welfare, mental health, juvenile justice, school, and healthcare systems. Led by a prominent researcher, the primary function of this partnership is to conduct research and generate knowledge.
- **Model 2** represents a partnership between researchers with practice experience and policymakers and practitioners affiliated with one of the largest child welfare systems in the United States. Led by the service system leaders, the primary function of this partnership is to provide long-term technical assistance and disseminate knowledge related to evidence-based interventions.
- **Model 3** represents a combination of the first two models. Research, technical assistance, knowledge generation, and knowledge dissemination for delivery of mental health services in state-supported clinics are undertaken in equal measure under the leadership of individuals with research, policy, and practice experience who act as an intermediary or 'culture broker'.

Source: Adapted from Palinkas et al (2017d)

These models are illustrated, based on the domains of activity, focus, and leadership, in Figure 8.1. Each model is illustrated by a case study of a particular partnership dedicated to child welfare and child mental health.

Model 1 Case study: Child and Adolescent Services Research Center and San Diego County Behavioral Health Services and Child Welfare Services

Introduction

The first case study, which involves an established research center partnering with county-level child welfare and child mental health service systems, illustrates the structure and operation of a research-dominant partnership. Although the partners view one another as equals, the researcher serves as the principal leader of this partnership. The primary function of this long-term partnership is to generate knowledge that is relevant to the development and implementation of EBPs and generalizable to the larger population of children and adolescents in need of services. The research agenda is driven primarily by extramural funding opportunities (predominately from the National Institutes of Health), as well as access to study participants afforded by the community partners. The partnership has also served an important secondary function of providing technical assistance to community-based child-serving systems for the purpose of improving service quality and outcomes.

Background

The Child and Adolescent Services Research Center (CASRC) at Rady Children's Hospital-San Diego is a consortium of over 100 investigators and staff from multiple academic institutions and research organizations in Southern California. CASRC has a strategic focus on improving child and adolescent mental healthcare through a program of research that spans clinical epidemiology studies linked to EBP, effectiveness and quality of care studies, and implementation studies that include organizational, financing and policy issues. Under the leadership of Director John Landsverk, the growth of the CASRC research agenda occurred in three phases (Landsverk et al, 2010). Initially

Figure 8.1: Successful research–practice–policy partnerships in child welfare and child mental health

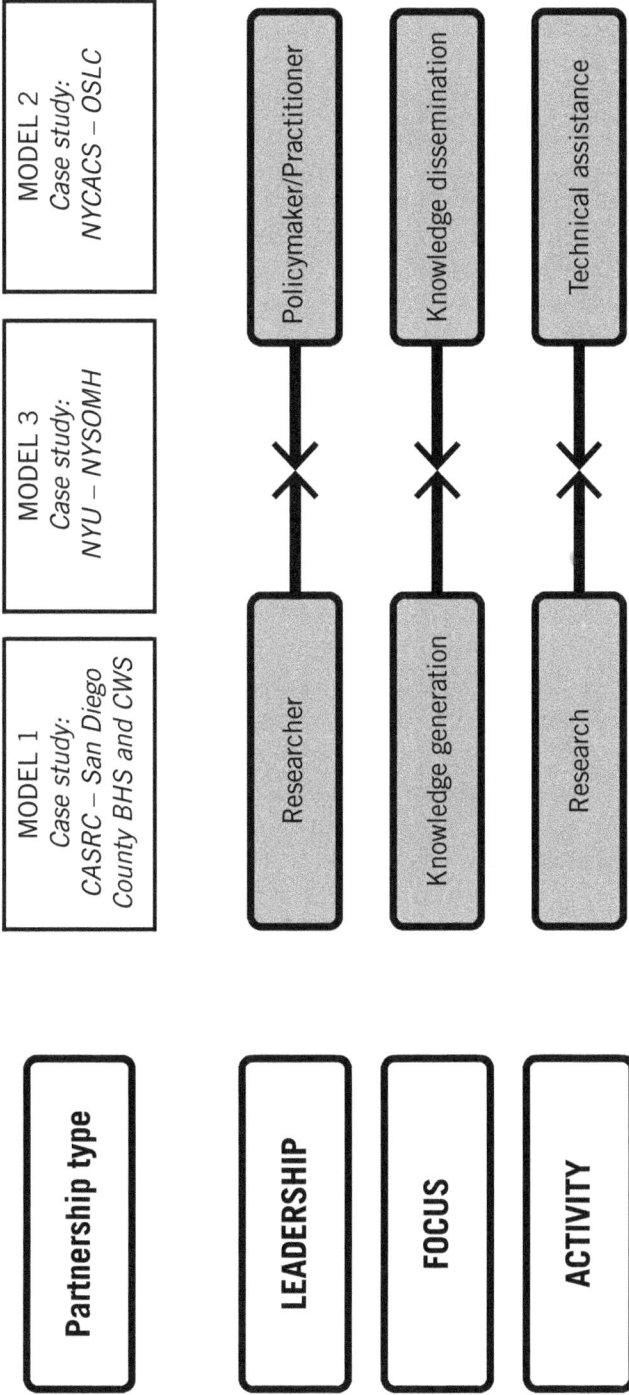

called the Child and Family Research Group (1989–94), early work focused primarily on the mental health needs of children in child welfare, and examined child, family, and system factors affecting access to and use of public child mental healthcare services. From 1994 to 2005, CASRC grew to be a nationally recognized center on pediatric mental health services, expanding the portfolio of studies to include children cared for across multiple public sector service systems. The third phase (2005 to present) saw the development of a robust program of research on the dissemination and implementation (D&I) of evidence-based interventions, "with a targeted focus on developing innovative design and measurement strategies and technology to address the formidable challenges of the emerging science of D&I" (Landsverk et al, 2010, p. 84). In all three phases, CASRC worked collaboratively with community service systems at the local, state, and national level. CASRC has a long history of partnering with local administrators and providers from multiple public agencies (for example, child welfare, mental health, Medicaid physical health, drug and alcohol education) and with community organizations (for example, the Foster Parent Association, Exceptional Family Resource Centers, Learning Disabilities Association, and local mental health advocacy groups (Landsverk et al, 2010).

Benefits to research: knowledge generation

One of the earliest studies resulting from these partnerships examined client crossover from the social services system to the mental health system in San Diego County (Blumberg et al, 1996). Public mental health service use was examined in 1,352 clients participating in a longitudinal study of children in foster care. Overall, 17.4 percent of the children in the social service system were also served in the mental health system. In another study (Leslie et al, 2003), administrative data from five different service systems in San Diego County were used to examine racial/ ethnic differences in caregiver reports of psychotropic medication use for a random stratified sample of 1,342 children who were served during the second half of fiscal year 1996–97. Caregivers of African American and Latino children were less likely to report past-year use compared to white children; caregivers of Latino children and 'others' were less likely to report lifetime use. Another study conducted in a partnership with San Diego County Child Welfare Services (CWS) (Price et al, 2008) examined the impact of a foster parent training and support intervention, KEEP (Keeping Foster Parents Trained and Supported), to determine whether the intervention mitigated placement disruption risks associated with children's placement histories in an ethnically diverse sample of 700 families with children between ages 5 and 12 years. Families were randomly assigned to the intervention or control condition. The intervention increased chances of a positive exit (for example, parent–child reunification) and mitigated the risk-enhancing effect of a history of multiple placements.

In all three of these studies, community partners provided access to the data, participated in data collection, and reviewed study findings. Agency staff received training in data collection by CASRC investigators. According to a CASRC investigator, agencies provided limited input as to what should be studied and how; rather, their primary function in these partnerships was to provide access to study participants. In the third study, child welfare case managers and foster parents received training in the intervention and used it with a cohort of families meeting study inclusion criteria.

Benefits to community: systems improvement

Although the primary function of these partnerships was to conduct research and generate knowledge that could be generalized to all service systems, a secondary function was to provide technical assistance to community organizations. The San Diego County System of Care Evaluation (SOCE) was developed through the System of Care Council with direct advisory support from the Super Outcomes Committee and collaborative partners. In 2004, a series of community stakeholder meetings were held to obtain input and feedback on the development of an evaluation system for San Diego County's Children, Youth and Families Behavioral Health Services (BHS). Stakeholders were involved from the beginning of the development process: clinicians, administrators, policymakers, and families. SOCE measures were chosen because of their assessment of System of Care goals as defined by the County and the availability of information to be analysed at multiple levels: the client level, the program level, and the system level. The specific objectives of the SOCE were to: 1) assure accountability for the delivery of results to consumers; 2) build and sustain the momentum of SOC accomplishments; and

3) effectively and efficiently move decision-making to action and results. CASRC investigators provided technical assistance in data collection and analysis under a contract to BHS. This arrangement was more focused on program evaluation than original research, but, in return for an evaluation of systems outcomes, CASRC investigators were granted access to county level services data for research purposes.

CASRC investigators routinely met with staff from the two service systems to review research findings and discuss possible issues for research. In meetings with BHS, participants would review results of CASRC studies and CASRC-produced Systems of Care reports to identify needs for additional information, such as county-wide patterns of drug and alcohol abuse. In meetings with CWS, CASRC researchers would share findings with agency leadership and program managers.

CASRC also has served as an intermediary between treatment developers and community-based practitioners. For instance, under the auspices of an RCT, foster and relative (kinship) families caring for a child received from San Diego County Child Welfare Services were trained by developers of the KEEP foster parent training intervention, designed to equip foster parents with strategies for managing externalizing behavior problems (Chamberlain et al, 2008a).

As an illustration of the benefits of the partnership to the community partners, one of the earliest findings from their partnered research was that two thirds of the youth in child welfare met screening criteria for developmental disabilities. Out of that finding came a long-term project that continues to focus on universal screening for developmental problems in youth served by CWS and a much stronger relationship between the developmental services offered at Rady Children's Hospital and the San Diego County child welfare system. In another instance, the results of a study conducted by CASRC investigators (Garland et al, 2010) were disseminated by BHS to all county-funded therapists, with the intention to improve delivery of services at the individual level. It was also used by CASRC investigators to advocate for changes in services delivery and the broader use of EBPs at the systems level. In both instances, the research findings were used to improve quality of services. The research conducted by CASRC and other investigators documenting the limited effectiveness of wraparound services was also used to support BHS's decision to reduce delivery of these services. The Systems of Care reports were used by the County to justify continued funding for services when findings pointed to successful outcomes, and for expansion of services when findings pointed to weaknesses or deficits in current service delivery. These reports were also used to respond to critics who argued that the County was not adequately responding to youth behavioral health needs in San Diego.

Model 2 Case study: New York City Administration for Children's Services and Oregon Social Learning Center

Introduction

The following case study illustrates a model of a practice-dominant partnership in which the relationship between researchers, practitioners, and policymakers is driven by a policy decision to improve the quality of care by using practices with demonstrable outcomes. In this model, the researcher assumes responsibility for dissemination of findings, and the policymaker serves as the principal leader of the partnership. The primary function of the partnership is to disseminate knowledge and provide technical assistance related to service delivery. This dissemination also requires and provides an opportunity to conduct research on EBP implementation and sustainment. In this instance, the research agenda is informed by the community partner's need to deliver high quality services to its clients.

Background

In 2012, the Administration for Children's Services (ACS) in New York City made a decision to use evidence-based and promising interventions to strengthen parenting for foster, biological, and adoptive parents involved in the child welfare system. By changing the role of case managers to support parents of children in foster care, ACS hoped to decrease placement disruptions, decrease the population in foster care, decrease recidivism, and increase permanency by 20 percent. The plan was to train over 300 case managers serving over 2,000 children and families in a number of parent-focused evidence-based interventions. The implementation of EBPs was a 'top-down' decision based on prior experience as part of the Children's Services Juvenile Justice Initiative.

To carry out this plan, ACS contacted Patricia Chamberlain, Senior Scientist at the Oregon Social Learning Center in Eugene, Oregon. A researcher with practice experience, Chamberlain had developed evidence-based parent training interventions, including TFCO (Chamberlain et al, 2007) and KEEP (Price et al, 2008). Although the agency had not previously worked with Chamberlain, she had implemented a number of TFCO programs in New York City and had familiarity with some of the agencies participating in the project.

ACS leadership asked Chamberlain if KEEP would be an appropriate intervention with their service population; they also solicited her advice on the choice of an appropriate training program for biological parents. These conversations led to the selection of KEEP, Parenting Through Change (PTC) (Forgatch and DeGarmo, 1999), and Youth Development Skills Coaching (a subcomponent of TFCO). In addition, ACS specified that they wished their case managers to be trained in Family Finding (Allen et al, 2011) in conjunction with Hillside Family Services. ACS also wanted staff trained in how to interact with the legal system.

Known as Child Success New York City (CSNYC), the project was planned so that it would be implemented in stages. The first stage would be a proof of concept and involve a cohort of five agencies selected by ACS, using data on length of stay, size, and rates of adoption. Subsequent stages involved training additional cohorts until every case manager within ACS agencies was trained.

Chamberlain negotiated directly with ACS to provide training and supervision in PTC and KEEP and overall project management. In turn, ACS negotiated directly with the five agencies to secure their participation. Chamberlain was responsible for training caseworkers and supervisors to fidelity in the five interventions; creating a team of trainers made up of case planners who had reached fidelity; and providing to ACS and the independent project evaluator data on attendance, engagement, child behavior problems, visitation observations, saturation, and participation in consultation. Chamberlain sent these reports to the agencies five days before sending them to ACS so that they could make corrections if necessary. She also participated in bi-weekly phone calls with executive directors of the five agencies and ACS.

Benefits to community: research-informed training and technical assistance

Implementation of CSNYS was but one component of an overall effort by the senior leadership of ACS to implement evidence-based interventions. Another benefit of the partnership for ACS was that they were relieved of the responsibility for managing different interventions and working with different treatment developers.

The partnership also resulted in certain benefits to the five community agencies being trained in the interventions. According to a deputy commissioner, all five agencies acknowledged the need for a program like CSNYC and admitted to certain benefits, especially with respect to the training of birth parents and foster parents. Training of staff and a reduction in caseloads were also perceived as benefits resulting from the program. The program also resulted in closer collaborations between parents and case managers. Echoing the view of ACS leadership, agencies saw the need for standardizing services delivered to clients due to the wide variation in outcomes based on agency assignment.

Benefits to research: evaluation and knowledge generation

ACS made it clear that the only research they were interested in was an evaluation of whether the project achieved benchmarks in placement stability, permanency, recidivism, and census. The agency contracted with the Chapin Hall Center at the University of Chicago for this purpose. For her part, Chamberlain viewed the project as an opportunity "to put the programs to the test in a way where we could have a public health impact." Her primary interest was in learning whether programs "make a difference at the population level." As part of that interest, she also wanted to know what was required to successfully implement the interventions: "We felt that, given our history with implementation research, we would try to find a way to map implementation research onto the primary agenda, which was New

York ACS's agenda." Chamberlain proposed training supervisors to integrate interventions into the daily practice culture by using an intervention known as R3 (reinforcing effort, relationships, and small steps), and then evaluating effectiveness (Saldana et al, 2016; Chamberlain, 2017). Chamberlain also proposed to implement a fidelity monitoring data system known as Computer Assisted Fidelity Environment (CAFE), originally developed to monitor implementation and fidelity of KEEP. In this project, as ACS found it to be appealing but wanted additional data collected, CAFE grew to have many more functions.

Model 3 Case study: New York University and New York State Office of Mental Health

Introduction

The following case study illustrates a type of a partnership in which research and technical assistance are given roughly equal weight. The primary function is to generate and disseminate knowledge related to the implementation of EBPs. In this model, policymakers and researchers share relatively equal responsibility for leadership of the partnership. What is especially distinctive about the leaders, however, is their experience as practitioners and policymakers, as well as researchers. In this instance, the research agenda is informed by the community partner's (a state agency) need to deliver high quality services to its clients, and by the researchers' desire to use the community as a 'natural laboratory' for developing, testing, and implementing EBPs in child mental health settings.

Background

The Center for Implementation-Dissemination of Evidence-Based Practices among States, known as the IDEAS Center, is an Advanced Center funded by the National Institute of Mental Health. Located at the New York University (NYU) Department of Child and Adolescent Psychiatry, IDEAS is dedicated to advancing implementation science in health and mental health systems serving children, adolescents, and their families. Its mission is to improve the effectiveness and efficiency of state roll-outs of EBPs and quality improvement initiatives. The Center's research activities are framed around three implementation challenges: 1) engagement in EBP initiatives at agency, provider, and consumer levels; 2) integration of data decision support systems for monitoring service delivery and outcomes; and 3) pragmatic mixed methods and measures to support efficient implementation in the dynamic policy environments of states. It carries out these activities in partnership with the New York State Office of Mental Health Division of Integrated Community Services for Children and Families. The Office of Mental Health (OMH) operates psychiatric centers across the state, and also regulates, certifies, and oversees more than 4,500 programs that are operated by local governments and nonprofit agencies. These programs include various inpatient and outpatient programs, and emergency, community support, residential, and family care programs.

The Director of the IDEAS Center is Kimberly Hoagwood, Vice Chair for Research in the Department of Child and Adolescent Psychiatry at the New York University School of Medicine. She also works with the Division of Child, Adolescent, and Family Services at OMH. Along with researchers and intervention developer Mary McKay, Professor and Dean of the George Warren Brown School of Social Work at Washington University in St. Louis, Hoagwood also directs the Community Technical Assistance Center (CTAC), funded by OMH, which provides technical assistance on how to improve the quality of children's care to the over 340 clinics operating throughout the state. According to Hoagwood, "the contract is for service provision, but because we have the support from NIH through our Advanced Center (IDEAS), we can use it as a laboratory to do the research that is important to the state in improving the quality of their services." Their multiple roles and experience has enabled Drs. Hoagwood and McKay to serve as intermediaries or culture brokers, bringing together researchers, practitioners, and policymakers to address child mental health issues of common interest. They are also able to incorporate both research and practice/policymaking perspectives when engaged in conducting research on child mental health issues or translating the results of that research into policy or practice.

Researchers meet with OMH administrators at least on a quarterly basis. During these interactions, researchers "don't wait to present results before all of the data are collected, analyzed, and verified," according to Hoagwood. "This is a difference with typical academic researchers. We're not going to wait until everything is spit-polished, you know—ready to go and out the door in press. You can't do that in this kind of policy environment." The foundation for this partnership is an iterative process that is atypical of academic research.

Benefits to community: technical assistance and systems improvement

The Center has provided numerous benefits to the Office of Mental Health through its technical assistance and research efforts. The CTAC is designed to help New York State clinics address the challenges associated with the recent changes in clinic regulations, financing, and overall healthcare reforms. CTAC's goal is to provide clinics with a set of technical assistance and training activities and tools that promote effective care through efficient practices. CTAC provides training on specific clinical skills and EBPs, and, importantly, helps clinics develop strong business and financial models to ensure sustainability. As part of these efforts, Center researchers have developed and implemented five system strategies driven by empirically based practices: 1) business practices, 2) use of health information technologies in quality improvement, 3) specific clinical interventions targeted at common childhood disorders, 4) parent activation, and 5) quality indicator development. This effort has been ongoing since 2002 in a partnership involving researchers, policymakers, providers, and family support specialists. Research partners also make themselves available to respond to specific requests from OMH staff. As explained by researcher McKay: "I think our job as researchers is to rapidly translate what is known about the headaches they have. They can't wait five years for us to figure it out."

In some instances, such technical assistance from researchers has led to the elimination of existing programs. OMH Deputy Commissioner Donna Bradbury cited as an example an initiative known as Child and Family Clinic Plus. "It was a multi-million-dollar investment. It was a big deal. It was statewide and highly publicised. Time was going by and we were hitting very specific barriers and not seeing the growth in outcomes that we were hoping to see." OMH requested one of their research partners to perform an evaluation of the program. Although the findings "didn't show us anything that we didn't already know, it was kind of confirming. It just validated our own gut instinct that we'd just have to stop this before it gets worse."

The benefits of the research conducted by the research partners extend beyond program evaluations and technical assistance, however. The policymakers also note the benefits that have been gained from NIH funded research, pointing to the family engagement interventions, especially NIH funded research.

Benefits to research: knowledge generation

As in the case study for Model 1, the partnership has provided researchers with numerous opportunities to examine key elements of implementation processes and outcomes, and to develop strategies to facilitate processes and outcomes. For instance, McKay asserts that the endorsement of her research by OMH was critical to convincing reviewers of an NIH RO1 application to which she could randomly assign a group of OMH-supported clinics. She states that OMH "offered us a platform to do a set of research studies, things that you only dream about when you are first starting out in your research career." In one such study, characteristics associated with participation in evidence-informed business and clinical practices training were examined in 346 outpatient mental health clinics licensed to treat youth in New York State (Olin et al, 2015). Clinics affiliated with larger, more efficient agencies and clinics that outsourced more clinical services had lower odds of participating in any business-practice trainings. Clinics with more full-time-equivalent clinical staff and a higher proportion of clients under age 18 had higher odds of participating in any clinical training. Participating clinics with larger proportions of youth clients had greater odds of being high adopters of clinical trainings. A second study prospectively examined the naturalistic adoption of clinical and business evidence-informed training by the same group of outpatient mental health clinics (Chor et al, 2014). The study used attendance data (September 2011–August 2013) from the CTAC to classify the clinics' adoption of 33 trainings. A total of 268 clinics adopted trainings, and business and clinical trainings were almost equally accessed (82% versus 78%). Participation was highest for hour-long webinars (96%), followed by learning collaboratives, which take 6 to 18 months to complete (34%). Most (73%–94%) adopters of business learning collaboratives, and all adopters of clinical learning collaboratives, had previously sampled a webinar, although maintaining participation in learning collaboratives was a challenge.

Core features of successful partnerships

Each of the case studies describes a specific model of a successful RPPP. The keys to their success lay in certain core features embedded in the individual participants, the relationships among partners, the organizations represented in the partnership, the environmental context in which the partnership exists, and the cultural systems that govern and emerge from these partnerships. These should not be viewed as mutually exclusive categories. A set of these features, grouped into categories of intrapersonal, interpersonal, organizational, environmental, and cultural characteristics, is presented in Figure 8.2.

Figure 8.2: Characteristics of successful research–practice–policy partnerships

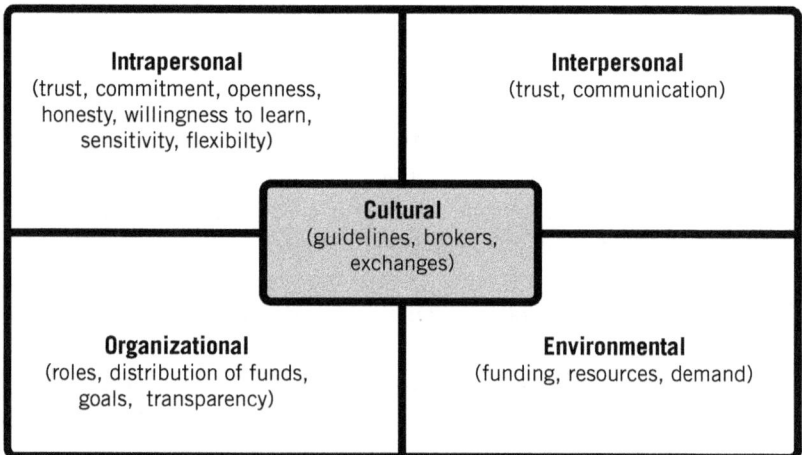

Intrapersonal
(trust, commitment, openness, honesty, willingness to learn, sensitivity, flexibilty)

Interpersonal
(trust, communication)

Cultural
(guidelines, brokers, exchanges)

Organizational
(roles, distribution of funds, goals, transparency)

Environmental
(funding, resources, demand)

Intrapersonal characteristics

Researchers, practitioners, and policymakers in all three case studies cited personality as being the most important ingredient of successful research–practice partnerships. As one community partner observed: "I would just like to emphasize that the key to a successful partnership is the personality, and [the research partner's] personality made it work."

Honesty and trustworthiness

The literature suggests that development of trust is one of the most important requirements for successful research–practice partnerships (Brinkerhoff, 2002; Garland et al, 2006; Jones and Wells, 2007). This development is viewed as requiring commitment, openness and honesty, respect and a willingness to learn about one another (Palinkas and Soydan, 2012). These elements are also embedded in the three models described above.

Developing trust requires transparency and honesty. According to one researcher, "policymakers do not want surprises, so frank conversations about the process and possible outcomes of research activities are discussed openly and often." A similar view was expressed by a policymaker who stated: "We're usually the one with the questions, but sometimes [the researchers] might need to tell us 'we can't answer that' or 'we can't answer it that way, but here is what we can do'."

Willingness to learn

The willingness to learn from one another is another feature of successful partnerships. In Case Study Two, an ACS administrator discussed her relationship with the researcher:

> We were curious and respectful of the other side. I really needed her advice. She is the world-renowned researcher and developer, and I really valued our partnership because I am a lawyer. I can't tell you the best way to engage with foster parents and effect behavior change. So I really needed her to do that. Conversely, she is not a lawyer. She couldn't do the pilot and handle all the logistics without someone like me. I think we both have a sort of intellectual curiosity to learn more about the other side. That was key.

Sensitivity

Willingness to learn from one another is also related to another common element of a successful partnership, which is being sensitive to the needs of the partner and ensuring that the partner derives some benefits from the collaboration (Israel et al, 2005; Minkler and Wallerstein, 2003; Wells et al, 2004). Those benefits accrue over the course of the relationship even if they are not always evident in any one specific project. One researcher asserted: "Any time they call you up and want something, you give it to them. That is an absolute rule. *Quid pro quo* is clearly it. You've got to figure out what they're going to get from it, and they'll tell you."

Sensitivity to the partner also requires an understanding of the factors that motivate a partner. Researchers and practitioners often possess negative stereotypes of each other that are often grounded in differences in organizational culture and previous experiences (Brinkerhoff, 2002; Minkler and Wallerstein, 2003; Wells et al, 2004; Israel et al, 2005; Garland et al, 2006; Palinkas and Soydan, 2012). Organizational cultures identify values, priorities, and normative and pragmatic rules for behavior. Although there is considerable overlap in the organizational cultures of researchers and practitioners, there are also important differences. Researchers, who are usually focused on tenure and promotion, give priority to scholarship, with its demands for scientific rigor, slow and methodical progress, and publication of results in peer-reviewed journals. Conversely, practitioners are usually focused on meeting the needs of their clients and thus give priority to expediency, efficiency, and client satisfaction. Successful partnerships must struggle to effectively "mesh the different missions."

Flexibility

Sensitivity is of little value to a partnership unless it is accompanied by a willingness and ability to be flexible. According to one of the researchers, "You have to go with the flow. You can't plan it all out. You have to be ready and willing to jump and respond to their needs as well as your own. It truly is an ad hoc process." Another researcher pointed to the necessity of having researcher participants who are flexible and open-minded: "I don't think this work is for everybody. You've got to be able to be very frank and very honest and not dogmatic." Flexibility is required because research operates in a very dynamic environment and that changes in the service systems are the norm rather than the exception. "We recognize the difficult environment [the policymakers] are in," according to one of the researchers. Another commented on the need for "flexibility of methods; choosing open source and low burden measures; and being really careful of design—not disrupting typical service flow, and not affecting billing and financing. There are a lot of practical considerations that you need to be really sensitive to, which a lot of researchers don't necessarily take into account."

Nevertheless, being flexible can come at a price. In Case Study Two, the desire by the ACS partners to use the CAFÉ fidelity monitoring system to collect additional data resulted in growing pains for both the researcher and the participating agencies, the latter of which were not provided with sufficient training to use CAFE.

Interpersonal characteristics

Trust

Attention to interpersonal relations is as important to the success of RPPPs as the personalities of individual partners. The two sets of characteristics are closely associated with one another. According to Garland and colleagues, "regardless of the level of the partnership, or its underlying structure, collaboration always relies heavily on interpersonal processes—specifically communication and trust building" (2006, p. 519). Identified above as an intrapersonal characteristic, trust must be mutual for a collaboration to be effective (Brinkerhoff, 2002; Muthusamy and White, 2005). Establishing mutual trust, in turn, requires explicit, clear, and comprehensive communication (Brinkerhoff, 2002). It also requires a long-term commitment. According to one researcher: "You have to think of it as a long-term relationship. It continues whether you are bringing in money or if you are without money, you just stay in there. It is absolutely built on personal relationships." The relationship between trust and a long-term commitment was echoed by another researcher: "I think that is one of the biggest issues—that is, having enough time for these frank conversations. I think that is true in any relationship. People have to have enough trust to be able to open up about what they are really worried about. It takes time."

Face-to-face communication

The importance of regular, face-to-face communication with each of the major stakeholders was evident in all three case studies. In Case Studies One and Three, researchers routinely gave presentations of their findings to their practitioner and policymaker partners. In Case Study Two, the researcher visited each of the five agencies and listened to their concerns regarding the implementation of the project. The interactions demonstrated that she was sensitive to those concerns and that their voices would be heard throughout the implementation. It also provided researchers with an opportunity to identify potential barriers to implementation and solutions for overcoming these barriers.

Organizational characteristics

Clarity of role

Perhaps the most important organization-level element is having a clear understanding of one's role in the partnership. Partnerships function by virtue of the willingness and ability of different partners to assume specific roles (Palinkas and Soydan, 2012). For instance, in Case Study Two, ACS made clear what decisions the researcher was responsible for. In trying to be responsive to both ACS and the agencies, the researcher also learned to avoid being the mediator between the two, as that was not her role: "I had to be careful not to overstep. I learned to stay in my lane."

Lack of clarity in assignment of roles and responsibilities can lead to assignments not being completed, tasks not being performed, and general uncertainty, confusion, and conflict. The obvious solution to addressing this challenge is to assign roles based on skills and resources. Researchers may assume responsibility for research design and quality control, whereas practitioner partners may assume responsibility for service delivery and logistics. Roles may be assigned based on other considerations, too, however. For instance, leadership of the partnership may be assigned to systems leaders, agency directors, or intermediaries who can gain the support of both researchers and practitioners. Partners may also assume different roles at different stages of the partnership in order to support different goals (for example, different phases of EBP implementation) (Minkler and Wallerstein, 2003; Wells et al, 2004; Israel et al, 2005). Protocols that document these roles and functions are highly recommended (Wong, 2006). Roles may also be assigned for the purpose of political expediency. For instance, a community partner may be assigned a role with greater visibility to secure community confidence.

Leadership

As illustrated in the case studies, leadership of successful RPPPs in child welfare and child mental health is not always shared equally—all partners must be willing to choose the role they play, and all partners must agree to that choice. Although co-leadership is often viewed as a key ingredient of a successful partnership, leadership may be exercised differently depending on the purpose of the partnership (for example, generating or disseminating knowledge, conducting research, or providing technical assistance) or the stage of partnership development (for example, transitioning from researcher leadership to community leadership) (Wells et al, 2004). In Case Study Two, both the researcher and the policymakers viewed the relationship as a partnership, albeit one where ACS exercised authority over the implementation of CSNYC. With respect to the partnership with County Behavioral Health Services in Case Study One, an agency administrator stated that he felt like a co-equal with the researcher. He noted this status was critical to the success of the partnership; each member assumed a particular role and set of responsibilities.

Culture broker

Community partners must play an active role in translating the relevance of the science and the need for rigorous methods to stakeholders at all levels (Palinkas and Soydan, 2012). As an intermediary between researchers, treatment developers, policymakers and practitioners, a 'culture broker' with research, practice and policy experience usually assumes this role by virtue of their familiarity with the different organizational cultures of the partners, and interpersonal characteristics of sensitivity, honesty, and communication. In Case Study One, the staff of the San Diego County child welfare services and behavioral health services acted as brokers between CASRC researchers and agency leaders and practitioners. In Case Study Two, the researcher assumed the role of intermediary between ACS senior leadership and agency case managers.

Distribution of resources

Another common element of successful partnerships is the distribution of funding and resources in a way that is acceptable to all stakeholders (Jones and Wells, 2007; Palinkas and Soydan, 2012). For instance, the director of the research center in Case Study One strived to ensure that community partners received some monetary benefit from the partnership. Although the child welfare partner stated at the outset that her agency had no interest in receiving funding to participate in a project, the researcher included in his proposal a full-time position in the mental health agency to support research-related activities. He also made it clear to both partners that he was not interested in obtaining funds from them to conduct research activities. Wishing to ease the burden of participation on his partners, the researcher had a principle of bringing money to them but not accepting money from them. A community partner also stressed the importance of availability of funding to support the community partners, citing as an example his involvement in a project led by researchers:

> At that time the National Institute of Mental Health was very interested in funding these kinds of partnerships. And they had service dollars in these grants. So they had research and service dollars; and their being able to provide both was critical. That project was very successful and very equal. We walked hand in hand. And so much of that had to do with getting both research dollars and service dollars.

Clear goals

It is critical that partners have clear, well defined, and measurable goals (Minkler and Wallerstein, 2003; Wells et al, 2004; Israel et al, 2005). In Case Study Two, ACS had a benchmark for each desired outcome. According to the researcher: "I think without that level of clarity, there is a lot more opportunity for drift. At the leadership level, I would say that ACS really had their act together. I had never worked on a project with that level of clarity before. They kept it simple—it was straightforward and measurable." According to the community partner: "We knew our goal: to improve outcomes for children and families; to expedite reunification and thereby reduce length of stay in foster care. We wanted our services to be much more intensive and much higher quality, and we wanted to get the children out quicker."

Written agreements that outline goals, roles, privileges, and rules of engagement are essential to all RPPPs (Minkler and Wallerstein, 2003; Wells et al, 2004; Israel et al, 2005; Jones and Wells, 2007). In all three models, these items were formalized through contracts and memoranda of understanding. However, as noted, even with written agreements, some flexibility is required.

Sensitivity

Successful partnerships require not only intrapersonal sensitivity to the needs of the partner, they also require organizational-level sensitivity to potential tensions and conflicts between participating organizations. For instance, a researcher in Case Study One noted that the issue of ethnic/racial disparities arose early in his relationship with the San Diego County child welfare system. Many of the African American case managers were reluctant to participate in the NIH-funded study out of concerns that it would merely reinforce stereotypes regarding poor parenting and bad behavior of youth in African American households. Another CASRC investigator knew many of the case managers and suggested that a meeting be held with them to address these concerns. At this meeting, the researchers acknowledged that they could not guarantee that the results would not reinforce those stereotypes, but that they would be sensitive to the implications of such findings. They also asked the African American case mangers if there was anything they could help them with. The discussion revealed that the case managers could benefit from CASRC assistance in using data to make a case for the existence of disparities in services received. Ultimately, the stalemate was resolved and the study was conducted with full participation.

Environmental characteristics

Supply of funding and resources and demand for partnership

The availability of adequate resources is essential to supporting and sustaining partnerships in all three models. In Case Study One, the partnership between CASRC investigators and county youth-serving systems was supported by funding from the National Institutes of Health and by the demand for high quality services from clients and community leaders. In Case Study Two, the long-term relationship between the researcher and the ACS was affected by the change in administration in New York City in 2014, resulting in a suspension of training activities for a time. In Case Study Three, the partnership between New York University researchers and OMH was supported and sustained by the availability of funding from the National Institutes of Health and from the state. Successful partnerships, therefore, require both a *supply* of funding and resources from external sources, and a *demand* for research and technical assistance from service consumers and policymakers.

Adaptation to changes in the environment

Partnerships also require the ability to adapt to changes in the environment. The research leader in Case Study Three noted that since she assumed her position at OMH, there have been three different Commissioners and three Deputy Commissioners for Children's Mental Health: "The state mental health system is changing in major ways. One of these changes is that services for low-income populations will be moved under managed care. Most of what we are trying to do is stay on top of these changes." One of the OMH partners also noted the impacts of a rapidly changing environment: "[We] sometimes joke that by the time we are ready to post an RFP (Request for Proposals), everything has changed about it and we want to do something different. Certainly [the researchers] have found themselves experiencing that firsthand."

Cultural system characteristics

Shared understanding

The importance of having a shared understanding between partners is evident in all three case studies. Community partners in all three case studies asserted there was no need to manage researcher expectations because "the relationship we had with them was a mature relationship; it was professional. They didn't come at us with 'we should do this or that'." In Case Study Three, for instance, community partners expressed a preference for working with researchers with a clear understanding of the constraints on and potential of child mental health services research. As one of these partners explained:

Just thinking about [the researchers] as individuals, what I find so valuable in them is that they have a really good understanding of what we deal with in state government, because one of them actually works for us. She has been part of the policy environment. [The other researcher] has also been involved in policy and implementation. And so I think they both have a really good handle on the day-to-day stuff that we deal with and what would be useful to us...What sets [the researchers] apart is that [we] don't really have to explain what we are dealing with and what we need. They get it pretty immediately, and the products they deliver to us are very relevant and useful.

In addition to sharing common understanding of the research, practice, and policy environments, the partnership itself must contain certain types of knowledge critical to achieving the partnerships goals and objectives. For instance, in Case Study Two, an agency administrator expressed the need to partner with researchers and treatment developers who have a firm grasp of the requirements for successful implementation of EBPs.

I think that having folks who have really thought through the implementation steps is key. I've talked to a number of developers who have these models, and they are just going to come and train, but they have no interest in understanding how it is going to end up working on the ground, how to know if people are going to retain the information, or how to know if they are actually using the model with their clients...And the other piece beyond the clinical fidelity piece is helping agencies figure out bigger pieces of how to support the model and what it takes for staff.

Common values

Partners must share common values. In Case Study Three, for instance, an OMH administrator made the following observation about her research partners:

They all want to do it for the right reasons. We come from different backgrounds and have a different focus, but we all do it for the same reasons. I have no doubt that [the researchers] absolutely care about kids and families. They just want to do what they can to make it better. [We] do our thing here and they do their thing there and we bring it all together.

Cultural exchange

Effectively creating and sustaining a common set of knowledge, attitudes, and beliefs requires individuals to assume the role of a culture broker. A researcher in Case Study Three stated that it is critical to respect the different values and drivers of the policy world and the science world. She finds herself doing "a lot of translating back and forth and helping people acknowledge and understand each other's points of view." In those instances where the two worlds diverge, she said, "as long as there is honesty and transparency, then you can find that sweet spot." This view was echoed by another researcher: "I think that what we have to do as academics is translate findings into things that are meaningful and easier to understand than the science itself."

Nevertheless, the attitudes and behaviors governing these partnerships are not static. They evolve as a consequence of the interactions among partners, and lead to various forms of cultural exchange. Cultural exchange is a transaction of knowledge, attitudes, and practices that occurs when two individuals or groups of individuals representing diverse cultural systems (ethnic, professional, organizational, national) interact and engage in a process of debate and compromise (Brekke et al, 2007; Palinkas and Soydan, 2012). It is a bidirectional process in which two or more stakeholders derive something from and are changed as a result of the transaction. Such an exchange requires an ability to communicate, compromise, and collaborate. Partners communicate with one another for the purpose of generating and sharing knowledge to improve the functioning of community organizations and the well-being of community members (Currie et al, 2005). Partners must also negotiate a balance between developing valid, generalizable knowledge and benefiting the community that is being researched (Macaulay et al, 1999). This negotiation is often facilitated by a culture broker, an individual who understands the cultural systems of research, practice, and/or policy, especially where they diverge and intersect (Soydan and Palinkas, 2014).

In Case Study One, a community partner pointed to a greater acceptance of the importance of research in public service systems:

"I think, pretty much across the board, the value of research is now accepted, as opposed to the early days. We had no dialogue. There was absolutely no relationship at all." For their part, CASRC investigators were provided with the opportunity to learn about how public youth-serving systems operated and both the opportunities and limitations to delivering evidence-based interventions to youth within the framework of these systems. As the Center director explained, "everything I know about child welfare and child mental health, I learned from working with these systems. Before coming to San Diego, I had worked entirely with adults. I knew almost nothing about working with kids." In Case Study Two, the cultural exchange was evidenced by a willingness of researchers and policymakers to learn from one another, as noted earlier. In Case Study Three, partners commented on the transformation of expectations resulting from the partnership. According to one of the researchers:

> It is important to communicate these constraints and opportunities to researchers outside of our Center who are unfamiliar with services research. I spend a lot of time explaining what services research is, how and why it is scientific, and how we get rigorous results. As for rigor, there are certain things you just cannot compromise. I am pretty clear of where those boundaries are and where there is room for maneuverability.

Change

Partnerships result in profound changes in knowledge, attitudes, and behaviors. As one researcher in Case Study Three noted about her partnership with OMH and the research resulting from that partnership:

> I have a huge appreciation for the gap in how scientists think about service, how families think about what they need, and what providers actually need to do when they are providing the service…I am deeply appreciative now of the kind of bridge functions that we really need to play. We have to bridge gaps between providers, organisations, and families, and between policymakers and academics. We still have pretty big gaps. We have to work together and understand each other. I'm more humble than anything else.

Common themes of successful implementation partnerships

The core features identified from the three case studies by no means capture all of the key ingredients of a successful RPPP in child welfare and child mental health. Other ingredients include adherence to scientific rigor (Israel et al, 2005; Brydon–Miller and Greenwood, 2006) the ethical conduct of research (Israel et al, 2005; Brydon–Miller and Greenwood, 2006), and balancing local relevance with scalability (Israel et al, 2005). The core features are also not unique to RPPPs in child welfare and child mental health. For instance, developing trust, maintaining effective communications, sensitivity to the priorities of researchers and practitioners, and possession of adequate resources are also core features of successful educational RPPPs at the district level (Coburn et al, 2013).

Nevertheless, the core features identified in these case studies reveal certain themes that characterize successful RPPPs in general and in child welfare and child mental health in particular. The theme of flexibility is illustrated at the intrapersonal, organizational, and environmental levels, and suggests that there should be an expectation that no context will remain the same for long. Partnerships should be prepared to respond to changes if they are to survive.

The ability to respond to such changes, however, requires a certain degree of sensitivity, a second theme linking these core features. This includes an awareness of the needs of individuals and the organizational cultures they represent. It also includes an awareness of features of the organizations and the external environments that may create constraints on or present opportunities for partnerships.

A third theme illustrated by the core features is clarity. This theme is evident in the intrapersonal element of openness and honesty associated with building and maintaining trust, with the interpersonal element of communications, and with the organizational elements of role definition and clear and measurable goals.

A fourth theme is mutualism. This theme is illustrated in the intrapersonal elements of sensitivity and humility and tolerance, the organizational element of equitable distribution of funding, and the cultural element of shared understandings.

A fifth theme is one of teaching and learning. This theme is illustrated by the intrapersonal element of learning from experience and from one another, the interpersonal element of communications, the organizational element of culture brokers, and the cultural element of cultural exchange. Successful RPPPs in child welfare and child mental health are learning organizations (Clancy et al, 2013; Shaw et al, 2013), where members are constantly learning from and teaching one another. This includes learning specific skills, like methods of data collection and analysis, and learning about the values and behaviors that characterize the organizational cultures to which partner members belong. In the partnerships profiled in the case studies, the culture broker plays an especially important role in teaching and learning because this individual is uniquely suited to translate and facilitate the exchange of knowledge that is critical to a learning organization.

Summary

- Successful RPPPs exist along various continua on dimensions of leadership (research–policymaker/practitioner), focus (knowledge generation–dissemination), and activity (research–technical assistance).
- In successful RPPPs, some aims are shared among all partners (for example, improved youth outcomes), while other aims are specific to each partner (for example, more publications for the researcher, reduced costs for policymaker, more satisfied clients for practitioner). Each partner is considered essential to achieving the aims of all.
- Successful partnerships in child welfare and child mental health yield improved outcomes, improved quality of services delivered, more cost-effective care, and innovative approaches to services delivery.
- Partnerships may be viewed as successful if there is sustainability of the products of the partnership (that is, an implemented evidence-based treatment).
- The keys to partnership success lay in certain core features embedded in the individual participants, the relationships among partners, the organizations represented in the partnership, the environmental context in which the partnership exists, and the cultural systems that govern and emerge from these partnerships.
- Successful partnerships are also characterized by the emphasis placed on flexibility, sensitivity, clarity, mutualism, and teaching and learning.
- Successful and sustainable RPPPs build upon the existing organizational cultures of research, policy, and practice that are transformed as a result of exchanges of understanding, values, attitudes, and rules of engagement between researchers, practitioners, and policymakers.

- This exchange occurs through a process of debate and compromise, requires identification of areas of convergence and a willingness to either eliminate or accommodate divergence, assumes that there is mutual self interest in learning how policymakers and practitioners view research and how researchers view policy and practice, and requires the ability to communicate in a common language and a willingness to collaborate and compromise.

9

Cultural exchange and EBP implementation

I think that in the community mental health sectors, so many of the clients we serve have multiple diagnoses, multiple problems, multiple risk factors and so much of the research seems focused on more single diagnoses, single risk factors, so I continue to think that it's important for researchers to do what they're doing but continue this trend of moving towards real-world situations and trying to find alternative methods of researching in real-world environments, or else the gulf between researchers and practitioners will continue. Practitioners will get research that is too removed from the clientele that they serve and just not be that impressed with it, and vice versa. I know researchers who view practitioners as not caring just one way or another about actual evidence will get frustrated. So I think there has been some great experience now with the federal system of care grants that have gone out and some of the other grant making processes where folks are learning more about how to do research and what outcomes are like and make it applicable to folks on the front line working in real community-based clinics. (Mental health services director)

Conceptual models of evidence use in policy and practice acknowledge that the URE to make or support decisions is often a collective and interactive endeavor rather than an activity performed by any one individual decision maker (Traynor et al, 2014; Edelstein, 2016). This collective endeavor involves the utilization of social capital (Spillane et al, 2001; Honig and Coburn, 2008), social networks (Foster-Fishman et al, 2001; Valente et al, 2015), a common language (Kothari et al, 2011), and the exchange of knowledge or information between researchers and practitioners and within networks of practitioners (Lomas, 2000; Mitton et al, 2007; Nutley et al, 2007).

As illustrated by the three case studies presented in the last chapter, the extent of collaboration between researchers and practitioners is often dependent upon the willingness and ability to exchange information and values through their interactions. This exchange is consistent with a conceptual model of evidence use in which decision makers are human information processors who interact with the evidence, interpret its meaning, and hence determine whether and how they will permit the evidence to influence them (Kennedy, 1984). It is also consistent with a model of collaborations that are predicated on some effort to align values, goals, structures and processes, leading to attempts in collective action in implementation that have a greater impact (Rycroft-Moore et al, 2016). These models view evidence use as an exchange between researchers and practitioners (users of evidence), and between practitioners and services consumers and community members. What is exchanged is evidence-based knowledge and local knowledge (Moll et al, 2005; Nutley et al, 2007). The product of this exchange is working knowledge, defined by Kennedy (1984, p. 1) as "the organised body of knowledge that administrators and policy makers spontaneously and routinely use in the context of their work." According to Honig and Coburn (2008, p. 592), "evidence never informs decisions directly but influences working knowledge which may shape decision making" through a process of sense making or interpretation (Spillane et al, 2002). In other words, this working knowledge becomes the foundation for a set of shared understandings that constitutes a cultural system.

In this chapter, we describe the process of exchanging knowledge, attitudes and behaviors held by various stakeholders in EBP implementation. We then examine the role of cultural exchange in the implementation of a modular approach to evidence-based treatments for child anxiety, depression and conduct disorders in Massachusetts and Hawaii and an EBP for treatment of behavioral problems in foster care youth in California and Ohio.

What is cultural exchange?

As noted in the last chapter, cultural exchange is a transaction of knowledge, attitudes and practices that occurs when two individuals or groups of individuals representing diverse cultural systems (ethnic, professional, organizational, national) interact and engage in a process of debate and compromise (Palinkas et al, 2005; Brekke et al, 2007). It offers potential as providing both a theory and a method of implementing EBPs (Palinkas et al, 2009) and bridging the gap between research and practice that impedes delivery of high quality services to those in need (Institute of Medicine, 2001). As a theory, it may explain when, how, and under what conditions research and practice-based evidence are used in policy and practice. As a method, it offers a set of guidelines for facilitating communication, collaboration, and compromise between various stakeholders committed to implementation. There are three forms of cultural exchange that occur in service systems that rely on research and practice-based evidence and global and local models of implementation to make decisions whether or not and how to implement evidence-based programs, practices, and interventions: 1) exchange between treatment developers and providers; 2) exchange between providers and organizations representing different systems of care (for example, healthcare, schools, child welfare, juvenile justice agencies; and 3) exchanges between each of these stakeholders and intermediary organizations tasked with disseminating EBPs.

The development of a cultural exchange model of implementation of EBPs in service systems takes as its starting point an understanding of agencies within these systems as organizational cultures. Cultural innovations like EBPs involve the translation, transformation and exchange of the cognitive (information) and affective (motivation) elements of meaning systems of the stakeholders involved in the EBP implementation process. The extent to which such innovations are adopted and disseminated and the research supporting such innovations is used within service systems is based on four conditions: 1) the status and skills of a change agent who introduces and advocates for the innovation; 2) the extent to which the proposed innovation supports or threatens the existing cultural system's hierarchy of value to practice orientations; 3) the extent to which that value to practice hierarchy is sustained and supported by the external environment; and 4) the interpersonal dynamics of the stakeholders involved in the innovative process (Bailey, 1973; Palinkas and Soydan, 2012).

The process of cultural exchange is illustrated in Figure 9.1. The process occurs in three stages. In the first stage, members of different cultural groups (national, ethnic, organizational) interact with one another and in so doing learn about and assess the 'other's' shared understandings of normative and pragmatic standards for belief and behavior. In this particular case, what is 'exchanged' is the global

Figure 9.1: Stages of cultural exchange

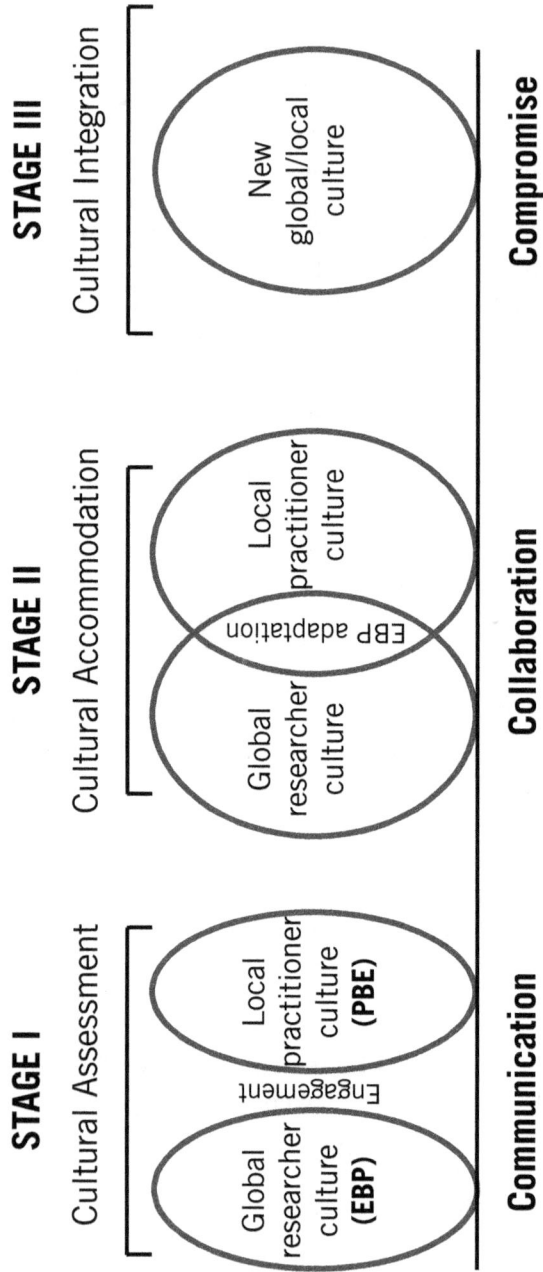

STAGE I
Cultural Assessment

Global researcher culture **(EBP)**

Engagement

Local practitioner culture **(PBE)**

STAGE II
Cultural Accommodation

Global researcher culture

EBP adaptation

Local practitioner culture

STAGE III
Cultural Integration

New global/local culture

Communication

Collaboration

Compromise

knowledge, attitudes and practices of the researcher on the one hand, and the local knowledge, attitudes and practices of the practitioner or policymaker on the other hand. This assessment is dependent on the willingness and ability of the stakeholders to communicate with one another.

In the second stage, the culturally influenced knowledge, attitudes and practices of researchers and practitioners/policymakers are subject to debate and compromise. Learning about the cultural systems of the other stakeholders in implementation forces each stakeholder to re-examine one's own knowledge, attitudes and practices. A set of understandings shared by both researchers and policymakers/practitioners begins to emerge. The focus on this set may involve an EBP representing the global culture of the researcher and preferences for adapting the EBP to suit the needs of a specific population and/or organizational setting representing the local culture of the practitioner or policymaker. This accommodation is dependent on the willingness and ability of the stakeholders to collaborate with one another.

In the third stage, a new culture consisting of a set of shared understandings reflecting the knowledge, attitudes and practices related to implementation and services delivery is created by the integration of elements of the cultural systems of each stakeholder. This new culture is dependent on the willingness and ability of the stakeholders to compromise with one another.

A key element of this process of cultural exchange is the presence of an individual or organization that can serve as culture broker or intermediary between researchers and practitioners/policymakers. As illustrated in the last chapter, that individual or organization may have experience in both research and policy or practice. That experience provides them with a familiarity with more than one set of shared understandings. The culture broker is fluent in the languages of research and policy/practice and is therefore able to translate the shared understandings of one stakeholder group for the benefit of the other group or groups. The culture broker is also a moderator of the debate between researchers and practitioners/policymakers. Experience, understanding differences in shared understandings, fluency, and mediation skills are important requirements for successful brokers of cultural exchanges.

Increasing capacity to serve high-needs children and adolescents with an evidence-based model requires a policy that will support strategies designed to facilitate EBP implementation, including the URE (Palinkas et al, 2017c) and interorganizational collaboration (Palinkas et al, 2014; Rycroft-Moore et al, 2016). Both of these strategies, in turn, are believed to be linked to shared understandings that constitute cultural systems of organizations tasked with delivering such EBPs and the exchanges that occur among the various stakeholders involved in EBP implementation.

Cultural exchange in Massachusetts and Hawaii

Analyses of field notes and interview transcripts from the CTP study revealed five sets of themes relating to the interactions among researchers and trainers and agency administrators and clinicians: interaction types, quality, content, outcomes, and requirements. Each of these themes will be examined in turn below.

Types of interactions

The CTP project involved two types of interactions. The first type comprised formal interactions between EBP propagators (researchers, trainers, and supervisors) and EBP end-users (agency directors, clinicians). In Boston and Honolulu, researchers met regularly with agency directors early on, and then the frequency of meetings was adjusted depending on the nature of the relationship, which was very individualized to each organization. For example, meetings were less frequent with some agencies due to schedule conflicts and other priorities. Directors of other organizations were content to meet with researchers over lunch every few months. Regular meetings were scheduled throughout the entire project period for still other agencies.

Formal interactions between EBP propagators and end-users also occurred during training and supervision phases of EBP implementation. In Boston and Honolulu, workshops were held where clinicians randomized into the SMT and MMT interventions received training from researchers, trainers and clinical supervisors for each of the three problem areas (anxiety, depression, and conduct problems). Each clinician attended one two-day workshop for each problem area over a three- to six-month period. The first day and a half of each workshop was devoted to the principles and practice of the evidence-based treatment for that specific problem, while the final half-day was devoted to implementation issues specific to either SMT or MMT, covered in separate groups. The next phase of training occurred with the clinical supervisors who met with therapists each week to address issues related to the application of each of the evidence-based treatments.

In addition to these formal interactions, CTP researchers, trainers, clinical supervisors, clinic directors and clinicians interacted with one another at dinners organized and sponsored by the researchers in Boston and Honolulu. Informal interactions also occurred frequently between clinical supervisors and clinicians. For instance, one CTP supervisor commented that during the hour of supervision, if the clinician did not have an active case or had just taken on a case, conversation extended to topics ranging from baseball to personal matters like caring for ailing parents, pregnancies, or children heading off to college. Conversations during this time also extended to professional issues outside the scope of the study. The extent of these non-project related discussions varied with CTP supervisors and the extent to which the clinician was making progress in his or her cases. Occasionally, these interactions extended beyond the hourly sessions of clinical supervisions and included meetings for coffee or lunch or organizing potluck picnics. Most of these meetings were initiated by clinicians, but their frequency appeared to be dependent upon the willingness and ability of supervisors to engage in such interactions.

Quality of interactions

For the most part, members of each of these groups reported interactions between EBP propagators and end-users to be positive. Researchers and trainers reported agency directors and staff to be cooperative in implementing the protocol and adhering to data collection requirements. In turn, administrators and clinicians reported being excited about participating in a research project, getting additional clinical supervision through their participation in the project, and learning new techniques for working with clients.

Not all interactions were viewed in a positive light, however. In the CTP, some of the clinical supervisors reported difficulties engaging with therapists. In one instance, a supervisor described the need to be thoughtful in the way she phrased things around a particular therapist "because she would get so tense and phrase things in a negative way." Another supervisor reported that a therapist had been upset with her and misunderstood what she was doing during the weekly sessions: "It turned out that she had felt misunderstood and had been angry with me." For their part, clinicians expressed concern that the EBPs and supervision would interfere with the task of building a therapeutic alliance with the client.

Content of interactions

An analysis of the content of interactions between EBP propagators and end-users revealed two types of exchange. The first type was access to resources. By agreeing to participate in these studies, agencies obtained funding for training for their staff, which they could then use for marketing, recruiting, and quality improvement; and a method for assessing program effectiveness. In turn, investigators obtained access to study participants (therapists and clients) and assistance in evaluating the effectiveness of the EBPs. The second was the exchange of knowledge. Researchers provided therapists with knowledge that was global in the sense that each of the EBPs was based on a well-grounded conceptual framework, supported by evidence gathered from rigorously conducted clinical trials, generalizable to different groups of clients, and offered a way of serving clients that was more systematic, ordered, and detailed than practices currently in use. Clinicians commented on the fact that the manuals helped to 'keep them on track' in working with their clients. Clinicians praised the EBPs for the structure offered by the interventions: "I really enjoyed using that structure with this, with the child who was rather vague otherwise, and this way, you know, was able to focus treatment with her" (modular therapist) (Palinkas et al, 2013a, p. 1113). In turn, clinicians provided researchers with knowledge that was local in the sense that it was based on personal experience in meeting the needs of a specific group of clients.

Propagators and end-users exchanged more than knowledge of a global or local approach to clinical practice, however; they also exchanged the attitudes and opinions that accompanied that knowledge, attitudes and opinions that revealed differences in values related to clinical practice possessed by either group. Researchers and trainers emphasized the scientific foundation of evidence supporting the EBPs being introduced, while clinicians emphasized the experiential foundation of the evidence supporting their treatment or practice as usual. Propagators emphasized the importance of standardization in practice as a means of improving quality of care, while end-users expressed doubts as to the validity of such an approach with clients who have unique clusters of issues needing to be addressed and the potential for loss of control of the therapeutic process by adopting a global approach to care that minimizes the importance of local variation in client need and clinician competence in addressing that need.

Outcomes of interactions

For the most part, these interactions produced three perspectives on EBP implementation. The first perspective is that the process as a whole has been successful. As one clinician in Boston asserted: "I think that it was done really well. So I had a really positive experience with it [the CTP]." Another Boston clinician cited her own experience of continuing to use the EBPs as evidence of the project's success:

> I think it gave me more tools to use with clients I was already seeing. It gave me a lot of practice doing it, and you have individual supervision once a week to go over it...I'm actually using the behavioral techniques a lot with the clients. And like, now, which is, you know, not part of the study.

A second outcome of the interaction was change in the attitudes of many clinicians towards using EBPs. As described by one of the clinicians in the modular condition:

> And a lot of us are psychodynamically trained, and so there was definitely some, uh, rumblings of, oh you know, "We're gonna, you know, jump full force with this, and we're on board, but it's gonna be hard." And then once we started using it, we, in general, we found that it was, you know, we all really embraced it and really liked it. And we felt, I mean, I think that we were given a lot of freedom to, you know, make it our own. (Palinkas et al, 2013a, p. 1113)

The most common outcome, however, was an adapted use of the EBPs. In the early stages of the study, all of the CTP supervisors felt that the majority of the therapists would continue to use some of the techniques, but "either they might select one of the protocols and use it, or use it for some of their clients, but not for the majority of them." One of the therapists in the SMT condition stated: "I would like to use them again, but not necessarily in the same order. I like some of these pieces a lot, and some of these not so much. I really like the relaxation part. I can use it for all my cases" (Palinkas et al, 2009, p.

1113). Preference for adapting the EBPs helped to explain why the modular approach produced significantly better outcomes in client behavior than treatment as usual and even the standard manualized approach (Weisz et al, 2012).

In a follow-up study at the conclusion of the CTP, 26 of the 28 participating therapists (93%) who had been assigned to the standard or the modular conditions reported using the techniques (for example, the fear ladder with anxiety cases; homework with disruptive conduct cases) with non-study cases subsequent to the conclusion of the trial. However, of the 26 therapists who had reported using the treatments with non-study clients, 24 (93%) reported making some form of adaptation or modification. This included all of the 14 modular therapists who were given a coordinating framework for how to make informed adaptations to the protocols, and 10 of the 12 standard therapists who were given explicit instruction in how to use the treatments as directed by the original manuals. Only two of the standard therapists (17%) indicated they were continuing to use the treatments as they had been trained to do so (Palinkas et al, 2013a). The most typical pattern of post-study use of the protocols was to use selected components/modules of a treatment (consistent with the modular approach) with all clients in need of that treatment or all modules (consistent with the standard approach) with some clients, but not the entire protocol with every client in need of a particular treatment (for example, depression). A second pattern of adaptation reported by 22 study participants was to use the protocols with clients who did not meet the criteria specified in the clinical trial itself. A third pattern of use reported by 19 therapists was to make changes in the presentation of the materials, either by rearranging the order in which the components were delivered, or making changes in the tools used to facilitate the presentation of the modules: "I definitely loved the tools that were there. I just don't necessarily use them in that order or necessarily all of them" (Standard therapist) (Palinkas et al, 2013a, p. 1113).

Interaction requirements

A review of the interactions in both case studies revealed four specific themes that appear to reflect requirements for interactions that led to productive exchanges among EBP propagators and end-users. The first requirement was accessibility of each group to the other.

Such accessibility requires effort on the part of both groups, however. According to one of the Honolulu clinicians, her research supervisor:

> was approachable as far as like, questions like, you know "Is this a dumb question?" I don't ever feel any kind of hesitation calling her…the supervision was excellent. I can't say enough about how valuable that was. And it was unlike blocks of counseling time. The supervisors really provided ample time for discussions. So I never felt like, you know, they were looking at a watch and saying: "Okay, well our time is up." You know, and that was really helpful, because sometimes I really wanted to talk things over. Sometimes I really wanted ideas about how to, you know, where to go next.

The second requirement for interaction was a sense of mutual respect. In Boston, for instance, a clinician in the modular condition commented on how much appreciation study participants had for the respect shown to them by the research team:

> the trainings were wonderful, the supervision was wonderful. I think, uhm…there's the other piece that I don't know if I emphasised, which is the amount of appreciation that was expressed by the research team, uhm, for people who were participating in the study. And, you know, we're in a culture where we often feel undervalued and underappreciated, and so, we were like, treated like royalty.

A third requirement for successful interaction was possession or creation of a shared language between EBP propagators and end-users. According to one of the CTP clinical supervisors, therapists "have different languages. I try to find their language for the things I'm talking about and kind of nudge it in the right direction. And I think we end up finding we have more commonalities than differences."

Finally, the willingness of all stakeholders to compromise and accommodate to the needs of the other appears to be a significant requirement for successful implementation. EBP propagators made it clear to end-users that some adaptations of the EBPs were desirable and perhaps necessary to meet the needs of their clients. During the CTP supervisory sessions, for instance, the role of the supervisor was to tailor the EBPs to the specific case and fit it into the therapist's own framework for working with clients. This willingness appeared to have alleviated end-user concern that there would be no flexibility in the use of the EBPs. As one Boston clinician stated:

> I definitely liked having that flexibility, but still with a lot of structure. There was so much flexibility that you didn't know which direction you were going, because the supervision was so positive…They went at the exact right pace. I never felt like we were going too fast or too slow. They had fabulous suggestions. They accommodated to my style and they were wonderful.

Such flexibility required a willingness to negotiate and a certain degree of compromise on the part of both EBP propagators and end-users. For instance, one of the Honolulu clinicians working in a school setting described an interaction with her research supervisor over the most appropriate intervention to use. Although the research protocol called for the use of the behavioral parent training intervention, the clinician felt that circumstances necessitated the use of the anxiety treatment intervention:

> There was one student I saw from start to finish. He actually started off with the disruptive behavior, the parent training. It was difficult because Mom was, uh, it was just very difficult for her. She was a homecare provider for children and it was just difficult to get the work done and for her to be consistent with our meetings. And my thoughts were, and I was working with my supervisor, Dr. [X], in that I personally, I had felt that the root of his problems were anxiety. And the reason he [the client] he was sent to the Parent Training Protocol was because that came up as his primary, the disruptive behavior came up as his primary difficulty. But my thoughts were that this was really more anxiety based. And we ended up switching protocols and we did the Anxiety Program from start to finish.

The CTP study revealed variations in the types, quality, outcomes, and requirements of interactions between EBP propagators and end-users. At the center of each of these variations, however, is the translation and transformation of the cognitive (information) and affective (motivation) elements of meaning systems of both groups through a process of cultural exchange. In the study clinics in Boston and Honolulu, there was an exchange of resources. Propagators provided funding, a means for measuring program effectiveness and quality control, prestige and potential staff recruitment associated with participation in a research project, and opportunities for valued staff training and clinical supervision. In turn, end-users provided access to study participants and assistance in conducting rigorous translational research in real world settings. There was also an exchange of knowledge. Propagators provided a global evidence-based approach to services found to be effective with other populations in other settings, thereby enhancing its generalizability to the target populations of the two projects. Clinicians provided a local knowledge of the specific needs of clients in the research sites as well as experience addressing these needs through long-established treatment strategies. The exchange of knowledge is central to EBP.

The exchange of global versus local knowledge reflects the challenge as well as the opportunity of EBP implementation. The challenge lies in attempting to integrate very different value orientations. For instance, EBP is often associated with a more positivistic tradition of clinical practice, while the distinctive, individualized practices and perspectives of many of the clinicians in both studies tend to reflect a more postmodernist, social constructivist orientation toward behavior and practice (Dodd and Epstein, 2012). The perspective of the propagators is oriented primarily toward the desire to advance and apply the science of mental health care, while the perspective of the end-users is oriented primarily toward the desire to advance practice through the application of theory and of practices consistent with their prior training and experience. In essence, the challenge faced by both groups is in accommodating to different priorities rooted in two different cultural systems (Palinkas et al, 2005), one academic and one clinical. As stated by one of the CTP supervisors when describing her interaction with one of the clinicians: "I really had to personally put my own world view right next to hers. And I had to be just as willing to have her ask me about how I see and feel things as I was asking her to be with me." Such accommodation requires a certain degree of collaboration, communication, and compromise.

Collaboration, communication and compromise are also critical to achieving a balance between fidelity to the intervention as designed and evaluated to create the evidence base and adaptation of the intervention to meet the specific needs of clients, provider organizations and communities. Preference for the modular approach to treating youth with evidence-based interventions in the CTP was based on the local knowledge of therapists in Boston and Honolulu, while fidelity to the standard manualized treatments was based on the global knowledge of researchers and treatment propagators. Fidelity is critical to successful implementation in two respects; first, careful measurement of fidelity enables researchers and program implementers to fully understand whether intervention outcomes are related to the characteristics of the intervention itself or to the quality and extent of its implementation; and second, "there is growing evidence that the fidelity to which an intervention is implemented is highly associated with success in achieving change in targeted outcomes" (Allen et al, 2018, p. 267). However, adaptation is also critical because interventions are "not implemented in a vacuum and contextual factors at multiple levels (for example, clients, providers, organizations, communities) influence its success" (Baumann et al, 2018, p. 286). Creating a better 'fit' between the intervention and the context or setting in which the intervention is implemented helps to ensure an increased likelihood of a positive outcome (Cabassa and Baumann, 2013). Thus, while fidelity and adaptation are often viewed as being two competing value orientations, both are critical to successful implementation (Chambers and Norton, 2016).

In the CTP, some of the researchers participated in the development of the EBPs being implemented. It may be hypothesized that the success of the researchers lay in the fact that they placed higher priority on utility and less of a priority on fidelity than some of their more 'scientifically-minded' academic colleagues. For their part, most of the clinicians were not necessarily representative of all clinicians because they had agreed to participate in the respective effectiveness trial. In both instances, neither represented a homogeneous or monolithic academic or clinical culture but represented to varying degrees a combination of both cultural systems. Change agents may also be an agency administrator wishing to improve the performance of his or her agency, a legislator wishing to support only programs with proven outcomes, a case manager or clinician respected for his or her ability to communicate and collaborate with other agency staff, or a biological parent or foster caregiver wishing to obtain a specific form of assistance.

The EBPs being implemented were also consistent with the agency's goals (for example, remission of symptoms of depression, anxiety or conduct problems), but required additional time and resources that burden existing personnel at all levels within the agency. In some instances, these EBPs conflicted with current patterns of service delivery viewed by staff as the most desirable approach given existing regulatory mandates and funding streams. For instance, some of the clinicians argued that implementing the EBPs constrained them in dealing with more immediate issues like parent substance abuse, mental health problems, financial hardship and imminent eviction from homes, or life-threatening situations. If the costs of adopting an innovation like EBP or specific EBPs are perceived to outweigh the benefits, its acceptance is likely to be more problematic (Bailey, 1973). Costs and benefits themselves are influenced by external factors such as demands for improved services or the inability of existing programs to meet goals and objectives. As noted in Chapter Seven, they are also influenced by principles of behavioral economics. A successful change agent in youth serving systems is thus likely to be an individual or group of individuals who possess both the status and skill to persuade other members of the agency that the benefits of the innovation outweigh the costs and are consistent with the existing hierarchy of the system's values and shared understandings.

The key to the cultural exchange process, however, lies in the dynamics of the interactions between the key stakeholders.

> Characteristics of collaborative stakeholder interpersonal dynamics that are likely to be associated with the extent of EBP implementation in youth serving organizations include the following: 1) possession of similar goals (for example, the well being of the child versus protection of 'turf' or academic advancement); 2) a sense of teamwork and shared control in the EBP implementation (for example, scheduling, training, monitoring of performance, adaptation to suit the needs of specific groups of clients); 3) perceived reciprocity (that is, do both get something desirable out of interaction?); and 4) frequency of communication with one another. (Palinkas et al, 2009, p. 610)

Cultural exchange in California and Ohio

In the CAL-OH study, variations in engagement in cultural exchanges with the treatment developers (and researchers), representatives of the intermediary organizations managing the community development teams, and other service system leaders suggested that some individuals are more likely than others to both exchange knowledge, attitudes and practices with others and change their own knowledge, attitudes and practices as a result of interactions and collaborations with other stakeholders in EBP implementation efforts (Palinkas et al, 2017b). The highest levels of cultural exchanges occurred with individuals from other agencies in the same county, and the lowest level of cultural exchanges occurred with individuals representing the two intermediary organizations.

Greater exchange interactions (that is, processes) with the treatment developer were significantly associated with less seniority in the agency and working in a probation department or other social service agency. Probation departments were significantly more likely than child welfare, child mental health, and other social service agency staff to report cultural exchanges with individuals representing agencies in other counties. Participants randomized to CDTs reported significantly higher levels of cultural exchanges with intermediary organizations and the treatment developer than participants in the control condition. Age, gender, ethnicity, State, education, type of agency and role in agency were all found to be unrelated to cultural exchanges with all four types of collaborators.

Greater exchange outcomes (that is, the knowledge, attitudes and behaviors that result from such exchanges) with the treatment developer were significantly associated with younger age, less education, less seniority in the agency, and working in a probation department or other social service agency. Probation department and other social service staff were significantly more likely than child welfare and mental health agency staff to report cultural exchange outcomes with individuals representing agencies in other counties. Participants randomized to CDTs reported significantly higher levels of cultural exchange outcomes with intermediary organizations and individuals representing agencies in other counties than participants in the control condition. Age, gender, ethnicity, State, education, type of agency and role in agency were all found to be unrelated to cultural exchange outcomes with intermediary organizations and other agencies in the same county.

Cultural exchange processes and outcomes with intermediary organizations were significantly associated with greater accessing of research evidence through documents, local networks, greater research acquisition in general (input) and greater engagement in URE in general. Exchange processes with the treatment developer were significantly associated with more access of research evidence through local networks, and exchange outcomes were significantly associated with more self-evaluations of the research evidence for validity and reliability and greater evaluation in general (research evidence process). Exchange outcomes with agencies in other counties were significantly associated with greater URE in decision-making and greater URE in general (research evidence output). Exchange outcomes with other agencies in the county were associated with acquisition of research evidence from local networks and total URE, and exchange outcomes with agencies in other counties were associated with greater URE in decision-making and greater URE in general.

When controlling for county, State, year of observation, and experimental condition, cultural exchange processes and outcomes in general and with intermediary organizations and the treatment developer in particular were significantly associated with furthest stage of implementation of TFCO and with the proportion of activities completed in the pre-implementation and implementation phases. Cultural exchange processes and outcomes with agencies in other counties were significantly associated with proportion of activities completed in the implementation phase.

Comparisons of the CEI process and outcomes scores across the four collaborators in the implementation of TFCO in California and Ohio revealed significantly greater exchanges between study participants and individuals with other agencies in the same county. In turn, they experienced significantly fewer exchanges with the intermediary organizations participating in the RCT. These differences are consistent with the roles of each of these organizations in the RCT. The intermediary organizations (California Institute of Mental Health [now called California Institute for Behavioral Health Solutions] in California and Center for Innovative Practices in Ohio) were responsible for conducting CDT meetings. As only half of the counties in each state were randomized to this condition, only half of the study participants would have had an opportunity to interact with and exchange knowledge, attitudes and practices with an intermediary organization in the context of the RCT. This is consistent with the finding that none of the participants randomized into the control condition reported any cultural exchanges with intermediary organizations or with representatives from agencies in different counties participating in the same CDT. In contrast, the study design called for collaboration among child welfare, child mental health and juvenile justice systems within the same county when feasible. Individuals representing agencies in the same county also reported more interaction with one another in delivering services and implementing innovative programs outside the context of the RCT as well. Thus, one would expect to see more cultural exchanges with organizations with which one has more interaction, as was the case in this particular study.

With few exceptions, we found no significant associations between the level of cultural exchanges and demographic characteristics of study participants. Exchange process was inversely associated with administrative seniority (that is, role), and exchange outcomes with the treatment developer were inversely associated with age, level of education, and administrative seniority. This is consistent with the observation that agency staff most likely to be in contact with treatment developers were those being trained in TFCO. Further research is required to determine why participants representing other social service agencies reported higher levels of cultural exchanges with the treatment developer and participants representing juvenile justice agencies reported higher levels of cultural exchanges with agencies in other counties.

Overall, URE was associated with cultural exchange process and outcomes with intermediary organizations and other agencies in the same county. The CDT strategy was facilitated by the intermediary organizations and designed to build networks among agencies and counties participating in the scaling up of TFCO. These organizations were also formed with the explicit responsibility for the dissemination of EBPs to county mental health service systems. Other agencies in the same county constitute the primary network used to acquire research evidence. Consequently, respondents reported changes in their own knowledge, attitudes and practices associated with these associations. However, what is interesting is that they perceived themselves to have an influence on the knowledge, attitudes and practices of the intermediary organization. This points to the role of the intermediary organization and the potential for bi-directional influence and exchange.

Finally, cultural exchange process and outcomes were both significant independent predictors of furthest stage of implementation and proportion of activities completed in the pre-implementation and implementation phases of the scale-up of TFCO. This was especially true in collaborations with the intermediary organizations and treatment developer. These two collaborations proved to be the most important sources of information about TCFO and the recourses necessary to implement the EBP. The perception of practitioners that interactions with these two collaborators could lead to changes in their knowledge, attitudes and practices also suggests that successful implementation may require changes in shared understandings of the practicalities of EBP implementation in specific contexts on the part of stakeholders charged with developing the EBP (that is, the treatment developer) and with facilitating its implementation (that is, the intermediary organization).

Summary

- Cultural exchanges may be critical to successful implementation as representatives of two different cultural systems, one academic-based and one practice-based, attempt to find common ground in their efforts to meet the needs of children and adolescents and create a new cultural system that incorporates the use of EBP through collaboration, communication, and compromise.
- Further research is required to develop means of measuring predictors and outcomes of these exchanges and to identify interventions that may facilitate these exchanges and thus lead to improved clinical care.
- Meeting the needs of vulnerable populations such as youth with mental and behavioral health problems through implementation of EBPs may require policies that support the bidirectional exchange of knowledge, attitudes and practices among all stakeholders.
- Policies are recommended that incentivize collaborating organizations to participate in activities that promote such exchanges as a means of increasing the likelihood of successful implementation of evidence-based policies and practices.
- Cultural exchanges among implementation stakeholders may also help to facilitate the acquisition, evaluation and application of research evidence in policy and practice settings.

10

A transactional model of implementing EBP

> We will use the results from the study, but it is not really about practice alone for us. The big benefit is that it begins to change the culture of the agency. It becomes a learning agency. We become an agency that has the wherewithal to develop new programs informed by research. We get to be a co-creator; we get to be an innovator. We get to be part of the group that advances the field. In addition, having your name on the research makes it easier to get funding to support the programs. It also has an impact on staff morale. Staff take pride when our own research demonstrates favorable results. (Program director)

Each of the previous five chapters focused on a specific component of EBP implementation, providing detail on how they manifest themselves in social and mental health services that target children and adolescents and their implications for the broader challenge of understanding and facilitating successful implementation of EBPs in any service setting. In Chapter Five, we examined social networks and inter-organizational collaboration and the role they played in the implementation of TFCO in California and Ohio. We then focused on URE as an illustration of both social interactions that facilitate URE and the shared understandings that comprise the organizational culture of URE. This was followed by another illustration of shared understandings, one that comprised the models of and for assessment of the barriers and facilitators of EBP implementation. We then returned to a focus on social relations and shared understandings that operate in the context of research–practice partnerships dedicated to the task of EBP implementation. This was followed by an examination of the exchanges of knowledge, attitudes and practices among implementation partners and the transformations in shared understandings that result from such exchanges.

This chapter summarizes the five components of a model for successful implementation of EBPs in child welfare and child mental health. It also examines the implications of this model in the design and implementation of three implementation 'facilitators' or support systems: 1) the development of policies that promote EBP use; 2) the development and use of strategies that facilitate EBP implementation; and 3) the formation and maintenance of partnerships that promote ongoing quality improvement in services delivery. It concludes by describing an agenda for future research and practice that will contribute to reducing the gap between these two important elements of child services.

Relationships, partnerships, evidence use, and cultural exchange

Although each of the studies described in this book had a distinct focus and set of research questions, collectively they helped to uncover a model for implementing EBPs that possesses five components: 1) social networks and collaborations; 2) use of research evidence (URE); 3) the integration of global and local models of evidence and implementation; 4) research–practice–policy partnerships (RPPP); and 5) cultural exchanges among stakeholders involved in implementation efforts. The results of the four studies reviewed (CAL-OH, IDEAS, RPPP, and CTP) point to three specific conclusions. First, EBP implementation is associated with the structure of social networks, URE and cultural exchanges among implementation stakeholders. The CAL-OH study demonstrated that stage of implementation was significantly associated with large, urban-based networks that exhibited a high level of in-degree centrality. This sociometric measure of networks was interpreted to mean that individuals in administrative jurisdictions that are further along in the process of successful implementation are more likely to be sought out for information and advice by individuals in jurisdictions that are considering implementation or not as far advanced in the process. In the CAL-OH study, URE in general (SIEU total) and acquisition of research evidence (Input) were significantly associated with furthest stage of implementation of TFCO and with the proportion of activities completed in the implementation and sustainment phases. Finally, the process and outcomes of exchanges among the various stakeholders engaged in implementing TFCO were significantly associated with furthest stage of implementation of TFCO and with the proportion of activities completed in the pre-implementation and implementation phases.

The second conclusion to be drawn from this collection of studies is that EBP implementation occurs in a certain context. In the CAL-OH study, the influence of social networks on stage of implementation was moderated by size and urbanicity of the county. URE was influenced by characteristics of the outer setting that influenced the supply and demand for research evidence and the fit with personal experience (that is, local evidence). In the IDEAS study, implementation occurs in the context of RPPPs that possess certain characteristics (intrapersonal, interpersonal, organizational, environmental, and cultural).

The third conclusion based on these studies is that the process of implementation involves an integration of global and local models of evidence and implementation. The CTP study demonstrated efforts by practitioners and researchers alike to integrate EBP with practice-based evidence. As noted earlier, the CAL-OH study demonstrated that URE was influenced by personal experience. The IDEAS study found that assessment of barriers and facilitators of EBP implementation by agency leaders exhibited principles of behavioral economics.

When considered together, these three conclusions point to two fundamental mechanisms underlying EBP implementation. The first mechanism is grounded in relationships among implementation stakeholders. These relationships are framed in terms of networks, partnerships, collaborations, and engagement in cultural exchanges (that is, process). The second mechanism is grounded in shared understandings of these stakeholders. These shared understandings are grounded in the URE, integration of global and local models of evidence and implementation, and transformation of knowledge, attitudes and practices resulting from cultural exchanges (that is, outcomes).

An illustration of the relationships between these two mechanisms and their predictors and outcomes is found in Figure 10.1. The mechanisms are influenced by implementation predictors found in most implementation models and frameworks, including the inner and outer context of implementation and characteristics of the EBP (Greenhalgh et al, 2004; Damschroder et al, 2009; Aarons et al, 2011). These mechanisms, in turn, influence implementation outcomes such as acceptability, adoption, appropriateness, costs, feasibility, fidelity, penetration, and sustainability (Proctor et al, 2011).

Figure 10.1: Transactional model of EBP implementation

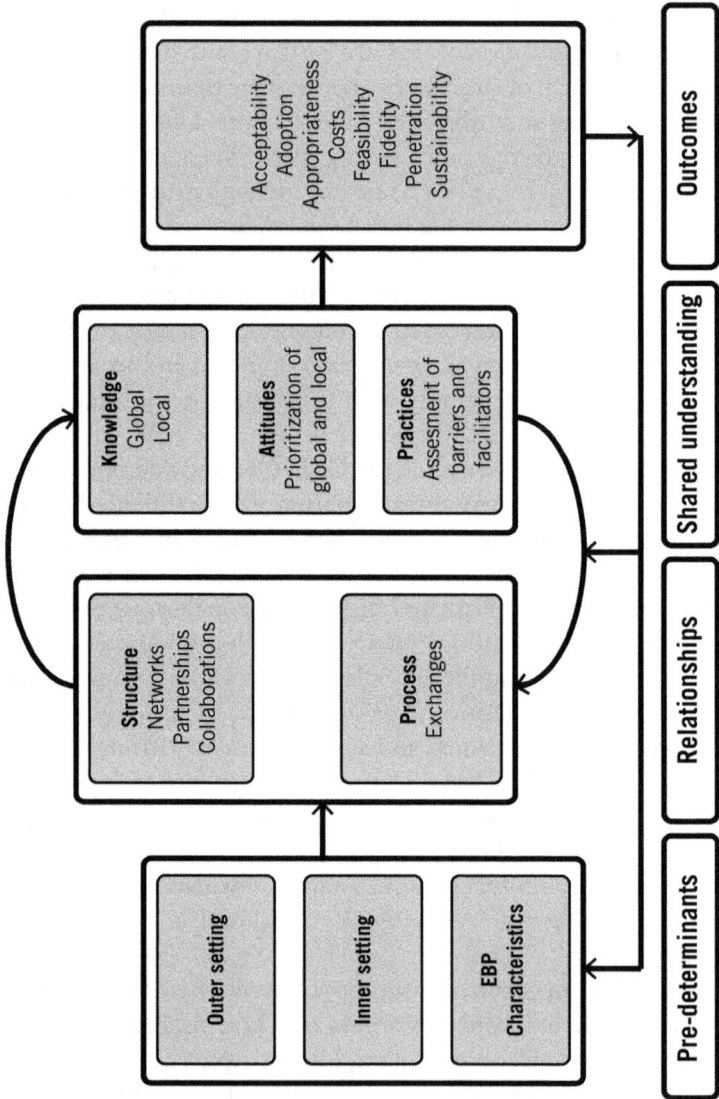

Development of relationships is viewed as key to the type of research being generated in RPPPs. Ellen and colleagues (2013, p. 17) note that "strong links between decision-makers and research producers can enhance the type of research being produced, that is, make it more relevant and highly applicable to the needs of the users, and ensure that the research addresses high priority issues" (Denis and Lomas, 2003). Among the chief obstacles to the development of these relationships, however, are "tradition-bound practitioners, who insist on practicing their way and believe they know their patients or populations best, and the smugness of scientists believing that if they publish it, practitioners and the public will use it" (Green et al, 2009, p. 154).

A focus on relationships pervades many of the existing implementation theories, models and frameworks. Frameworks like the EPIS (Aarons et al, 2011) and the CFIR (Damschroder et al, 2009) emphasize the structure of networks but not the process of relationships among network members. The Diffusion of Innovation theory (Rogers, 2003) gives emphasis to both structure and process and acknowledges the bidirectional nature of relationships between innovators and their audiences. Development of relationships is also fundamental to efforts to promote URE in health system management, policy- and decision-making. These relationships and their products are highlighted in 'interactive' models of research use such as Huberman's (1994) 'dissemination effort' model and Tyden's (1993) 'synthesis pedagogics' model. As Ellen and colleagues note, "exchange activities focus on building and maintaining relationships between researchers and health system managers and policymakers" (2013, p. 2). What is different about this model is that it elaborates on the structure (that is, role of the early adopter and in-degree centrality in disseminating the EBP, partnerships and collaboratives), the process (how exchanges occur, what is exchanged), and the context (how inner and outer context shape relationships). The model expands on the emphasis placed in other models and frameworks on relationships by defining a "culture of implementation" as a set of shared understandings that constitute a model of as well as a model for two specific sets of behaviors critical to the process of implementation: URE and the integration of global and local models of evidence and implementation.

Ellen and colleagues (2013, pp. 14–16) found that "linkage and exchange efforts" within and across organizations and networks was highlighted by managers and staff of health system organizations in Canada as essential to URE:

since it facilitated ease of access to necessary research, enhanced dialogues between researchers and users, and assisted in the establishment of a culture that valued research evidence, even if the research was not immediately relevant. It essentially provided a network of contacts and experts that could be accessed to obtain relevant research to incorporate into the decision-making process.

Patterns and processes of the diffusion and adoption of ideas, values, products and behavior have been extensively examined under various rubrics, including socioeconomic development, acculturation, modernization, and sociocultural change (Hatch, 1993; Rogers, 2003). The development of a cultural exchange model of research–operational collaboration takes as its starting point an understanding of a health or social service system as an organizational culture. Like cultural systems in general, the organizational culture of child welfare, child mental health, juvenile justice and other child-service systems represents a structure comprising learned systems of meaning, communicated by means of a language and other symbol systems, having representational, directive, and affective functions, and capable of creating cultural entities and particular senses of reality (D'Andrade, 1984). Cultural systems also represent:

> a moral process of interpretation and collective experience, composed of many voices, created by and, in turn, creator of social action, and located not in the minds of individuals, but between people, in the medium of intersubjective engagements that spread through the social world of families, work settings, networks, and whole communities. (Lewis-Fernandez and Kleinman, 1995, p. 434)

Both the structure and process of cultural systems are encapsulated in a set of shared understandings or value orientations. Value orientations are complex but definitely patterned, resulting from the traditional interplay of basic values (normative values), social values (prescriptive ethics) and their physical expression (artifacts). These give order and direction to human organization. The cultural logic that articulates the normative values explains why an agency does what it does (that is, to treat mental and behavioral health problems in children and adolescents), while the social knowledge that is embedded in the prescriptive ethics explains how it is done (that is, to use EBPs with fidelity). The artifacts of the normative and prescriptive values explain what is done, who does it, when it is done, and where (Hatch, 1993). These three elements are arranged in hierarchical fashion with the normative truths at the top and the artifacts at the bottom (Bailey, 1973). The higher the element, the more resistant it is to change from the outside.

Cultural innovations like EBPs involve the translation, transformation and exchange of the cognitive (information) and affective (motivation) elements of meaning systems of the stakeholders involved in EBP implementation. As noted in the last chapter, the extent to which such innovations are adopted and disseminated within an organization like a child welfare or child mental health system/agency is based on four conditions: 1) the status and skills of a change agent who introduces and advocates for the innovation; 2) the extent to which the proposed innovation supports or threatens the existing cultural system's hierarchy of value orientations; 3) the extent to which that value hierarchy is sustained and supported by the external environment; and 4) the interpersonal dynamics of the stakeholders involved in the innovative process. For instance, if the costs of adopting an innovation such as an evidence-based treatment for depression are perceived to outweigh the benefits:

> the more ramifying the expected consequences of introducing an item into a system, the more difficult is likely to be its acceptance; it ramifies more widely in so far as it is defined by the people concerned as having an effect upon items which approach the status of a premise, that is, which hold a position relatively high in their hierarchy of values. (Bailey, 1973, p. 8)

Costs and benefits themselves are influenced by external factors such as demands for improved services or the inability of existing programs to meet goals and objectives. A successful change agent is likely to be a member or members of an organization who possess both the status and skill to persuade other members of the organization that the benefits of the innovation outweigh the costs and are consistent with the existing hierarchy of values and shared understandings (Rogers, 2003).

Classic models of behavioral change assume individuals choose among alternative behaviors by performing cost–benefit analyses using payoff-relevant information (that is, data about costs and benefits). This is referred to as the Environmental Learning Model (Henrich, 2001). A farmer who currently plants wheat variety A and then decides to plant a small patch of land with a novel wheat seed, variety B, as an experiment is an example of the environmental learning model (Henrich, 2001, p. 35). The decision to continue planting the variety B wheat is based on whether it results in a greater yield per hectare than variety A. However, this model is not consistent with empirical data of rates of diffusions of innovations. Instead, because humans rely on social learning or cultural transmission to acquire their behaviors, the dynamics of diffusion demand primary reliance on some form of biased cultural transmission. This process contains a number of biases: direct bias—people attracted to specific qualities of idea, belief, practice or value; prestige bias—people copy ideas or practices from individuals with specific qualities or attributes (role models, change agents); and conformist bias—people imitate ideas or behaviors expressed by a majority of the group (Henrich, 2001). For instance, the Stanford Heart Disease Prevention Program conducted in the 1970s and 1980s in several California communities engaged in a series of communication campaigns to recruit at-risk individuals into small group-training classes such as aerobic exercise and smoking cessation, using highly credible individuals who had lost weight through dieting and exercise as positive role models (Rogers, 2003). The success of this program, as measured by indicators of risk reduction in the target communities, was attributed to the self-selection of individuals who were predisposed to a health promotion message reinforced by the role models and the presence of individuals participating in the classes who had a similar predisposition. From the perspective of services for children and adolescents, biased cultural transmission of an EBP is likely to occur when practitioners, policymakers and consumers find that it resonates with their own beliefs and experience, when its chief advocate is a senior practitioner, and when other practitioners begin to accept and adopt the EBP. As noted in Chapter Seven, those beliefs and experience are also informed by principles of behavioral economics in which precedence in the decision to implement EBPs is given to temporal discounting, risk aversion, use of heuristics, decision fatigue, framing and manipulation.

Finally, the adoption of innovations by the entire organization occurs as a result of a negotiation process involving conflict and compromise (Bailey, 1973; Huberman, 1994). However, once adopted, innovations themselves are likely to have an impact on the hierarchical order of shared understandings. These impacts are reflected in changes in the knowledge, attitudes and behaviors of individual members of the organization and in the degree of consensus as to the prioritization of value orientations within the organization itself (Martin, 2002).

From this perspective, successful collaboration between the key stakeholders in delivering services to children and adolescents would involve a process whereby knowledge, attitudes and behaviors related to treatment and prevention rooted in their respective organizational or professional cultures are exchanged and transformed through debate and compromise. In contrast to unidirectional models of innovation that are dependent upon the efforts of the innovator (in this case, the researcher), cultural exchange presupposes a bidirectional process in which innovators and consumers (patients, clients, clinicians, administrators, policymakers) derive something from and are changed as a result of the transaction (Bailey, 1973; Tyden, 1993). Using the mechanisms of debate and compromise, a bidirectional process targets the construction of a commonly accepted value hierarchy (that is, a prioritization of the goals and objectives of child welfare and child mental health), the assignment of the normative and pragmatic components of a specific EBP to that value hierarchy, specification of the role of each stakeholder in this assignment, and the leveling of status between and among stakeholders. For such a process to operate effectively, however, both the rules and opportunities for engaging in debate and compromise must be clearly defined.

Implications for implementation science

In the first chapter, we noted three central debates in the field of implementation science. Each debate focused on the best means for striking a balance between three seemingly contradictory perspectives: fidelity and adaptation, internal and external validity, and global and local evidence. The experience of developing a scientific approach to understanding and facilitating the delivery of EBPs to at-risk youth suggests that a transactional model highlighting relationships and cultural exchanges may create opportunities for striking such balances. In Chapters Six and Seven, we examined how such interactions facilitated the use of global forms of research evidence within the context of local evidence generated by personal experience and internal and external setting influences on such use, including the principles of behavioral economics. In Chapter Eight, we examined how variations in the priorities given to assigning responsibilities for partnership leadership, knowledge generation and application and conducting research and providing technical assistance might help to resolve the tension between giving priority to internal versus external validity when implementing EBPs. In Chapter Nine, we described how such interactions operated to achieve compromises with respect to implementing EBPs with fidelity and adapting them to meet the needs of both practitioners and their clients. In each of these instances, an emphasis on a transactional model of EBP implementation may help to resolve these and similar debates that dominate in the field of implementation science.

Implications for research

A model such as this is only as good as the evidence supporting it. To create such evidence, a number of suggestions are offered for the creation of a research agenda that pays particular attention to the social relations and shared understandings of EBP implementation. One potential avenue for future research might involve the incorporation of relationship building and social networking interventions in KTE strategies designed for facilitating URE. Future research might examine how changes in the knowledge, attitudes and practices of knowledge generators (that is, researchers) results from engagement in RPPPs and/or collaborations between researchers and knowledge consumers. Research should also document whether and how such changes increase the likelihood of successful implementation.

Another potential avenue for future research based on the proposed model would be in the development of new tools for the assessment of the process and outcomes of cultural exchange. Such assessment might build upon existing instruments such as the Cultural Exchange Inventory (CEI) (Palinkas et al, 2017b) or integrate measures of cultural exchange in existing measures of implementation process and outcomes such as the Stages of Implementation Completion (SIC) (Chamberlain et al, 2011).

A third avenue for future research would involve the integration of the transactional model into existing D&I theories, models and frameworks. For example, the frameworks like EPIS (Aarons et al, 2011) and CFIR (Damschroder et al, 2009) describe the inner and outer context that potentially influence the operation of relationship building and development of shared understandings of evidence and implementation. The transactions involved in relationship building and shared understandings might help to move the D&I process and action models (Grol and Wensing, 2004) from description to explanation. The use of a model based on transactional theory might provide greater emphasis to the bidirectional character of diffusion of innovations (Rogers, 2003), as well as outlines the 'rules' for the practice of observation (a model for behavior) as well as the cognitive models resulting from such observation (a model of behavior) found in social learning theory (Bandura, 1986).

Implications for policy and practice

A model such as the one proposed here that is rooted in fundamental mechanisms of relationships and cultural change has several important implications for the development of policies and practices directed at the mental and behavioral health needs of youth in general and youth involved in child welfare in particular. One such implication is that it provides a better understanding of how to build and sustain effective relationships for the purpose of EBP implementation. The model tells us, for example, whom to target within networks (for example, opinion leaders, structural holes), how to build networks (for example, quality improvement collaboratives such as community development teams), and how to build partnerships and collaborations (for example, building trust, establishing transparency). Another implication is that the model provides us with a better understanding of how to use research evidence in policy and practice for the purpose of implementing specific EBPs and for building support (capacity and acceptability) for the EBP. Finally, the model provides a better understanding of how to facilitate implementation by integrating global and local models of evidence and implementation through RPPPs and using principles of behavioral economics to influence the decisions of practitioners and policymakers. For instance, policies that promote EBP use might include provisions for the development and maintenance of community coalitions that are tasked with the responsibility for sustaining an EBP once the initial funding or investment from a government agency has expired. Similarly, policies of funding agencies might mandate the use of specific strategies that build stakeholder capacity for communication, collaboration and compromise. Existing management-based interventions designed to build effective teams and promote interdisciplinary and inter-organizational diversity and inclusion could potentially facilitate EBP implementation. Policy might also provide guidance on formation and maintenance of partnerships that promote ongoing quality improvement in services delivery through more efficient URE and integration of global and local models of evidence and implementation.

Final thoughts

It could be argued that the model presented here is too simplistic to achieve any of these three sets of understandings. However, they do indicate that both relationships and the development of shared understandings through cultural exchange are complex phenomena, shaped by characteristics of the inner and outer context in which implementation occurs. These phenomena will inevitably require more detailed examination, as well as validation through rigorous hypothesis testing. Nevertheless, it is important to keep in mind what is at stake here, that is, the health and well-being of youth, older adults, patients with chronic disease, military veterans, disaster victims, and anyone else in need who would benefit from an EBP.

References

Aarons, G. A. and Palinkas, L.A. (2007) 'Implementation of evidence-based practice in child welfare: service provider perspectives', *Administration and Policy in Mental Health*, 34: 411–19.

Aarons, G. A. and Sawitzky, A.C. (2006) 'Organizational culture and climate and mental health provider attitudes toward evidence-based practices', *Psychological Services*, 3(1): 61–72.

Aarons, G. A., Hurlburt, M. and Horwitz, S. M. (2011) 'Advancing a conceptual model of evidence-based practice implementation in public sector services', *Administration and Policy in Mental Health*, 38: 4–23.

Aarons, G. A., Ehrhart, M. G., Moullin, J. C., Torres, E. M. and Green, A. E. (2017) 'Testing the leadership and organizational change for innovation intervention in substance abuse treatment: a cluster randomized trial study protocol', *Implementation Science*, 12: 29.

Abram, K., Teplin, L., Charles, D., Longworth, S., McClelland, G. and Dulcan, M. (2004) 'Posttraumatic stress disorder and trauma in youth in juvenile detention', *Archives of General Psychiatry*, 61: 403–10.

Agency for Healthcare Research and Quality (2014) *Strategies to improve mental health care for children and adolescents*, Rockville, MD: U.S. Department of Health and Human Services.

Alexander, J. A., Waldron, H. B., Robbins, M. S. and Neeb, A. (2013) *Functional Family Therapy for adolescent behavior problems*, Washington, DC: American Psychological Association.

Alisic, E., Zalta, A. K., van Wesel, F., Larsen, S. E., Hafstad, G. S., Hassanpour, K. and Smid, G. E. (2014) 'Rates of posttraumatic stress disorder in trauma-exposed children and adolescents: meta-analysis', *British Journal of Psychiatry*, 204: 335–40.

Allen, J. D., Shelton, R. C., Emmons, K. M. and Linnan, L. A. (2018) 'Fidelity and its relationship to implementation effectiveness, adaptation, and dissemination', in R. C. Brownson, G. A. Colditz and E. K. Proctor (eds) *Dissemination and implementation research in health: Translating science to practice* (2nd edn), New York: Oxford University Press, pp 267–284.

Allen, T., Malm, K., Williams, S. C. and Ellis, R. (2011) 'Piecing together the puzzle: tips and techniques for effective discovery in family finding', *Child Trends Research Brief*, Publication #2011-31, http://childtrends.org/?publications=piecing-together-the-puzzle-tips-and-techniques-for-effective-discovery-in-family-finding

Armstrong, N., Herbert, G. and Brewster, L. (2016) 'Contextual barriers to implementation in primary care: an ethnographic study of a programme to improve chronic kidney disease care', *Family Practice*, 33(4): 426–31.

Atkins, D., Best, D. and Shapiro, E. N. (2001) 'The Third U.S. Preventive Services Task Force: background, methods and first recommendations', *American Journal of Preventive Medicine*, 20: 1–108.

Atkins, D., Eccles, M., Flottorp, S., Henry, D., Hill, S., Liberati, A., O'Connell, D., Oxman, A. D., Phillips, B., Schunsmann, H., Edejer, T. T., Vist, G. E., Williams, J. W. Jr, and The GRADE Working Group (2004) 'Systems for grading the quality of evidence and the strength of recommendations I: critical appraisal of existing approaches The GRADE Working Group', *BMC Health Services Research*, 4: 38.

Ayers, L., Beyea, S., Godfrey, M., Harper, D., Nelson, E. and Batalden, P. (2005) 'Quality improvement learning collaboratives', *Quality Management in Healthcare*, 14(4): 234–47.

Bachmann, M. O., O'Brien, M., Husbands, C., Shreeve, A., Jones, N., Watson, J., Reading, R., Thoburn, J., Mugford, M. and the National Evaluation of Children's Trusts Team (2009) 'Integrating children's services in England: national evaluation of children's trusts', *Child: Care, Health and Development*, 35: 257–65.

Bai, Y., Wells, R. and Hillemeier, M. (2009) 'Coordinaton between child welfare agencies and mental health services providers, children's service use, and outcomes', *Child Abuse & Neglect*, 33: 372–81.

Bailey, F. G. (1973) 'Promethian fire: right and wrong', in F. G. Bailey (ed) *Debate and compromise: The politics of innovation*, Totowa NJ: Rowman & Littlefield, pp 1–15.

Balas, E. A. and Boren, S. A. (2000) 'Managing clinical knowledge for healthcare improvement', *Yearbook of Medical Informatics*, Bethesda, MD: National Library of Medicine, pp 65–70.

Bandura, A. (1986) *Social foundations of thought and action: A social cognitive theory*, Englewood Cliffs, NJ: Prentice Hall.

Bandura, A. (1997) *Self-efficacy: The exercise of control*, New York: W.H. Freeman.

Barkley, R. A. (1997) *Defiant children: A clinician's manual for assessment and parent training* (2nd edn), New York: Guilford.

Baron-Cohen, S., Scott, F. J., Allison, C., Williams, J., Bolton, P., Matthews, F. E. and Brayne, C. (2009) 'Prevalence of autism-spectrum conditions: UK school-based population study', *British Journal of Psychiatry*, 194(6): 500–9.

Barth, F. (1959) *Political leadership among Swat Pathans*, London: The Athlone Press.

Baumann, A. A., Cabassa, L. J. and Wiltsey Stirman S. (2018) 'Adaptation in dissemination and implementation science', in R. C. Brownson, G. A. Colditz and E. K. Proctor (eds) *Dissemination and implementation research in health: Translating science to practice* (2nd edn), New York: Oxford University Press, pp 285–300.

Beesdo, K., Knappe, S. and Pine, D. S. (2009) 'Anxiety and anxiety disorders in children and adolescents: developmental issues and implications for DSM-V', *Psychiatric Clinics of North America*, 32: 483–524.

Beidas, R. S. and Kendall, P. C. (eds) (2014) *Dissemination and implementation of evidence-based practices in child and adolescent mental health*, New York: Oxford University Press.

Beidas, R. S., Adams, D. R., Kratz, H. E., Jackson, K., Berkowitz, S., Zinny, A., Cliggitt, L. P., DeWitt, K. L., Skriner, L. and Evans, A. Jr. (2016) 'Lessons learned while building a trauma-informed public behavioral health system in the City of Philadelphia', *Evaluation and Program Planning*, 59: 21–32.

Bentley, H., O'Hagan, O., Brown, A., Vasco, N., Lynch, C., Peppiate, J., Webber, M., Ball, R., Miller, P., Byrne, A., Hafizi, M. and Letendrie, F. (2017) *How safe are our children? The most comprehensive overview of child protection in the UK 2017*, London: NSPCC.

Bhattacharyya, O., Reeves, S., Garfinkel, S. and Zwarenstein, M. (2006) 'Designing theoretically-informed implementation interventions: fine in theory, but evidence of effectiveness in practice is needed', *Implementation Science*, 1, 5.

Bickel, W. K., Green, L. and Vuchinich, R. E. (1995) 'Behavioral economics', *Journal of Experimental Analysis of Behavior*, 64: 257–62.

Bickman, L., Lambert, E. W., Andrade, A. R. and Penaloza, R. V. (2000) 'The Fort Bragg continuum of care for children and adolescents: mental health outcomes over 5 years', *Journal of Consulting and Clinical Psychology*, 68: 710–16.

Blumberg, E., Landsverk, J., Ellis-MacLeod, E., Ganger, W. and Culver, S. (1996) 'Use of the public mental health system by children in foster care: client characteristics and service use patterns', *Journal of Mental Health Administration*, 23: 389–405.

Brekke J. S., Ell, K. and Palinkas, L. A. (2007) 'Translational science at the National Institutes of Mental Health: can social work take its rightful place?', *Research on Social Work Practice*, 17: 123–33.

Breslau, N., Davis, G. C., Andreski, P. and Peterson, E. (1991) 'Traumatic events and posttraumatic stress disorder in an urban population of young adults', *Archives of General Psychiatry*, 48: 216–22.

Brinkerhoff, J. M. (2002) 'Assessing and improving partnership relations and outcomes: a proposed framework', *Evaluation and Program Planning*, 25, 215–31.

Bronsard, G., Assandrini, M., Fond, G., Loundou, A., Auquier, P., Tordjman, S. and Boyer, L. (2016) 'The prevalence of mental disorders among children and adolescents in the child welfare system: a systematic review and meta-analysis', *Medicine*, 95(7): e2622.

Brooks, F., Magnusson, J., Klemera, E., Spencer, N. and Morgan, A. (2011) *HBSC England National Report*, Hatfield: University of Hertfordshire.

Brown, C. H., Chamberlain, P., Saldana, L., Padgett, C., Wang, W. and Cruden, G. (2014) 'Evaluation of two implementation strategies in 51 child county public service systems in two states: results of a cluster randomized head-to-head implementation trial', *Implementation Science*, 9: 134.

Brown, C. H., Curran, G., Palinkas, L. A., Wells, K. B., Jones, L., Collins, L. M., Duan, N., Mittman, B. S., Wallace, A., Tabak, R. G., Ducharme, L., Chambers, D., Neta, G., Wiley, T., Landsverk, J., Cheung, K., and Cruden, G. (2017) 'An overview of research and evaluation designs for dissemination and implementation', *Annual Review of Public Health*, 38: 1–22.

Brownson, R. C., Colditz, G. A. and Proctor, E. K. (2018) 'Future issues in dissemination and implementation research', in R. C. Brownson, G. A. Colditz and E. K. Proctor (eds) *Dissemination and implementation research in health: Translating science to practice* (2nd edn), New York: Oxford University Press, pp 481–490.

Brydon-Miller, M. and Greenwood, D. (2006) 'A re-examination of the relationship between action research and human subjects review processes', *Action Research*, 4(1), 117–28.

Bryson, S. A., Akin, B. A., Blase, K. A., McDonald, T. and Walker, S. (2014) 'Selecting an EBP to reduce long-term foster care: lessons from a university–child welfare agency partnership', *Journal of Evidence-Based Social Work*, 11: 208–21.

Buckley, H., Tonmyr, L., Lewig, K. and Jack, S. (2013) 'Factors influencing the uptake of research evidence in child welfare: a synthesis of findings from Australia, Canada, and Ireland', *Child Abuse Review*, 23: 5–16.

Buescher, A. V., Cidav, Z., Knapp, M. and Mandell, D. S. (2014) 'Costs of autism spectrum disorders in the United Kingdom and the United States', *JAMA Pediatrics*, 168(8), 721–28.

Bunger, A. C., Hanson, R. F., Doogan, N. J., Powell, B. J., Cao, Y. and Dunn, J. (2016) 'Can learning collaboratives support implementation by rewiring professional networks?', *Administration and Policy in Mental Health*, 43(1): 79–92.

Burns, B. (2003) 'Children and evidence-based practice', *Psychiatric Clinics of North America*, 26: 955–70.

Burns, B. J., Phillips, S. D., Wagner, H. R., Barth, R. P., Kolko, D. J., Campbell, C. and Landsverk, J. (2004) 'Mental health need and access to mental health services by youths involved with child welfare: a national survey', *Journal of the American Academy of Child and Adolescent Psychiatry*, 43: 960–70.

Burstein, M., He, J. P., Kattan, G., Albano, A. M., Avenevoli, S. and Merikangas, K. R. (2011) 'Social phobia and subtypes in the national comorbidity survey—adolescent supplement: prevalence, correlates, and comorbidity', *Journal of the American Academy of Child and Adolescent Psychiatry*, 50: 870–80.

Burstein, M., Beesdo-Baum, K., He, J. P. and Merikangas, K. R. (2014) 'Threshold and subthreshold generalized anxiety disorder among US adolescents: prevalence, sociodemographic, and clinical characteristics', *Psychological Medicine*, 44: 2351–62.

Burt, R. S. (1999) 'The social capital of opinion leaders', *Annals of the American Academy of Political and Social Sciences*, 566: 37–54.

Cabassa, L. J. and Baumann, A. A. (2013) 'A two-way street: bridging implementation science and cultural adaptations of mental health treatments', *Implementation Science*, 8: 90.

Caplan, N. (1979) 'The two-communities theory and knowledge utilization', *American Behavioral Scientist*, 22: 459–71.

CDC (Centers for Disease Control and Prevention) (2014) 'Prevalence and characteristics of autism spectrum disorders among children aged 8 years – Autism and Developmental Disabilities Monitoring Network, 11 Sites, United States, 2012', *Morbidity and Mortality Weekly Report (MMWR) Surveillance Summary* 65 (#SS-3): 1–23.

CDC (Centers for Disease Control and Prevention) (2015a) 'Suicide trends among persons aged 10–24 years—United States, 1994–2012', *Morbidity and Mortality Weekly Report*, 64(8): 201–05.

CDC (Centers for Disease Control and Prevention) (2015b) 'Underlying cause of death 1999–2014 on CDC WONDER online database, released 2015. Data are from the Multiple Cause of Death Files, 1999–2014, as compiled from data provided by the 57 vital statistics jurisdictions through the Vital Statistics Cooperative Program', http://wonder.cdc.gov/ucd-icd10.html.

CEBC (California Evidence-Based Clearinghouse for Child Welfare) (2018) *Scientific Rating Scale*, www.cebc4cw.org/ratings/scientific-rating-scale/

CEBC (California Evidence-Based Clearinghouse for Child Welfare) (n.d.) Website, www.cebc4cw.org/

Chamberlain, P. (2017) 'Toward creating synergy among policy, procedures, and implementation of evidence-based models in child welfare systems: two case examples', *Clinical Child and Family Psychology Review*, 20(1): 78–86.

Chamberlain, P. and Reid, J. B. (1998) 'Comparison of two community alternatives to incarceration for chronic juvenile offenders', *Journal of Consulting and Clinical Psychology*, 66(4): 624–33.

Chamberlain, P., Leve, L. D. and Degarmo, D. S. (2007) 'Multidimensional treatment foster care for girls in the juvenile justice system: 2-year follow-up of a randomized clinical trial', *Journal of Consulting and Clinical Psychology*, 75: 187–93.

Chamberlain, P., Price, J., Leve, L., Laurent, H., Landsverk, J. and Reid, J. (2008a) 'Prevention of behavior problems for children in foster care: outcomes and mediation effects', *Prevention Science*, 9: 17–27.

Chamberlain, P., Brown, C. H., Saldana, L., Reid, J., Wang, W., Marsenich, L., Sosna, T., Padgett, C. and Bouwman, G. (2008b) 'Engaging and recruiting counties in an experiment on implementing evidence-based practice in California', *Administration and Policy in Mental Health*, 35: 250–60.

Chamberlain, P., Brown, C. and Saldana, L. (2011) 'Observational measure of implementation progress in community-based settings: the stages of implementation completion (SIC)', *Implementation Science*, 6: 116.

Chamberlain, P., Roberts, R., Jones, H., Marsenich, L., Sosna, T. and Price, J. (2012) 'Three collaborative models for scaling up evidence-based practice', *Administration and Policy in Mental Health*, 39: 278–90.

Chambers, D. A. and Norton, W. E. (2016) The adaptome: advancing the science of intervention adaptation', *American Journal of Preventive Medicine*, 51: S124–S131.

Children's Bureau (2017) *Child welfare outcomes 2010–2014: Report to Congress*, Administration for Children and Families, www.acf.hhs.gov/cb/resource/cwo-10-14

Children's Society (2008) *The good childhood inquiry: Health research evidence*, London: Children's Society.

Chor, K. H., Olin, S. C., Weaver, J., Cleek, A. F., McKay, M. M., Hoagwood, K. E. and Horwitz, S. (2014) 'Adoption of clinical and business trainings by child mental health clinics in New York State', *Psychiatric Services*, 65(12): 1439–44.

Chorpita, B. F. and Weisz, J. R. (2005) *Modular approach to therapy for children with anxiety, depression, or conduct problems*, Honolulu, HI and Boston, MA: University of Hawaii at Manoa and Judge Baker Children's Center, Harvard Medical School.

Chorpita, B. F., Yim, L. M., Donkervoet, J. C., Arensdorf, A., Amundsen, M., McGee, C, Serrano, A., Yates, A., Burns, J. A. and Morelli, P. (2002) 'Toward large-scale implementation of empirically supported treatments for children', *Clinical Psychology: Science and Practice*, 9: 165–90.

Chorpita, B. F., Daleiden, E. and Weisz, J. R. (2005) 'Modularity in the design and application of therapeutic interventions', *Applied and Preventive Psychology*, 11: 141–156.

Chorpita, B. F., Bernstein, A. D., Daleiden, E. L. and Research Network on Youth Mental Health (2008) 'Driving with roadmaps and dashboards: using information resources to structure the decision models in service organizations', *Administration and Policy in Mental Health, 35*, 114–123.

Chuang, E. and Wells, R. (2010) 'The role of inter-agency collaboration in facilitating receipt of behavioral health services for youth involved with child welfare and juvenile justice', *Children and Youth Services Review*, 32: 1814–22.

Clancy, C. M., Margolis, P. A. and Miller, M. (2013) 'Collaborative networks for both improvement and research', *Pediatrics*, 131(Suppl 4): S210–14.

Clara, F. Garcia, K. Y. and Metz, A. (2017) *Implementing evidence-based child welfare: The New York City experience*. Baltimore, MD: Casey Family Programs, www.casey.org/media/evidence-based-child-welfare-nyc.pdf

Coburn, C., Penuel, W. and Geil, K. (2013) *Research-practice partnerships: A strategy for leveraging research educational improvement in school districts*, New York. William T. Grant Foundation, http://wtgrantfoundation.org/library/uploads/2015/10/Research-Practice-Partnerships-at-the-District-Level.pdf

Cohen, J. A., Deblinger, E., Mannarino, A. P. and Steer, R. A. (2004) 'A multisite, randomized controlled trial for children with sexual abuse-related PTSD symptoms', *Journal of the American Academy of Child and Adolescent Psychiatry*, 43(4): 393–402.

Cohen, J. A., Mannarino, A. P. and Deblinger, E. (2006) *Treating trauma and traumatic grief in children and adolescents*, New York: Guilford Press.

Cohen, J. A., Mannarino, A. P. and Iyengar, S. (2011) 'Community treatment of posttraumatic stress disorder for children exposed to intimate partner violence: a randomized controlled trial', *Archives of Pediatric and Adolescent Medicine*, 165(1): 16–21.

Collins, L. M., Murphy, S. A., Nair, V. N. and Strecher, V. J. (2005) 'A strategy for optimizing and evaluating behavioral interventions', *Annals of Behavioral Medicine*, 30(1): 65–73.

Cooke, R. A. and Rousseau, D. M. (1988) 'Behavioral norms and expectations: a quantitative approach to the assessment of organizational culture', *Group & Organization Management*, 13(3): 245–73.

Copeland, W. E., Keeler G, Angold, A. and Costello, E. J. (2010) 'Posttraumatic stress without trauma in children', *American Journal of Psychiatry*, 167: 1059–65.

Costello, E. J., Angold, A., Burns, B. J., Stangl, D. K., Tweed, D. L., Erkanli, A. and Worthman, C. M. (1996) 'The Great Smoky Mountains study of youth: goals, design, methods, and the prevalence of DSM-III-R disorders', *Archives of General Psychiatry*, 53: 1129–36.

Costello, E. J., Erkanli, A. and Angold, A. (2006) 'Is there an epidemic of child or adolescent depression ?', *Journal of Child Psychology and Psychiatry*, 47(12) : 1263–71.

Costello, E. J., He, J., Sampson, N. A., Kessler, R. C. and Merikangas, K. R. (2014) 'Services for adolescents with psychiatric disorders: 12-month data from the National Comorbidity Survey – Adolescent', *Psychiatric Services*, 65: 1–8.

Cottrell, D., Lucey, D., Porter, I. and Walker, D. (2000) 'Joint working between child and adolescent mental health services and the department of social services: the Leeds model', *Clinical Child Psychology and Psychiatry*, 5(4): 481–9.

Couturier, J., Kimber, M., Jack, S., Niccols, A., Van Blyderveen, S. and McVey, G. (2014) 'Using a knowledge transfer framework to identify factors facilitating implementation of family-based treatment', *International Journal of Eating Disorders*, 47: 410–17.

Crabtree, B. F., and Miller W. L. (1992) 'A template approach to text analysis: developing and using codebooks', in B. F. Crabtree and W. L. Miller (eds) *Doing Qualitative Research, Vol. 3*. Thousand Oaks, CA: Sage Press, pp 93–109.

Creswell, J. W. and Plano Clark, V. L. (2011) *Designing and conducting mixed method research* (2nd edn), Thousand Oaks, CA: Sage.

Cross-Disorder Group of the Psychiatric Genomics Consortium (2013) 'Identification of risk loci with shared effects on five major psychiatric disorders: a genome-wide analysis', *Lancet*, 381(9875): 1371–79.

Curran, G. M., Bauer, M., Mittman, B., Pyne, J. M. and Stetler, C. (2012) 'Effectiveness-implementation hybrid designs: combining elements of clinical effectiveness and implementation research to enhance public health impact', *Medical Care*, 50(3): 217–26.

Currie, M., King, G., Rosenbaum, P., Law, M., Kertoy, M. and Specht, J. (2005) 'A model of impacts of research partnerships in health and social services', *Evaluation and Program Planning*, 28(4), 400–12.

Damanpour, F. (1991) 'Organizational innovation: a meta-analysis of effects of determinants and moderators', *Academy of Management Journal*, 34(3): 555–90.

Damschroder, L. J., Aron, D. C., Keith, R. E., Kirsh, S. R., Alexander, J. A. and Lowery, J. C. (2009) 'Fostering implementation of health services research findings into practice: a consolidated framework for advancing implementation science', *Implementation Science*, 4: 50.

D'Andrade, R. G. (1984) 'Cultural meaning systems', in R. A. Shweder and R. A. LeVine (eds) *Culture theory: Essays on mind, self, and emotion*, New York: Cambridge University Press, pp 88–122.

Davies, H. T. O., Nutley, S. M. and Mannion, R. (2000) 'Organisational culture and quality of health care', *Quality in Health Care*, 9: 111–9.

Davies, H., Nutley, S. and Walter, I. (2008) 'Why "knowledge transfer" is misconceived for applied social research', *Journal of Health Services and Policy*, 13(3): 188–90.

Davis, K. E. (2014) 'Expenditures for treatment of mental health disorders among children, ages 5–17, 2009–2011: estimates for the US civilian noninstitutionalized population', *Statistical brief no. 440; Medical Expenditure Panel Survey*, Rockville (MD): Agency for Healthcare Research and Quality.

Davis, M., Koroloff, N. and Johnsen, M. (2012) 'Social network analysis of child and adult interorganizational connections', *Psychiatric Rehabilitation Journal*, 35: 265–272.

Demakis, J.G., McQueen, L., Kizer, K. W. and Fuessner, J. R. (2000) 'Quality Enhancement Research Initiative (QUERI): a collaboration between research and clinical practice', *Medical Care*, 38: 17–25.

Deming, W. E. (1986) *Out of the crisis*, Cambridge, MA: MIT Press.

Denis, J. L. and Lomas, J. (2003) 'Convergent evolution: the academic and policy roots of collaborative research' *Journal of Health Services Research and Policy*, 8(Suppl 2): 1–6

Diehle, J., Opmeer, B. C., Boer, F., Mannarino, A. P. and Lindauer, R. J. (2015) 'Trauma-focused cognitive behavioral therapy or eye movement desensitization and reprocessing: what works in children with posttraumatic stress symptoms? A randomized controlled trial', *European Child and Adolescent Psychiatry*, 24(2): 227–36.

Dodd, S. J. and Epstein, I. (2012) *Practice-based research in social work: A guide for reluctant researchers*, Abingdon: Routledge.

dosReis, S., Zito, J. M., Safer, D. J. and Soeken, K. L. (2001) 'Mental health services for youths in foster care and disabled youths', *American Journal of Public Health*, 91: 1094–9.

Driedger, S. M., Kothari, A., Graham, I. D., Cooper, E., Crighton, E. J., Zahab, M., Morrison, J. and Sawada, M. (2010) 'If you build it, they still may not come: outcomes and process of implementing a community-based integrated knowledge translation mapping innovation', *Implementation Science*, 5: 47.

Ebert, L., Amaya-Jackson, L., Markiewicz, J., Kisiel, C. and Fairbank, J. (2011) 'Use of the Breakthrough Series Collaborative to support broad and sustained use of evidence-based trauma treatment for children in community practice settings', *Administration and Policy in Mental Health*, 39(3): 187–99.

Eccles, M. P. and Mittman, B. S. (2006) 'Welcome to implementation science', *Implementation Science*, 1: 1.

Edelstein, H. (2016) 'Collaborative research partnerships for knowledge mobilization', *Evidence & Policy*, 12: 199–216.

Ehrle, J., Andrews Scarcella, C. and Geen, R. (2004) 'Teaming up: collaboration between welfare and child welfare agencies since welfare reform', *Children and Youth Services Review*, 26(3): 265–85.

Eichler, M. (2007) *Consensus organizing: Building communities of mutual self interest*, Newbury Park, CA: Sage.

Ellen, M. E., Leon, G., Bouchard, G. I, Lavis, J. N. and Ouimet, M. (2013) 'What supports do health system organizations have in place to facilitate evidence-informed decision-making? A qualitative study', *Implementation Science*, 8: 84.

Epstein, J. M. (2007) *Generative social science: Studies in agent-based computational modeling*, Princeton, NJ: Princeton University Press.

Evans, G. W. (2016) 'Childhood poverty and adult psychological well-being', *Proceedings of the National Academy of Sciences*, 113(52): 14949–52.

Fixsen, D. L., Naoom, S. F., Blase, K. A., Friedman, R. M. and Wallace, F. (2005) *Implementation research: A synthesis of the literature*, Tampa, FL: University of South Florida, Louis de la Parte Florida Mental Health Institute, The National Implementation Research Network, FMHI Publication #231.

Ford, T., Goodman, R. and Meltzer, H. (2003) '*The* British child and adolescent mental health survey 1999: the prevalence of DSM-IV disorders', *Journal of the American Academy Child and Adolescent Psychiatry,* 42: 1203–11.

Forgatch, M. S. and DeGarmo, D. S. (1999) 'Parenting through change: an effective parenting training program for single mothers', *Journal of Consulting and Clinical Psychology*, 67: 711–24.

Foster-Fishman, P. G., Salem, D. A., Allen, N. A. and Fahrbach, K. (2001) 'Facilitating interorganizational collaboration: the contribution of interorganizational alliances', *American Journal of Community Psychology*, 29(6): 875–905.

Frambach, R. T. and Schillewaert, N. (2002) 'Organizational innovation adoption: a multi-level framework of determinants and opportunities for future research', *Journal of Business Research*, 55(2): 163–76.

Froehlich, T. E., Lanphear, B. P., Epstein, J. N., Barbaresi, W. J., Katusic, S. K. and Kahn, R. S. (2007) 'Prevalence, recognition, and treatment of attention-deficit/hyperactivity disorder in a national sample of US children', *Archives of Pediatrics and Adolescent Medicine,* 161: 857–64.

Fuller, E. (2013) *Smoking, drinking and drug use among young people in England in 2012*, Leeds: Health and Social Care Information Centre.

Garber, A. M. and Meltzer, D. O. (2009) 'Setting priorities for comparative effectiveness research', in *Implementing comparative effectiveness research: Priorities, methods, and impact*, Washington, DC: Brookings Institution, pp 15–34. www.hamiltonproject.org/assets/legacy/files/downloads_and_links/Implementing_Comparative_Effectiveness_Research-_Priorities_Methods_and_Impact.pdf

Gardner, F., Burton, J. and Klimes, I. (2006) 'Randomized controlled trial of a parenting intervention in the voluntary sector for reducing child conduct problems: outcomes and mechanisms of change', *Journal of Child Psychology and Psychiatry*, 47(11): 1123–32.

Garland, A. F., Plemmons, D. and Koontz, L. (2006) 'Research-practice partnership in mental health: lessons from participants', *Administration and Policy in Mental Health*, 33: 517–28.

Garland, A. F., Brookman-Frazee, L., Hurlburt, M., Accurso, E. C., Zoffness, R., Haine, R. A. and Granger, W. (2010) 'Mental health care for children with disruptive behavior problems: a view inside therapists' offices', *Psychiatric Services*, 61, 788–95.

Garmy, P., Jakobsson, U., Carlsson, K. S., Berg, A. and Clausson, E. K. (2015) 'Evaluation of a school-based program aimed at preventing depressive symptoms in adolescents', *Journal of School Nursing*, 31(2): 117–25.

Gill, K. J., Campbell E., Gauthier, G., Xenocostas, S., Charney, D. and Macauley, A. C. (2014) 'From policy to practice: implementing frontline community health services for substance dependence—study protocol', *Implementation Science*, 9: 108.

Glasgow, R. E., Vogt, S. M. and Bowles, T. M. (1999) 'Evaluating the public health impact of health promotion interventions: the RE-AIM framework', *American Journal of Public Health*, 89(9): 1322–7.

Glasgow, R. E., Lichtenstein, E. and Marcus, A. C. (2003) 'Why don't we see more translation of health promotion research to practice? Rethinking the efficacy to effectiveness transition', *American Journal of Public Health*, 93(8): 1261–7.

Glasgow, R. E., Magid, D. J., Beck, A., Ritzwoller, D. and Estabrooks, P. A. (2005) 'Practical clinical trials for translating research to practice: design and measurement recommendations', *Medical Care*, 43(6): 551–7.

Gleacher, A. A., Olin, S. S., Nadeem, E., Pollock, M., Ringle, V., Bickman, L., Douglas, S. and Hoagwood, K. (2016) 'Implementing a measurement feedback system in community mental health clinics: a case study of multilevel barriers and facilitators', *Administration and Policy in Mental Health*, 43(3): 426–40.

Glisson, C. (2002) 'The organizational context of children's mental health services', *Clinical Child and Family Psychology Review*, 5: 233–53.

Glisson, C. and Green, P. (2006) 'The effects of organizational culture and climate on the access to mental health care in child welfare and juvenile justice systems', *Administration and Policy in Mental Health*, 33(4): 433–48.

Glisson, C. and Hemmelgarn, A. (1998) 'The effects of organizational climate and interorganizational coordination on the quality and outcomes of children's service systems', *Child Abuse & Neglect*, 22: 401–21.

Glisson, C. and James, L. R. (2002) 'The cross-level effects of culture and climate in human service teams', *Journal of Organizational Behavior*, 23(6): 767–94.

Glisson, C. and Schoenwald, S. K. (2005) 'The ARC organizational and community intervention strategy for implementing evidence-based children's mental health treatments', *Mental Health Services Research*, 7(4): 243–59.

Glisson, C., Dukes, D. and Green, P. (2006) 'The effects of the ARC organizational intervention on caseworker turnover, climate, and culture in children's service systems', *Child Abuse & Neglect*, 30(8): 855–80.

Glisson, C., Landsverk, J., Schoenwald, S., Kelleher, K., Hoagwood, K. E., Mayberg, S. and Green, P. (2008a) 'Assessing the organizational social context (OSC) of mental health services: implications for research and practice', *Administration and Policy in Mental Health*, 35: 98–113.

Glisson, C., Schoenwald, S. K., Kelleher, K., Landsverk, J., Hoagwood, K. E., Mayberg, S., Green, P. and the Research Network on Youth Mental Health (2008b) 'Therapist turnover and new program sustainability in mental health clinics as a function of organizational culture, climate, and service structure', *Administration and Policy in Mental Health*, 35(1–2): 124–33.

Glisson, C., Schoenwald, S. K., Hemmelgarn, A., Green, P., Dukes, D., Armstrong, K. S. and Chapson, J. E. (2010) 'Randomized trial of MST and ARC in a two-level evidence-based treatment strategy', *Journal of Consulting and Clinical Psychology*, 78(4): 537–50.

Gorman, D. M. (2017) 'Has the National Registry of Evidence-Based Programs and Practices (NREPP) lost its way?', *International Journal of Drug Policy*, 45, 40–41.

Gottsman, D. and Schwarz, S. (2011) *Juvenile justice in the U.S.: Facts for policymakers*, New York: National Center for Children in Poverty.

Graham, I. D. and Logan. J. (2004) 'Innovations in knowledge transfer and continuity of care', *Canadian Journal of Nursing Research*, 36(2): 89–103.

Graham, I. D., Logan, J., Harrison, M. B., Strauss, S. E., Tetroe, J., Caswell, W. and Robinson, N. (2006) 'Lost in knowledge translation: time for a map?', *Journal of Continuing Education in the Health Professions*, 26(1): 13–24.

Green, B. L., Rockhill, A. and Burrus, S. (2008) 'The role of interagency collaboration for substance-abusing families involved with child welfare', *Child Welfare*, 87(1): 29–61.

Green, H., McGinnity, A., Meltzer, H., Ford, T., Goodman, R. (2005) *Mental health of children and young people in Great Britain: 2004*, New York: Palgrave Macmillan.

Green, J. G., McLaughlin, K. A., Berglund, P. A., Gruber, M. J., Sampson, N. A., Zaslavsky, A. M. and Kessler, R. C. (2010) 'Childhood adversities and adult psychiatric disorders in the National Comorbidity Survey replication I', *Archives of General Psychiatry*, 67: 113–23.

Green, L. W., Ottoson, J. M., Garcia, C. and Hiatt, R. A. (2009) 'Diffusion theory and knowledge dissemination, utilization, and integration in public health', *Annual Review of Public Health*, 30: 151–74.

Greenhalgh, T., Robert, G., Macfarlane, F., Bate, P. and Kyriakidou, O. (2004) 'Diffusion of innovations in service organizations: systematic review and recommendations', *Milbank Quarterly*, 82(4): 581–629.

Greer, D., Grasso, D. J., Cohen, A. and Webb, C. (2013) 'Trauma-focused treatment in a state system of care: is it worth the cost?', *Administration and Policy in Mental Health*, 41: 317–23.

Grol, R. (2001) 'Successes and failures of the implementation of evidence-based guidelines for clinical practice', *Medical Care*, 39: 1146–54.

Grol, R. and Wensing, M. (2004) 'What drives change? Barriers to and incentives for achieving evidence-based practice', *Medical Journal of Australia*, 180(6 Suppl): S57–60.

Gupta-Singh K., Singh R. R. and Lawson, K. A. (2017) 'Economic burden of attention/deficit hyperactivity disorder among pediatric patients in the United States', *Value in Health*, 20(4): 602–9.

Hanson, R. F., Self-Brown, S., Rostad, W. L. and Jackson, M. C. (2016) 'The what, when and why of implementation frameworks for evidence-based practices in child welfare and child mental health service systems', *Child Abuse & Neglect*, 53: 51–63.

Harris, V. V. and Sherman, J. A. (1973) 'Use and analysis of the "Good Behavior Game" to reduce disruptive classroom behavior', *Journal of Applied Behavior Analysis*, 6: 405–17.

Hatch, J., Moss, N., Saran, A., Presley-Cantrell, L. and Mallory, C. (1993) 'Community research: partnership in black communities', *American Journal of Preventive Medicine*, 9(6 Suppl.): 27–31.

Hatch, M. J. (1993) 'The dynamics of organizational culture', *Academy of Management Review*, 18(4): 657–93.

Havlicek, J. R., Garcia, A. R. and Smith, D. C. (2013) 'Mental health and substance use disorders among foster youth transitioning to adulthood: past research and future directions', *Children and Youth Services Review*, 35: 194–203.

Haynes, A. S., Gillispie, J. A., Derrick, G. E., Hall, W. D., Redman, S., Chapman, S. and Sturk, H. (2011) 'Galvanizers, guides, champions, and shields: the many ways that policymakers use public health researchers', *Milbank Quarterly*, 89: 564–98.

Haynes, R. B., Devereaux, P. J. and Guyatt, G. H. (2002) 'Clinical expertise in the era of evidence-based medicine and patient choice', *Evidence-Based Medicine*, 7: 36–8.

Hemmelgarn, A. L., Glisson, C. and Dukes, D. (2001) 'Emergency room culture and the emotional support component of family-centered care', *Children's Health Care*, 30(2): 93–110.

Henggeler, S. W., Schoenwald, S. K., Borduin, C. M., Rowland, M. D. and Cunningham, P. B. (1998) *Multisystemic treatment of antisocial behavior in children and adolescents*, New York: Guilford Press.

Henrich, J. (2001) 'Cultural transmission and the diffusion of innovations: adoption dynamics indicate that biased cultural transmission is the predominate force in behavioral change', *American Anthropologist*, 103: 992–1013.

Himmelman, A. (2001) 'On coalitions and the transformation of power relations: collaborative betterment and collaborative empowerment', *American Journal of Community Psychology*, 29: 277–84.

Hoagwood, K. and Olin, S. S. (2002) 'The NIMH blueprint for change report: research priorities in child and adolescent mental health', *Journal of the American Academy of Child and Adolescent Psychiatry*, 41: 760–7.

Hoagwood, K., Burns, B. J., Kiser, L., Ringeisen, H. and Schoenwald, SK. (2001) 'Evidence-based practice in child and adolescent mental health services', *Psychiatric Services*, 52: 1179–89.

Hodgkinson, S., Godoy, L., Beers, L. S. and Lewin, A. (2017) 'Improving mental health access for low-income children and families in the primary care setting', *Pediatrics*, 139(1), pii: e20151175.

Hoertel, N., Franco, S., Wall, M. M., Oquendo, M. A., Wang, S., Limosin, F. and Blanco, C. (2015) 'Childhood maltreatment and risk of suicide attempt: a nationally representative study', *Journal of Clinical Psychiatry*, 76(7): 916–23.

Hoffman, T., Bennett, S. and Del Mar, C. (2013) *Evidence-based practice: Across the health professions* (2nd edn), Chatswood, NSW: Elsevier.

Holden, S. E., Jenkins-Jones, S., Poole, C. D., Morgan, C. L., Coghill, D. and Currie, C. J. (2013) 'The prevalence and incidence, resource use and financial costs of treating people with attention deficit/ hyperactivity disorder (ADHD) in the United Kingdom (1998 to 2010)', *Child and Adolescent Psychiatry and Mental Health* 7: 34.

Honig, M. I. and Coburn, C. (2008) 'Evidence-based decision making in school district central offices: toward a policy and research agenda', *Educational Policy*, 22(4): 578–608.

Horwath, J. and Morrison, T. (2007) 'Collaboration, integration and change in children's services: critical issues and key ingredients', *Child Abuse & Neglect*, 31(1): 55–69.

Horwitz, S. M., Hurlburt, M. S., Goldhaber-Fiebert, J. D., Heneghan, A. M., Zhang, J., Rolls-Reutz, J., Fisher, E., Landsverk, J. and Stein, R. E. (2012) 'Mental health services use by children investigated by child welfare agencies', *Pediatrics*, 130: 861–9.

Horwitz, S. M., Hurlburt, M. S., Goldhaber-Fiebert, J. D., Palinkas, L. A., Rolls-Reutz, J., Zhang, J., Fisher, E. and Landsverk, J. (2014) 'Exploration and adoption of evidence-based practices by child welfare agencies', *Child and Youth Services Review* 39: 147–52.

Howell, E. (2004) *Access to children's mental health services under Medicaid and SCHIP*, Washington, DC: The Urban Institute.

Hoyert, D. L. and Xu, J. (2012) 'Division of Vital Statistics. Deaths: preliminary data for 2011', *National Vital Statistics Reports*, 61(6): 1–51.

Huberman, M. (1994) 'Research utilization: the state of the art', *Knowledge and Policy*, 7(4): 13–33.

Hukkinen, J. I. (2016) 'A model for the temporal dynamics of knowledge brokerage in sustainable development', *Evidence & Policy*, 12: 321–40.

Hutchings, J., Bywater, T., Daley, D., Gardner, F., Whitaker, C., Jones, K., Eames, C. and Edwards, R. (2007) 'Parenting intervention in Sure Start services for children at risk of developing conduct disorder: pragmatic randomised controlled trial', *BMJ*, 334(7595): 678.

IHI (Institute for Healthcare Improvement) (2003) *The Breakthrough Series: IHI's collaborative model for achieving breakthrough Improvement*, Boston, MA: Institute for Healthcare Improvement.

Incredible Years (2017) *The Incredible Years® parents, teachers, and children training series*, www.incredibleyears.com/

Institute of Medicine (2001) *Crossing the quality chasm: A new health system for the 21st century*. Washington, DC: National Academy Press.

Intervention Central (2017) *Good Behavior Game*. www.interventioncentral.org/behavioral-interventions/schoolwide-classroommgmt/good-behavior-game

Israel, B. A., Eng, E., Schulz, A. J. and Parker, E. A. (eds) (2005) *Methods in community-based participatory research for health*, San Francisco, CA: Jossey-Bass.

Jensen, T. K., Holt, T. and Ormhaug, S. M. (2017) 'A follow-up study from a multisite, randomized controlled trial for traumatized children receiving TF-CBT', *Journal of Abnormal Child Psychology*, 45(8): 1587–97.

Johnson, L. J., Zorn, D., Tam, B. K. Y., Lamontaigne, M. and Johnson, S. A. (2003) 'Interagency and interprofessional collaboration in community care: the interdependence of structures and values', *Journal of Interprofessional Care*, 17: 69–83.

Johnston, L. D., O'Malley, P. M., Bachman, J. G. and Schulenberg, J. E. (2013) *Monitoring the future national results on drug use: 2012 overview, key findings on adolescent drug use*, Ann Arbor, MI: Institute for Social Research, University of Michigan.

Jones, L. and Wells, K. B. (2007) 'Strategies for academic and clinician engagement in community-participatory partnered research', *Journal of the American Medical Association*, 297(4): 407–10.

Jones, N., Thomas, P. and Rudd, L. (2004) 'Collaborating for mental health services in Wales: a process evaluation', *Public Administration*, 82: 109–21.

Josefiak, T., Kayed, N. S., Rimehaug, T., Wormda, A. K., Brubakk, A. M. and Wichstrøm, L. (2016) 'Prevalence and co-morbidity of mental disorders among adolescents living in residential youth care', *European Child and Adolescent Psychiatry*, 25: 33–47.

Juran, J. M. (1964) *Managerial breakthrough*, New York: McGraw-Hill.

Kahneman, D. (2011) *Thinking fast and slow*, New York: Farrar, Strauss and Giroux.

Kahneman, D. and Tversky, A. (1979) 'Prospect theory: an analysis of decision under risk', *Econometrica*, 47: 263–92.

Kann, L., McManus, T., Harris, W. A., Shanklin, S. L., Flint, K. H., Hawkins, J., Queen, B., Lowry, R., Olsen, E., Chyen, D., Whittle, L., Thornton, J., Lim, C., Yamakawa, Y., Brener, N. and Zaza, S. (2016) 'Youth risk behavior surveillance—United States, 2015', *Morbidity and Mortality Weekly Review, Surveillance Summaries*, June 10, 65(6): 1–174.

Kataoka, S. H., Zhang, L. and Wells, K. B. (2002) 'Unmet need for mental health care among U.S. children: variation by ethnicity and insurance status', *American Journal of Psychiatry*, 159(9): 1548–55.

Keifer, L., Frank, J., Di Ruggiero, E., Dobbins, M., Manuel, D., Gully, P. R. and Mowat, D. (2005) 'Fostering evidence-based decision-making in Canada: examining the need for a Canadian public health evidence centre and research network', *Canadian Journal of Public Health*, 96(3): I1–I19.

Kellam, S. G., Brown, C. H., Poduska, J. M., Ialongo, N. S., Wang, W., Toyinbo, P., Petras, H., Ford, C., Windham, A. and Wilcox, H. C. (2008) 'Effects of a universal classroom behavior management program in first and second grades on young adult behavioral, psychiatric, and social outcomes', *Drug and Alcohol Dependence*, 95(Suppl 1): S5–S28.

Kellam, S. G., Wang, W., Mackenzie, A. C., Brown, C. H., Ompad, D. C., Or, F., Ialongo, N. S., Poduska, J. M. and Windham, A. (2014) 'The impact of the Good Behavior Game, a universal classroom-based preventive intervention in first and second grades, on high-risk sexual behaviors and drug abuse and dependence disorders into young adulthood', *Prevention Science*, 15(Suppl 1): S6–18.

Kendall, P. C. (1990) *The coping cat workbook*, Ardmore, PA: Workbook Publishing.

Kendler, K. S., Kuhn, J. W. and Prescott, C. A. (2004) 'Childhood sexual abuse, stressful life events and risk for major depression in women', *Psychological Medicine*, 34(8): 1475–82.

Kennedy, M. M. (1984) 'How evidence alters understanding and decisions', *Educational Evaluation and Policy Analysis*, 6(3): 207–26.

Kessler, R. C., Chiu, W. T., Demler, O., Merikangas, K. R. and Walters, E. E. (2005) 'Prevalence, severity, and comorbidity of 12-month DSM-IV disorders in the National Comorbidity Survey Replication', *Archives of General Psychiatry*, 62(6): 617–27.

Kessler, R. C., McLaughlin, K. A., Green, J. G., Gruber, M. J., Sampson, N. A., Zaslavsky, A. M., Aguilar-Gaxiola, S., Alhamzawi, A. O., Alonso, J., Angermeyer, M., Benjet, C., Bromet, E., Chatterji, S., de Girolamo, G., Demyttenaere, K., Fayyad, J., Florescu, S., Gal, G., Gureje, O., Haro, J. M., Hu, C. Y., Karam, E. G., Kawakami, N., Lee, S., Lépine, J.P., Ormel, J., Posada-Villa, J., Sagar, R., Tsang, A., Üstün, T. B., Vassilev, S., Viana, M. C. and Williams, D. A. (2010) 'Childhood adversities and adult psychopathology in the WHO world mental health surveys', *British Journal of Psychiatry*, 197: 378–85.

Kessler, R. C., Avenevoli, S., Costello, J., Georgiades, K., Green, J. G., Gruber, M. J., He, J. P., Koretz, D., McLaughlin, K. A., Petukhova, M., Sampson, N. A., Zaslavsky, A. M. and Merikangas, K. R. (2012) 'Prevalence, persistence, and sociodemographic correlates of DSM-IV disorders in the National Comorbidity Survey Replication Adolescent Supplement', *Archives of General Psychiatry*, 69(4): 372–80.

Kim-Cohen, J., Caspi, A., Moffitt, T. E., Harrington, H., Milne, B.J. and Poulton, R. (2003) 'Prior juvenile diagnoses in adults with mental disorder: developmental follow-back of a prospective-longitudinal cohort', *Archives of General Psychiatry*, 60(7): 709–17.

Knight, C. and Lightowler, C. (2010) 'Reflection on 'knowledge exchange professionals' in the social sciences: emerging opportunities and challenges for university-based knowledge brokers', *Evidence & Policy*, 6: 543–56.

Kothari, A., Birch, S. and Charles, C. (2005) 'Interaction and research utilization in health policies and programs: does it work?', *Health Policy*, 71: 117–25.

Kothari, A., MacLean, L., Edwards, N. and Hobbs, A. (2011) 'Indicators at the interface: managing policymaker-researcher collaboration', *Knowledge Management Research and Practice*, 9: 203–14.

Kumpfer, K. L., Alvarado, R., Smith, P. and Bellamy, N. (2002) 'Cultural sensitivity and adaptation in family-based prevention interventions', *Prevention Science*, 3(3): 241–6.

Landry, R., Amara, N. and Lamari, M. (2001) 'Climbing the ladder of research utilization: evidence from social science research', *Science Communication*, *22*, 396–422.

Landry, R., Lamari, M. and Amara, N. (2003) 'The extent and determinants of the utilization of university research in government agencies', *Public Administration Review*, 63: 192–205.

Landsverk, J., Garland, A., Rolls Reutz, J. and Davis, I. (2010) 'Bridging science and practice in child welfare and children's mental health service system through a two-decade research center trajectory', *Journal of Social Work*, 11(1): 80–98.

Landsverk, J., Brown, C. H., Rolls Reutz, J., Palinkas, L. and Horwitz, S. M. (2011) 'Design elements in implementation research: a structured review of child welfare and child mental health studies', *Administration and Policy in Mental Health*, 38(1): 54–63.

Landsverk, J., Brown, C. H., Smith, J. D., Curran G. M., Palinkas, L. A., Ogihara, M., Czaja, S., Goldhaber-Fiebert, J., Vermeer, W., Saldana, L., Rolls-Reutz, J. A. and Horwitz, S. M. (2018) 'Design and analysis in dissemination and implementation research', in R. C. Brownson, G. A. Colditz and E. K. Proctor (eds), *Dissemination and implementation research in health: Translating science to practice* (2nd edn), New York: Oxford University Press, pp. 201–60.

Lavelle, T. A., Weinstein, M. C., Newhouse, J. P., Munir, K., Kuhthau, K. A. and Prosser, L. A. (2014) 'Economic burden of childhood autism spectrum disorders', *Pediatrics*, 133(3): e520–9.

Lavis, J., Ross, S., Hurley, J., Hohenadal, J., Stoddart, G., Woodward, C. and Abelson, J. (2002) 'Examining the role of health services research in public policymaking', *Milbank Quarterly*, 80: 125–54.

Lavis, J. N., Robertson, D., Woodside, J. M., McLeod, C. B., Abelson, J. and The Knowledge Transfer Group (2003) 'How can research organizations more effectively transfer research knowledge to decision makers?', *Milbank Quarterly*, 81(2): 221–49.

Lavis, J., Lomas, J., Hamid, M. and Sewankambo, N. (2006) 'Assessing country-level efforts to link research to action', *Bulletin of the World Health Organization*, 84: 620–8.

Leslie, L. K., Weckerly, J., Landsverk, J., Hough, R. L., Hurlburt, M. S. and Wood, P. A. (2003) 'Racial/ethnic differences in the use of psychotropic medication in high-risk children and adolescents', *Journal of the American Academy of Child and Adolescent Psychiatry*, 42: 1433–42.

Leve, L. D. and Chamberlain, P. (2005) 'Association with delinquent peers: intervention effects for youth in the juvenile justice system', *Journal of Abnormal Child Psychology*, 33(3): 339–47.

Lewis-Fernandez, R. and Kleinman, A. (1995) 'Cultural psychiatry: theoretical, clinical and research issues', *Psychiatric Clinics of North America*, 18: 433–48.

Lindblom, C. E. and Cohen, D. K. (1979) *Usable knowledge: Social science and social problem solving*, New Haven, CT: Yale University Press.

Little, M., Berry, V., Morpeth, L., Blower, S., Axford, N., Taylor, R., Bywater, T., Lehtonen, M. and Tobin, K. (2012) 'The impact of three evidence-based programmes delivered in public systems in Birmingham, UK', *International Journal of Conflict and Violence*, 6(2): 260–72.

Lochman, J. E., Boxmeyer, C., Powell, N., Qu, I., Wells, K. and Windle, M (2009) 'Dissemination of the coping power program: importance of intensity of counselor training', *Journal of Consulting and Clinical Psychology*, 77(3): 397–409.

Logan, J. and Graham I. D. (1998) 'Toward a comprehensive interdisciplinary model of health care research use', *Science Communications*, 20(2): 227–46.

Lomas, J. (2000) 'Using "linkage and exchange" to move research into policy at a Canadian foundation', *Health Affairs*, 19(1): 236–40.

Lutzker, J. R. (1990) 'Behavioral treatment of child neglect', *Behavior Modification*, 14: 301–15.

Macaulay, A. C., Commanda, L. E., Freeman, W. L., Gibson, N., McCabe, M. L., Robbins, C. M. and Twohig, P.L. (1999) 'Participatory research maximises community and lay involvement', *British Medical Journal*, 319(7212): 774–78.

Manuel, J. I., Mullen, E. J., Fang, L., Bellamy, J. L. and Bledsoe, S. E. (2009) 'Preparing social work practitioners to use evidence-based practice: a comparison of experiences from an implementation project', *Research on Social Work Practice*, 19(5): 613–27.

Martin, J. (2002) Organiz*ational culture: Mapping the terrain*, Thousand Oaks, CA: Sage.

May, C. and Finch, T. (2009) 'Implementation, embedding and integration: an outline of normalization process theory', *Sociology*, 43: 535–54.

Medland, M. B. and Stachnik, T. J. (1972) 'Good-behavior Game: a replication and systematic analysis', *Journal of Applied Behavior Analysis*, 5: 45–51.

Melnyk, B., Fulmer, T., Van Orman, S. and Thorpe, K. (2015) 'The forgotten chronic disease: mental health among teens and young adults', *Health Affairs Blog* http://healthaffairs.org/blog/2015/10/01/the-forgotten-chronic-disease-mental-health-among-teens-and-young-adults/

Menting, A. T. A., de Castro, B. O. and Matthys, W. (2013) 'Effectiveness of the Incredible Years parent training to modify disruptive and prosocial child behavior: a meta-analytic review', *Clinical Psychology Review*, 33: 901–13.

Merikangas, K. R., Nakamura, E. F. and Kessler, R. C. (2009) 'Epidemiology of mental disorders in children and adolescents', *Dialogues in Clinical Neuroscience*, 11: 7–20.

Merikangas, K. R., He, J. P., Burstein, M., Swanson, S. A., Avenevoli, S., Cui, L., Benjet, C., Georgiades, K. and Swendsen, J. (2010) 'Lifetime prevalence of mental disorders in U.S. adolescents: results from the National Co-morbidity Replication—Adolescent Supplement (NCR—AS)', *Journal of the American Academy of Child Adolescent Psychiatry*, 49(10): 980–9.

Meyer, M. (2010) 'The rise of the knowledge broker', *Science Communication*, 32: 118–27.

Minkler, M. and Wallerstein, N. (eds) (2003) *Community-based participatory research for health*, San Francisco, CA: Jossey-Bass.

Mitton, C., Adair, C. E., McKenzie, E., Patten, S. B. and Waye Perry, B. (2007) 'Knowledge transfer and exchange: review and synthesis of the literature', *Milbank Quarterly*, 85: 729–68.

Mojtabai, R., Olfson, M. and Han, B. (2016) 'National trends and the prevalence and treatment of depression in adolescents and young adults', *Pediatrics*, 138(6), pii: e20161878.

Moll, L., Amanti, C. and Gonzalez, N. (eds) (2005) *Funds of knowledge: Theorizing practices in households and communities*, Mahwah, NJ: Lawrence Earlbaum.

Murray, L. K., Skavenski, S., Kane, J. C., Mayeya, J., Dorsey, S., Cohen, J. A., Michalopoulos, L. T., Imasiku, M. and Bolton, P. A. (2015) 'Effectiveness of trauma-focused cognitive behavioral therapy among trauma-affected children in Lusaka, Zambia: a randomized clinical trial', *JAMA Pediatrics*, 169(8): 761–9.

Muthusamy, S. K. and White, M. A. (2005) 'Learning and knowledge transfer in strategic alliances: a social exchange view', *Organization Studies*, 26(3): 415–41.

Myers, E. F., Trostler, N., Varsha, V. and Voet, H. (2017) 'Insights from the Diabetes in India Nutrition Guidelines Study: adopting innovations using a knowledge transfer model', *Topics in Clinical Nutrition*, 32(1): 69–86.

Nadeem, E., Olin, S. S., Campbell, L., Hoagwood K. E and Horwitz, S. M. (2013) 'Understanding the components of quality improvement collaboratives: a systematic literature review', *Milbank Quarterly*, 91(2): 354–94.

Nadeem, E., Weiss, D., Olin, S. S., Hoagwood, K. E. and Horwitz, S. M. (2016) 'Using a theory-guided learning collaborative model to improve implementation of EBPs in a state children's mental health system: a pilot study', *Administration and Policy in Mental Health*, 43: 978–90.

NCCMT (National Collaborating Center for Methods and Tools) (2010) *Ottawa model of research use: A framework for adopting innovations*, Hamilton, ON: McMaster University (Updated August 29 2017), www.nccmt.ca/knowledge-repositories/search/65

Nembhard, I. M. (2012) 'All teach, all learn, all improve?: the role of interorganizational learning in quality improvement collaboratives', *Health Care Management Review*, 37(2): 154–64.

Neta, G., Sanchez, M. A., Chambers, D. A., Phillips, S. M., Leyva, B., Cynkin, L., Farrell, M. M., Heurtin-Roberts, S. and Vinson, C. (2015) 'Implementation science in cancer prevention and control: a decade of grant funding by the National Cancer Institute and future directions', *Implementation Science*, 10: 4.

NIDA (National Institute on Drug Abuse) (2012) *Principles of drug abuse treatment: A research based guide* (3rd edn), USDHHS/NIH Publication #12-4180. Washington, DC: Government Printing Office.

Nieva, V. F., Murphy, R., Ridley, N., Donaldson, N., Combes, J., Mitchell, P., Kovner, C., Hoy, E. and Carpenter, D. (2005) 'From science to practice: A framework for the transfer of patient safety research into practice', in K. Henriksen, J. B. Battles, E. S. Marks and D. I. Lewin (eds) *Advances in patient safety: From research to implementation* (Volume 2: Concepts and methodology), Rockville (MD): Agency for Healthcare Research and Quality.

Nilsen, P. (2015) 'Making sense of implementation theories, models and frameworks', *Implementation Science*, 10: 53.

NIRN (National Implementationn Research Network) (n.d.) *The Exploration Stage: Assessing Readiness*, http://nirn.fpg.unc.edu/learn-implementation/implementation-stages/exploration-readiness

Nutley, S. M., Walter, I. and Davies, H. T. O. (2007) *Using evidence: How research can inform public services*, Bristol: The Policy Press.

O'Connell, M. E., Boat, T. and Warner, K. E. (2009) *Preventing mental, emotional and behavioral disorders among young people: progress and possibilities*, Washington, DC: National Academies Press.

Olesen, J., Gustavsson, A., Svensson, M., Wittchene, H-U. and Jönsson, B. on behalf of the CDBE2010 study group and the European Brain Council (2012) 'The economic cost of brain disorders in Europe', *European Journal of Neurology*, 19: 155–62.

Olin, S. C., Chor, K. H., Weaver, J., Duan, N., Kerker, B. D., Clark, L. J., Cleek, A. F., Hoagwood, K. E. and Horwitz, S. M. (2015) 'Multilevel predictors of clinic adoption of state-supported trainings in children's services', *Psychiatric Services*, 66(5): 484–90.

Orr, K. and Bennett, M. (2012) 'Public administration scholarship and the politics of coproduction academic–practitioner research', *Public Administration Review*, 72: 487–96.

Ouimet, M., Bedard, P-O, Turgeon, J., Lavis, J. N., Gelineau, F., Gagnon, E. and Dallaire, C. (2010) 'Correlates of consulting research evidence among policy analysts in government ministries: a cross-sectional survey', *Evidence & Policy*, 6: 433–60.

Oxman, A. D., Fretheim, A. and Flottorp S. (2005) 'The OFF theory of research utilization', *Journal of Clinical Epidemiology*, 58: 113–16.

Palinkas, L. A. (2014) 'Qualitative and mixed methods in mental health services and implementation research', *Journal of Clinical Child and Adolescent Psychology*, 43: 851–61.

Palinkas, L. A. and Aarons, G. A. (2009) 'A view from the top: executive and management challenges in a statewide implementation of an evidence-based practice to reduce child neglect', *International Journal of Child Health and Human Development*, 2: 47–55.

Palinkas, L. A. and Soydan, H. (2012) *Translation and implementation of evidence-based practice*, New York: Oxford University Press.

Palinkas, L. A., Allred, C. A. and Landsverk, J. (2005) 'Models of research-operational collaboration for behavioral health in space', *Aviation, Space and Environmental Medicine*, 76(Suppl 6): B52–60.

Palinkas, L. A, Schoenwald, S. K., Hoagwood, K., Landsverk, J., Chorpita, B. F., Weisz, J. R. and Research Network on Youth Mental Health (2008) 'An ethnographic study of implementation of evidence-based treatment in child mental health: first steps', *Psychiatric Services*, 59: 738–46.

Palinkas, L. A., Aarons, G. A., Chorpita, B. F., Hoagwood, K., Landsverk, J., Weisz, J. R. and the Research Network on Youth Mental Health (2009) 'Cultural exchange and the implementation of evidence-based practice: two case studies', *Research on Social Work Practice*, 19: 602–12.

Palinkas, L. A., Holloway, I. W., Rice, E., Fuentes, D., Wu, Q. and Chamberlain, P. (2011a) 'Social networks and implementation of evidence-based practices in public youth-serving systems: a mixed methods study', *Implementation Science*, 6: 113.

Palinkas, L. A., Aarons, G. A., Horwitz, S. M., Chamberlain, P., Hurlburt, M. and Landsverk, J. (2011b) 'Mixed method designs in implementation research', *Administration and Policy in Mental Health*, 38: 44–53.

Palinkas, L. A., Weisz, J. R., Chorpita, B., Levine, B., Garland, A., Hoagwood, K. E. and Landsverk, J. (2013a) 'Use of evidence-based treatments for youth mental health subsequent to a randomized controlled effectiveness trial: a qualitative study', *Psychiatric Services*, 64: 1110–18.

Palinkas, L. A., Holloway, I. W., Rice, E., Brown, C. H., Valente, T. and Chamberlain, P. (2013b) 'Influence network linkages across treatment conditions in a randomized controlled trial of two implementation strategies for scaling up evidence-based practices in public youth-serving systems', *Implementation Science*, 8: 133.

Palinkas, L. A., Fuentes, D., Garcia A. R., Finno, M., Holloway, I. W. and Chamberlain P. (2014) 'Inter-organizational collaboration in the implementation of evidence-based practices among agencies serving abused and neglected youth', *Administration and Policy in Mental Health*, 41: 74–85.

Palinkas, L. A., Short, C. and Wong, M. (2015) *Research–practice–policy partnerships for implementation of evidence-based practices in child welfare and child mental health*, New York: William T Grant Foundation, http://blog.wtgrantfoundation.org/post/125440468772/new-report-partnerships-and-evidence-based

Palinkas, L. A., Garcia, A. R., Aarons, G. A., Finno-Velasquez, M., Holloway, I. W., Mackie, T., Leslie, L. K. and Chamberlain, P. (2016) 'Measuring use of research evidence in child-serving systems: the Structured Interview for Evidence Use (SIEU)', *Research on Social Work Practice*, 26(5): 550–64.

Palinkas, L. A., Um, M. Y., Jeong, C. H., Chor, K. H. B., Olin, S., Horwitz, S. M. and Hoagwood, K. E. (2017a) 'Adoption of innovative and evidence-based practices for children and adolescents in state-supported mental health clinics: a qualitative study', *Health Research Policy and Systems*, 15: 27, doi: 10.1186/s12961-017-0190-z.

Palinkas, L. A., Garcia, A. R., Aarons, G. A., Finno-Velasquez, M., Fuentes, D. and Chamberlain P. (2017b) 'Measuring collaboration and communication to increase implementation of evidence-based practices in public youth-serving systems in California and Ohio: the Cultural Exchange Inventory', *Evidence & Policy*,14: 35–61.

Palinkas, L. A., Wu, Q., Fuentes, D., Finno-Velasquez, M., Holloway, I. W., Garcia, A. and Chamberlain, P. (2017c) 'Innovation and the use of research evidence in youth-serving systems: a mixed methods study', *Child Welfare*, 94(2): 57–85.

Palinkas L. A., He, A. S., Choy Brown, M. and Hertel, A. L. (2017d) 'Operationalizing social work science through research–practice partnerships: lessons from implementation science', *Research on Social Work Practice*, 27(2): 181–8.

Panzano, P. C. and Roth, D. (2006) 'The decision to adopt evidence-based and other innovative mental health practices: risky business?', *Psychiatric Services*, 57: 1153–61.

Petras, H., Kellam, S. G., Brown, C. H., Muthén, B. O., Ialongo, N. S. and Poduska, J. M. (2008) 'Developmental epidemiological courses leading to antisocial personality disorder and violent and criminal behavior: effects by young adulthood of a universal preventive intervention in first- and second-grade classrooms', *Drug and Alcohol Dependence*, 95(Suppl 1): S45–59.

Peyre, H., Hoertel, N., Stordeur, C., Lebeau, G., Blanco, C., McMahon, K., Basmaci, R., Lemogne, C., Limosin, F. and Delorme, R. (2017) 'Contributing factors and mental health outcomes of first suicide attempt during childhood and adolescence: results from a nationally representative study', *Journal of Clinical Psychiatry*, 78(6): e622–e630.

Phillips, N. K., Hammen, C. L., Brennan, P. A., Najman, J. M. and Bor, W. (2005) 'Early adversity and the prospective prediction of depressive and anxiety disorders in adolescents', *Journal of Abnormal Child Psychology*, 33(1): 13–24.

Phipps, D. and Morton, S. (2013) 'Qualities of knowledge brokers: reflections from practice', *Evidence & Policy*, 9: 255–65.

Pinto, A., Benn, J., Burnett, S., Parand, A. and Vincent, C. (2011) 'Predictors of the perceived impact of a patient safety collaborative: an exploratory study', *International Journal for Quality in Health Care*, 23(2): 173–81.

Poduska, J., Kellam, S., Brown, C.H., Ford, C., Windham, A., Keegan, N. and Wang, W. (2009) 'Study protocol for a group randomized controlled trial of a classroom-based intervention aimed at preventing early risk factors for drug abuse: integrating effectiveness and implementation research', *Implementation Science*, 4: 56.

Polanczyk, G. V., Salum, G. A., Sugaya, L. S., Caye, A. and Rohde, L. A. (2015) 'Annual research review: a meta-analysis of the worldwide prevalence of mental disorders in children and adolescents', *Journal of Child Psychology and Psychiatry*, 56(3): 345–65.

Powell, B. J., McMillen, J. C., Proctor, E. K., Carpenter, C. R., Griffey, R. T., Bunger, A. C., Glass, J. E. and York, J. L. (2012) 'A compilation of strategies for implementing clinical innovations in health and mental health', *Medical Care Research and Review*, 69(2): 123–57.

Price, J. M., Chamberlain, P., Landsverk, J., Reid, J. B., Leve, L. D. and Laurent, H. (2008) 'Effects of a foster parent training intervention on placement changes of children in foster care', *Child Maltreatment*, 13: 64–75.

Price, J., Chamberlain, P., Landsverk, J. and Reid, J. (2010) 'KEEP foster parent training intervention: model description and effectiveness', *Child and Family Social Work*, 4: 233–42.

Proctor, E. K., Landsverk, J., Aarons, G., Chambers, D., Glisson, C. and Mittman, B. (2009) 'Implementation research in mental health services: emerging science with conceptual, methodological, and training challenges', *Administration and Policy in Mental Health*, 36: 24–34.

Proctor, E. Silmere, H., Raghavan, R., Hovmand, P., Aarons, G., Bunger, A., Griffey, R. and Hensley, M. (2011) 'Outcomes for implementation research: conceptual distinctions, measurement challenges, and research agenda', *Administration and Policy in Mental Health*, 38: 65–76.

Proctor, E. K., Powell, B. J. and McMillan, C. (2013) 'Implementation strategies: recommendations for specifying and reporting', *Implementation Science*, 8: 139.

Pynoos, R. S., Steinberg, A. M., Layne, C. M., Briggs, E. C., Ostrowski, S. A. and Fairbank, J. A. (2009) 'DSM-V PTSD diagnostic criteria for children and adolescents: a developmental perspective and recommendations', *Journal of Traumatic Stress*, 22(5): 391–8.

Raghavan, R., Inoue, M., Ettner, S. L., Hamilton, B. H. and Landsverk, J. (2010) 'Preliminary analysis of the receipt of mental health services consistent with national standards among children in the child welfare system', *American Journal of Public Health*, 100(4): 742–49.

Research Impact (2014) 'So what the heck is knowledge mobilization and why should I care?', http://researchimpact.ca/so-what-the-heck-is-knowledge-mobilization-and-why-should-i-care/

Rhoades, K. A., Chamberlain, P., Roberts, R. and Leve, L. (2013) 'MTFC for high-risk adolescent girls: a comparison of outcomes in England and the United States', *Journal of Child & Adolescent Substance Abuse*, 22: 435–49.

Rice, E. R., Holloway, I. W., Barman-Adhikari, A., Fuentes, D., Brown, C. H. and Palinkas, L. A. (2014) 'A mixed methods approach to network data collection', *Field Methods*, 26(3): 252–68.

Rice, T. (2013) 'The behavioral economics of health and health care', *Annual Review of Public Health*, 34, 431–47.

Roberts, Y. H., Maher, E., Killos, L. F., O'Brien, K. and Pecora, P. J. (2017) 'Strategies to promote research use in child welfare', www.casey.org/media/strategies-promote-research.pdf

Rogers, E. M. (2003) *Diffusion of innovations* (5th edn), New York: Free Press.

Rosen, A. and Proctor, E. K. (1981) 'Distinctions between treatment outcomes and their implications for treatment evaluation', *Journal of Consulting and Clinical Psychology*, 49(3): 418–25.

Russell, G., Rodgers, L. R., Ukoumunne, O. C. and Ford, T. (2014) 'Prevalence of parent-reported ASD and ADHD in the UK: findings from the Millennium Cohort Study', *Journal of Autism and Developmental Disorders*, 44: 31–40.

Ryan, B. and Gross, N. C. (1943) 'The diffusion of hybrid seed corn in two Iowa communities', *Rural Sociology*, 8: 15–24.

Rycroft-Moore, J., Burton, C. R., Wilkinson, J., Harvey, G., McCormack, B., Baker, R., Dopson, S., Graham, I. D., Staniszweska, S., Thompson, C., Ariss, S., Melville-Richards, L. and Williams, L. (2016) 'Collective action for implementation: a realist evaluation of organizational collaboration in healthcare', *Implementation Science*, 11: 17.

Sackett, D. L., Rosenberg, W., Gray, J. A. M., Haynes, R. B. and Richardson, W. S. (1996) 'Evidence-based medicine: what it is and what it isn't', *Lancet*, 312: 71–2.

Sacks, J. J., Gonzales, K. R., Bouchery, E. E., Tomedi, L. E. and Brewer, R. D. (2015) '2010 national and state costs of excessive alcohol consumption', *American Journal of Preventive Medicine*, 249: e73–9.

Saldana, L. and Chamberlain, P. (2012) 'Supporting implementation: the role of community development teams to build infrastructure', *American Journal of Community Psychology*, 50, 334–46.

Saldana, L., Chamberlain, P., Wang, W. and Brown, C. H. (2012) 'Predicting program start-up using the stages of implementation measure', *Administration and Policy in Mental Health*, 39(6): 419–25.

Saldana, L., Chamberlain, P. and Chapman, J. (2016) 'A supervisor-targeted implementation approach to promote system change: the R3 model. *Administration and Policy in Mental Health*, 43(6): 879–92.

SAMHSA (Substance Abuse and Mental Health Services Administration) (2018) 'Statement of Elinore F. McCance-Katz, MD, PhD, Assistant Secretary for Mental Health and Substance Use regarding the National Registry of Evidence-based Programs and Practices and SAMHSA's new approach to implementation of evidence-based practices (EBPs)', www.samhsa.gov/newsroom/press-announcements/201801110330

SAMHSA (Substance Abuse and Mental Health Services Administration) (2016) 'Model Programs Guide', www.samhsa.gov/capt/tools-learning-resources/model-programs-guide

SAMHSA (Substance Abuse and Mental Health Services Administration) (2015) *Behavioral health trends in the United States: Results from the 2014 National Survey on Drug Use and Health*, HHS Publication #SMA 15-4927, NSDUH Series H-50, Center for Behavioral Health Statistics and Quality, www.samhsa.gov/data/

Schneider, S. J., Grilli, S. F. and Schneider, J. R. (2013) 'Evidence-based treatments for traumatized children and adolescents', *Current Psychiatry Reports*, 15(1): 332.

Schoenwald, S. K. and Hoagwood, K. (2001) 'Effectiveness, transportability, and dissemination of interventions: what matters when?', *Psychiatric Services*, 52: 1190–7.

Schoenwald, S. K., Garland, A., Chapman, J. E., Frazier, S. L., Shaidow, A. J. and Southam-Gerow, M. A. (2011) 'Toward the effective and efficient measurement of implementation fidelity', *Administration and Policy in Mental Health*, 38: 32–43.

Seffrin, B., Panzano, P. C. and Roth, D. (2009) 'What gets noticed: how barrier and facilitator perceptions relate to the adoption and implementation of innovative mental health practices', *Community Mental Health Journal*, 45: 260–9.

Shadish, W. R., Cook, T. D. and Campbell, D. T. (2002) *Experimental and quasi-experimental designs for generalized causal inference*, Boston, MA: Houghton Mifflin.

Shaw, J. S., Norlin, C., Gillispie, R. J., Weissman, M. and McGrath, J. (2013) 'The national improvement partnership network: state-based partnerships that improve primary care quality', *Academic Pediatrics*, 13(Suppl 6): S84–94.

Shin, H. S., Valente, T. W., Riiggs, N. R., Huh, J., Spruijt-Metz, D., Chou, C. P. and Pentz, M. A. (2014) 'The interaction of social networks and child obesity prevention program effects: the pathways trial', *Obesity*, 22(6): 1520–6.

Simon, H. A. (1955) 'A behavioral model of rational choice', *Quarterly Journal of Economics*, 69: 99–118.

Simpson, D. D. (2002) 'A conceptual framework for transferring research to practice', *Journal of Substance Abuse Treatment*, 22(4): 171–82.

Smith, P., Yule, W., Perrin, S., Tranah, T., Dalgleish, T. and Clark, D. M. (2007) 'Cognitive-behavioral therapy for PTSD in children and adolescents: a preliminary randomized-controlled trial', *Journal of the American Academy of Child and Adolescent Psychiatry*, 46(8): 1051–61.

Snell, T., Knapp, M., Healey, A., Guglani, S., Evans-Lacko, S., Fernández, J-L. and Ford, T. (2013) 'Economic impact of childhood psychiatric disorder on public sector services in Britain: estimates from national survey data', *Journal of Child Psychology and Psychiatry*, 54: 977–85.

Soydan, H. and Palinkas, L. A. (2014) *Evidence-based practice in social work: Development of a new professional culture*, London: Routledge.

Spillane, J. P., Diamond, J. B., Walker, L. J., Halverson, R. and Jita, L. (2001) 'Urban school leadership for elementary science instruction: identifying and activating resources in an undervalued school subject', *Journal of Research in Science Teaching* 38(8): 918–40.

Spillane, J. P., Reiser, B. J. and Reimer, T. (2002) 'Policy implementation and cognition: Reframing and refocusing implementation research', *Review of Educational Research*, 72(3): 387–431.

Stallard, P. (2016) 'Suicide rates in children and young people increase', *Lancet*, 387(10028): 1618.

Strupp, H. H. and Anderson, T. (1997) 'On the limitations of therapy manuals', *Clinical Psychology: Science and Practice*, 4: 76–82.

Tabak, R. G., Khoong, E. C., Chambers, D. A. and Brownson, R. C. (2012) 'Bridging research and practice: models for dissemination and implementation research', *American Journal of Preventive Medicine*, 43: 337–50.

Tabak, R. G., Chambers, D. A., Hook, M. and Brownson, R. C. (2018) 'The conceptual basis for dissemination and implementation research', in R. C. Brownson, G. A. Colditz and E. K. Proctor (eds) *Dissemination and implementation research in health: Translating science to practice* (2nd edn), New York: Oxford University Press, pp 73–88.

Taylor, E. (2017) 'Attention deficit hyperactivity disorder: overdiagnosed or diagnoses missed?', *Archives of Diseases of the Child*, 102(4): 376–79.

Teddlie, C. and Tashakkori, A. (2003) 'Major issues and controversies in the use of mixed methods in the social and behavioral sciences', in A. Tashakkori and C. Teddlie (eds) *Handbook of mixed methods in the social and behavioral sciences*, Thousand Oaks, CA: Sage, pp 3–50.

Ten Have, T. R., Coyne, J., Salzer, M. and Katz, I. (2003) 'Research to improve the quality of care for depression: alternatives to the simple randomized clinical trial', *General Hospital Psychiatry*, 25(2): 115–23.

Teplin, L. A., Abram, K. M., McClelland, G. M., Dulcan, M. K. and Mericle, A. A. (2002) 'Psychiatric disorders in youth in juvenile detention', *Archives of General Psychiatry*, 59: 1133–43.

Teplin, L., Abram, K., McClelland, G., Mericle, A., Dulcan, M. and Washburn, D. (2006) *Psychiatric disorders of youth in detention*, Washington, DC: Office of Juvenile Justice and Delinquency Prevention.

Tobias, C., Downes, A., Eddens. S. and Ruiz, J. (2012) 'Building blocks for peer success: lessons learned from a train-the-trainer program', *AIDS Patient Care and STDs*, 26(1): 53–59.

Trautman, S., Rehm, J. and Wittchen, H-U. (2016) 'The economic costs of mental disorders', *EMBO Reports*, 17(9): 1245–49.

Traynor, R., Dobbins, M. and DeCorby, K. (2014) 'Challenges of partnership research: insights from a collaborative partnership in evidence-based public health decision-making', *Evidence & Policy*, 11(1): 99–109.

Tseng, V. (2012) 'The use of research in policy and practice', *Social Policy Report*, 26: 1–16.

Tyden, T. (1993) *Knowledge interplay: User oriented research dissemination through synthesis pedagogics*, Uppsala Studies in Education 50. Uppsala, Sweden: Uppsala University.

Tyrka, A. R., Ridout, K. K. and Parade, S. H. (2016) 'Childhood adversity and epigenetic regulation of glucocorticoid signaling genes: associations in children and adults', *Development and Psychopathology*, 28(4pt2): 1319–31.

Valente, T. W. (2006) 'Opinion leader intervention in social networks can change HIV risk behavior in high risk communities', *British Medical Journal*, 333: 1082–3.

Valente, T.W. (2010) *Social networks and health: Models, methods, and applications*, New York: Oxford University Press.

Valente, T. W. (2012) 'Network interventions', *Science*, 337: 49–53.

Valente, T. W. and Pumpuang, P. (2007) 'Identifying opinion leaders to promote behavior change', *Health Education and Behavior*, 34: 881–96.

Valente, T. W., Hoffman, B. R., Rin-Olson, A., Lichtman, K. and Johnson, C. A. (2003) 'The effects of a social network method for group assignment strategies on peer led tobacco prevention programs in schools', *American Journal of Public Health*, 93: 1837–43.

Valente, T. W., Chou, C. P. and Pentz, M. A. (2007) 'Community coalitions as a system: effects of network change and adoption of evidence-based substance abuse prevention', *American Journal of Public Health*, 97: 880–6.

Valente, T., Palinkas, L. A., Czaja, S., Chu, K. H. and Brown, C. H. (2015) 'Social network analysis for program implementation (SNAPI)', *PLOS One*, 10(6): e0131712.

Visser, S. N., Bitsko, R. H., Danielson, M. L. and Perou, R. (2010) 'Increasing prevalence of parent-reported attention-deficit/hyperactivity disorder among children—United States, 2003 and 2007', *Morbidity Mortality Weekly Reports*, 59: 1439–43.

Wang, W., Saldana, L., Brown, C. H. and Chamberlain, P. (2010) 'Factors that influenced county system leaders to implement an evidence-based program: a baseline survey within a randomized controlled trial', *Implementation Science*, 5: 72.

Wasserman, G. A., McReynolds, L. S., Lucas, C. P., Fisher, P. and Santos, L. (2002) 'The voice DISC-IV with incarcerated male youths: prevalence of disorder', *Journal of the American Academy of Child and Adolescent Psychiatry*, 41: 314–21.

Webster-Stratton, C., Reid, J. R. and Hammond, M. (2004) 'Treating children with early-onset conduct disorder: intervention outcomes for parent, child, and teacher training', *Journal of Clinical Child and Adolescent Psychology*, 31: 168–80.

Webster-Stratton, C. and Herman, K. C. (2008) 'The impact of parent behavior-management training on child depressive symptoms', *Journal of Counseling Psychology*, 55(4): 473–84.

Webster-Stratton, C. H., Reid, M. J., and Beauchaine, T. (2011) 'Combining parent and child training for young children with ADHD', *Journal of Clinical Child and Adolescent Psychology*, 40(2): 191–203.

Weinberg, L. A., Zetlin, A. and Shea, N. M. (2009) 'Removing barriers to educating children in foster care through interagency collaboration: a seven county multiple-case study', *Child Welfare*, 88(4): 77–111.

Weiner, B. J., Lewis, C. C., Stanick, C., Powell, B. J., Dorsey, C. N., Clary, A. S., Boynton, M. H. and Halko, H. (2017) 'Psychometric assessment of three newly developed implementation outcome measures', *Implementation Science*, 12: 108.

Weiss, B. and Garber, J. (2003) 'Developmental differences in the phenomology of depression', *Development and Psychopathology*, 15: 403–30.

Weisz, J. R. and Gray, J. S. (2008) 'Evidence-based psychotherapy for children and adolescents: data from the present and a model for the future', *Child and Adolescent Mental Health*, 13(2): 54–65.

Weisz, J. R. and Jensen, P. (1999) 'Efficacy and effectiveness of child and adolescent psychotherapy and pharmacotherapy', *Mental Health Services Research*, 1: 125–57.

Weisz, J. R., Weiss, B., Han, S. S., Granger, D. A. and Morton, T. (1995) 'Effects of psychotherapy with children and adolescents revisited: a meta-analysis of treatment outcome studies', *Psychological Bulletin*, 117: 450–68.

Weisz, J. R., Thurber, C. A., Sweeney, L., Proffitt, V. D. and LeGagnoux, G. L. (1997) 'Brief treatment of mild-to-moderate child depression using primary and secondary control enhancement training', *Journal of Consulting and Clinical Psychology*, 65: 703–7.

Weisz, J. R., Hawley, K. and Jensen-Doss, A. (2004) 'Empirically tested psychotherapies for youth internalizing and externalizing problems and disorders', *Child and Adolescent Psychiatric Clinics of North America*, 13: 729–815.

Weisz, J. R., Jensen-Doss, A. and Hawley, K. M. (2006) 'Evidence-based youth psychotherapies versus usual clinical care: a meta-analysis of direct comparisons', *American Psychologist*, 61(7): 671–89.

Weisz, J. R., Chorpita, B., Palinkas, L. A., Schoenwald, S. K., Miranda, J., Bearman, S. K., Daleiden, E. L., Ugueto, A. M., Ho, A., Martin, J., Gray, J., Alleyne, A., Langer, D. A., Southam-Gerow, M. A., Gibbons, R. D. and the Research Network on Youth Mental Health (2012) 'Testing standard and modular designs for psychotherapy treating depression, anxiety and conduct problems in youth: a randomized effectiveness trial', *Archives of General Psychiatry*, 69: 274–82.

Wells, K. B., Miranda, J., Bruce, M. L., Alegria, M. and Wallerstein, N. (2004) 'Bridging community intervention and mental health services research', *American Journal of Psychiatry*, 161(6), 955–63.

West, S. G., Duan, N., Pequegnat, W., Gaist, P., Des Jarlais, D. C., Holtgrave, D., Szapocnik, J., Fishbein, M., Rapkin, B., Clatts, M. and Mullen, P. D. (2008) 'Alternatives to the randomized controlled trial', *American Journal of Public Health*, 98(8): 1359–66.

Westen, D., Novotny, C. M. and Thompson-Brenner, H. (2004) 'The empirical status of empirically supported psychotherapies: assumptions, findings, and reporting in controlled clinical trials', *Psychological Bulletin*, 130(4): 631–63.

Whiteford, H. A., Degenhardt, L., Rehm, J., Baxter, A. J., Ferrari, A. J., Erskine, H. E., Charlson, F. J., Norman, R. E., Flaxman, A. D., Johns, N., Burstein, R., Murray, C. J. and Vos, T. (2013) 'Global burden of disease attributable to mental and substance use disorders: findings from the Global Burden of Disease Study 2010', *Lancet*, 382: 1575–86.

WHO (World Health Organization) (2006) *Bridging the 'know–do' gap*, Geneva: World Health Organization.

Widom, C. S., DuMont, K. and Czaja, S. J. (2007) 'A prospective investigation of major depressive disorder and comorbidity in abused and neglected children grown up', *Archives of General Psychiatry*, 64(1): 49–56.

Wilcox, H. C., Kellam, S. G., Brown, C. H., Poduska, J. M., Ialongo, N. S., Wang, W. and Anthony, J. C. (2008) 'The impact of two universal randomized first- and second-grade classroom interventions on young adult suicide ideation and attempts', *Drug and Alcohol Dependence*, 95(Suppl 1): S60–S73.

Wilson, T., Berwick, D. M. and Cleary, P. (2004) 'What do collaborative improvement projects do? Experience from seven countries', *Joint Commission Journal on Quality and Patient Safety*, 30(Supplement 1): 25–33.

Wong, M. (2006) 'Commentary: building partnerships between schools and academic partners to achieve a health-related research agenda', *Ethnicity and Disease*, 16(1, Suppl. 1): S149–53.

Wyman, P. A., Brown, C. H., LoMurray, M., Schmeelk-Cone, K., Petrova, M., Yu, Q., Walsh, E., Tu, X. and Wang, W. (2010) 'An outcome evaluation of the Sources of Strength suicide prevention program delivered by adolescent peer leaders in high schools', *American Journal of Public Health*, 100(9): 1653–61.

Yoshikawa, H., Aber, J. L. and Beardslee, W. R. (2012) 'The effects of poverty on the mental, emotional, and behavioral health of children and youth: implications for prevention', *American Psychologist*, 67(4): 272–84.

Zazzali, J. L., Sherbourne, C., Hoagwood, K. E., Greene, D., Bigley, M. F. and Sexton, T. L. (2008) 'The adoption and implementation of an evidence based practice in child and family mental health services organizations: a pilot study of functional family therapy in New York State', *Administration and Policy in Mental Health*, 35, 38–49.

Index

Note: page numbers in italic type refer to Figures; those in bold type refer to Tables.

www.ingramcontent.com/pod-product-compliance
Lightning Source LLC
Chambersburg PA
CBHW070918030426
42336CB00014BA/2460